HEAVEN'S DESIGN TEAM

VOL.06

BY ▶ HEBI-ZOU & TSUTA SUZUKI

ART BY ▶ TARAKO

HEAVEN'S DESIGN TEAM

CHARACTER PROFILES

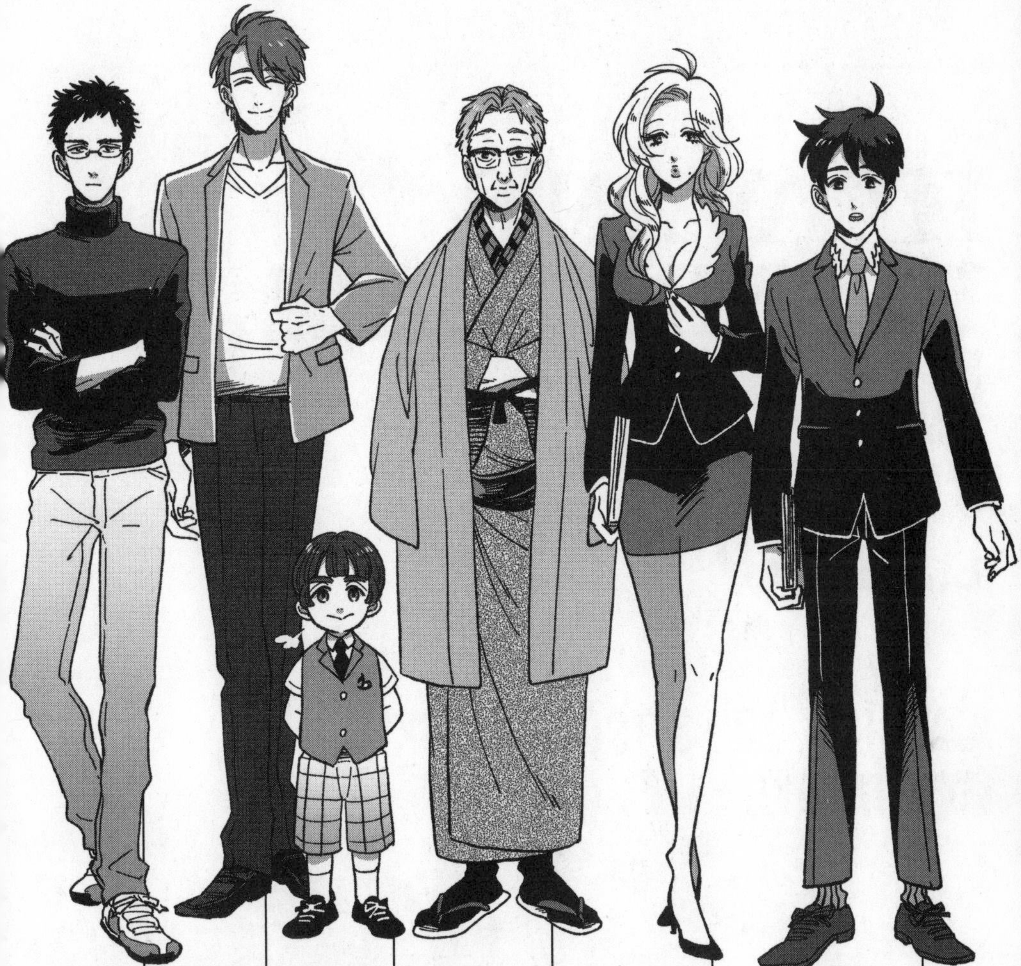

MERCURY

A designer. His masterpiece: the snake.

JUPITER

A designer. His masterpiece: the cow.

MR. SATURN'S GRANDSON

Mr. Saturn's grandson, Kenta. A horse fan, just like his grandpa.

MR. SATURN

A designer and the head of the Design Department. His masterpiece: the horse.

UEDA

Shimoda's supervisor. An angel who acts as a liaison between God and the Design Department.

SHIMODA

The new angel. Serves as the liaison between God (the client) and the Design Department.

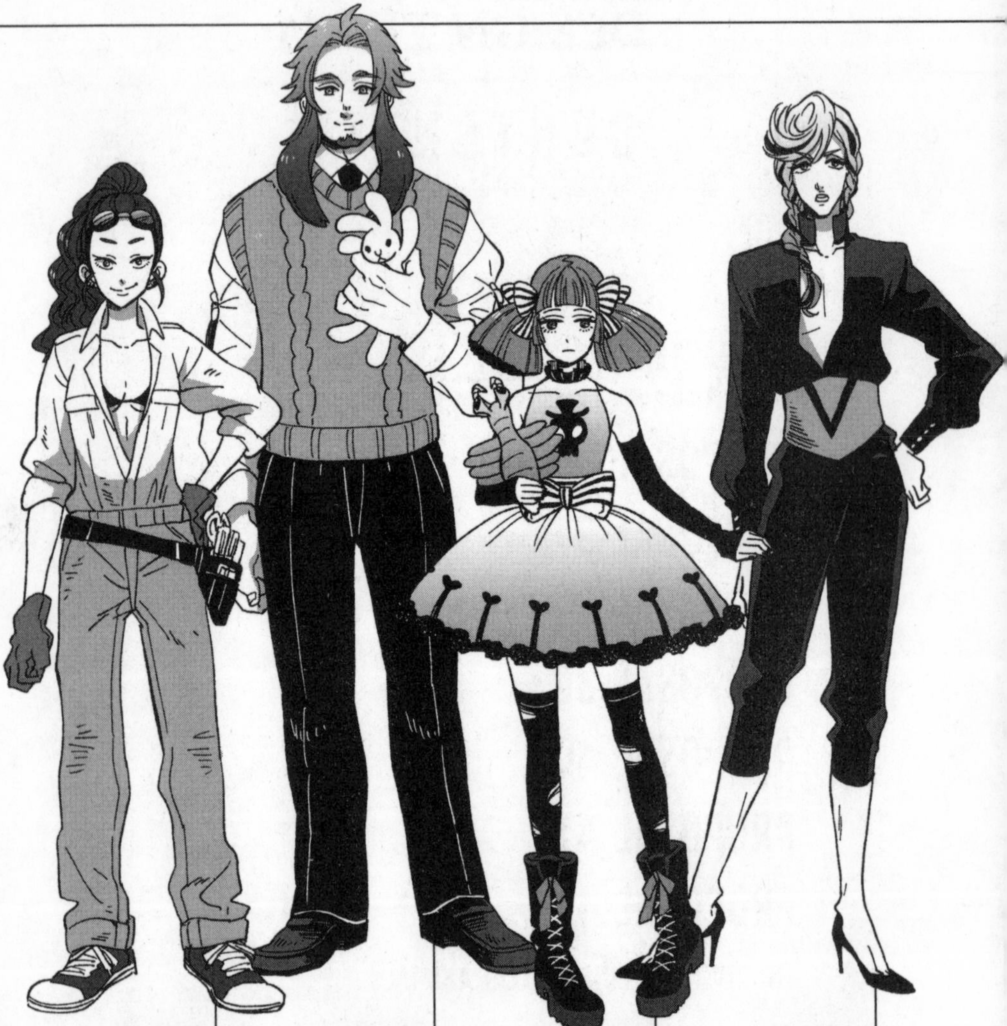

MARS

An engineer. Tests whether the animal designs will actually function in the physical world. The hardest worker in the office.

NEPTUNE

A designer. His masterpiece: the kangaroo.

PLUTO

A designer. Her masterpiece: the poisonous frog.

VENUS

A designer. Nicknamed "Ven." Their masterpiece: the bird.

HEAVEN'S DESIGN TEAM

✦

CONTENTS

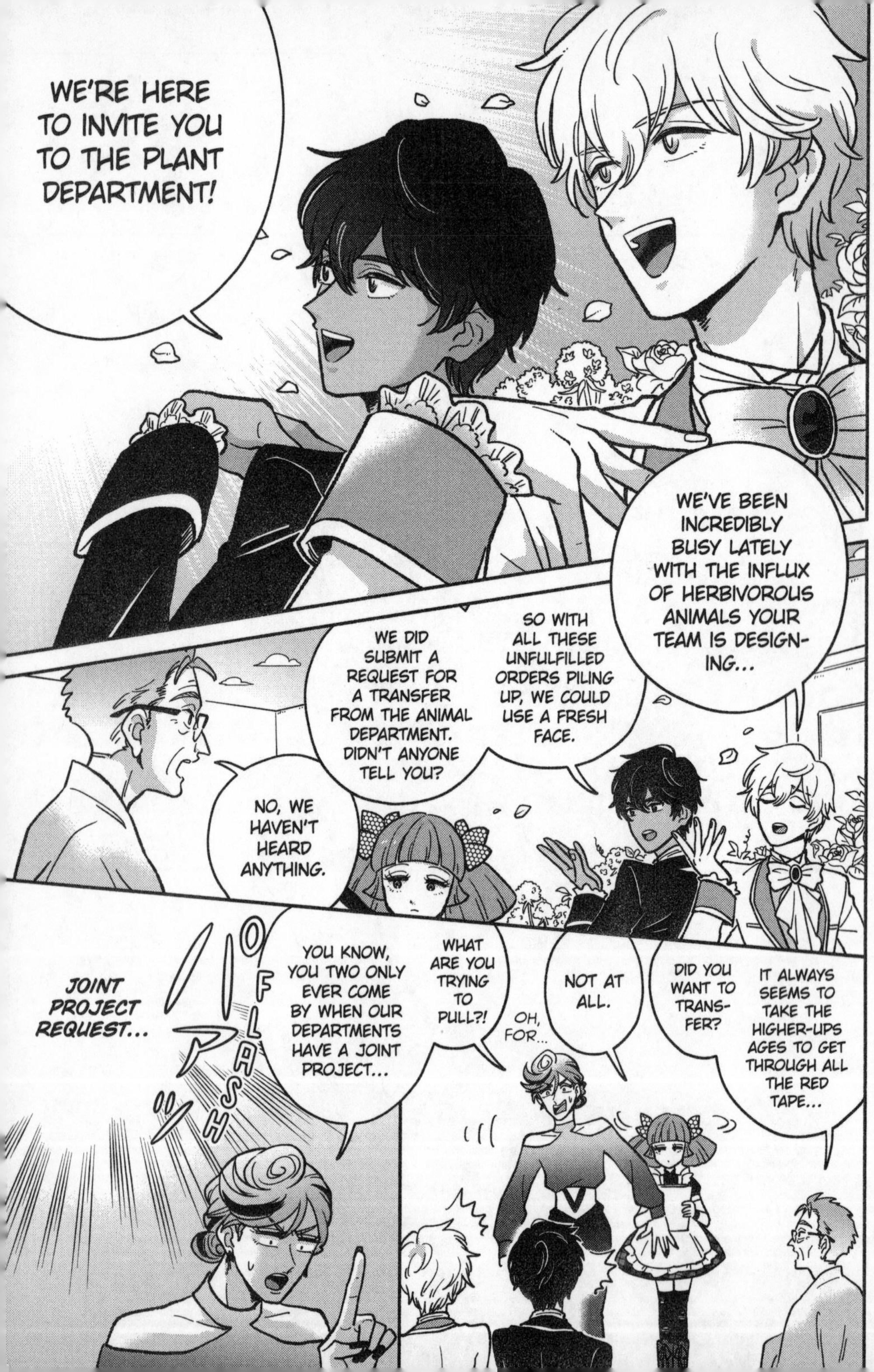
WE'RE HERE TO INVITE YOU TO THE PLANT DEPARTMENT!
WE'VE BEEN INCREDIBLY BUSY LATELY WITH THE INFLUX OF HERBIVOROUS ANIMALS YOUR TEAM IS DESIGN-ING...
SO WITH ALL THESE UNFULFILLED ORDERS PILING UP, WE COULD USE A FRESH FACE.
WE DID SUBMIT A REQUEST FOR A TRANSFER FROM THE ANIMAL DEPARTMENT. DIDN'T ANYONE TELL YOU?
NO, WE HAVEN'T HEARD ANYTHING.
IT ALWAYS SEEMS TO TAKE THE HIGHER-UPS AGES TO GET THROUGH ALL THE RED TAPE...
DID YOU WANT TO TRANS-FER?
NOT AT ALL.
OH, FOR...
WHAT ARE YOU TRYING TO PULL?!
FLASH
YOU KNOW, YOU TWO ONLY EVER COME BY WHEN OUR DEPARTMENTS HAVE A JOINT PROJECT...
JOINT PROJECT REQUEST...

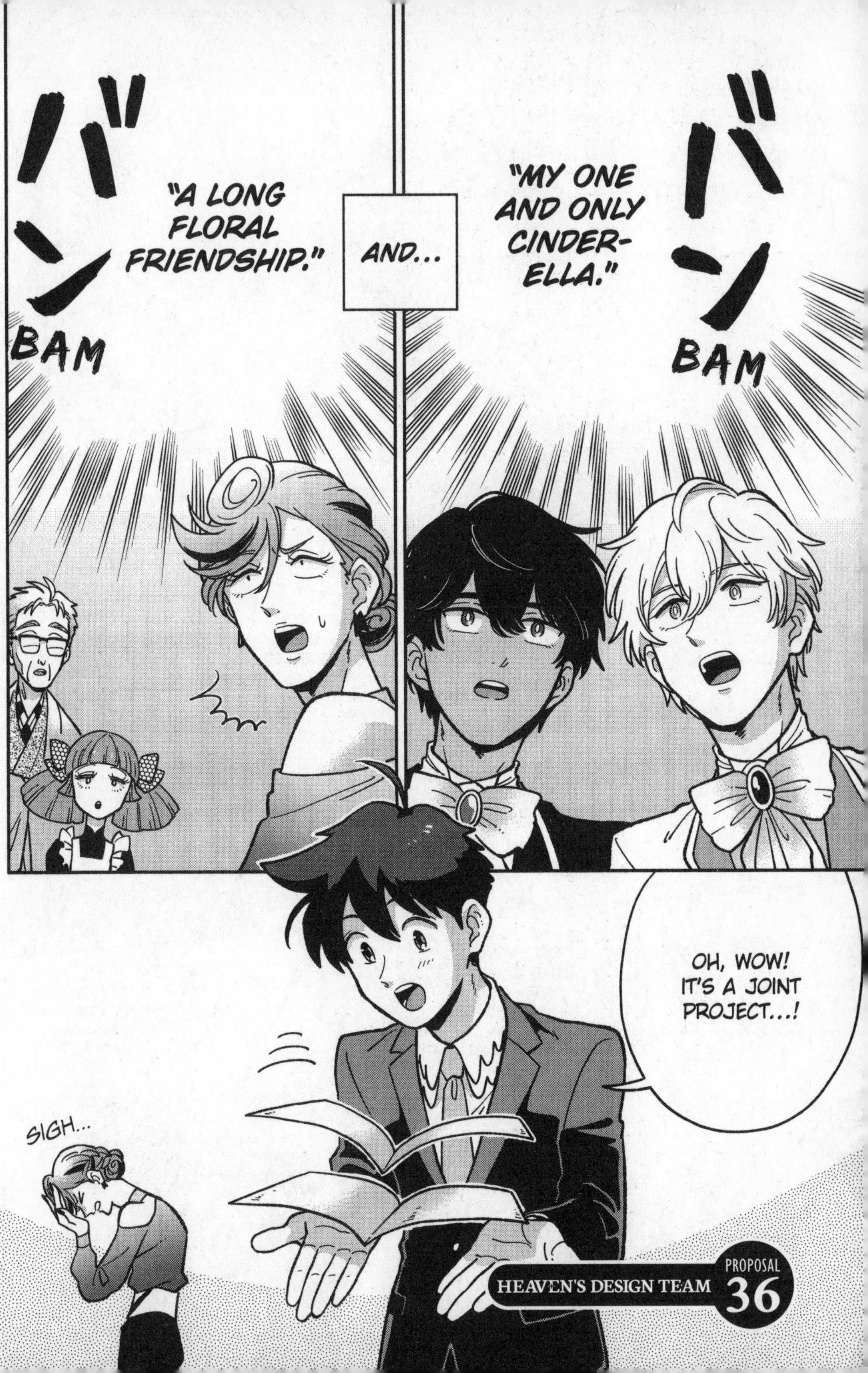
バン
BAM
"MY ONE AND ONLY CINDER-ELLA."
AND...
"A LONG FLORAL FRIENDSHIP."
バン
BAM
OH, WOW! IT'S A JOINT PROJECT...!
SIGH...
HEAVEN'S DESIGN TEAM
PROPOSAL 36

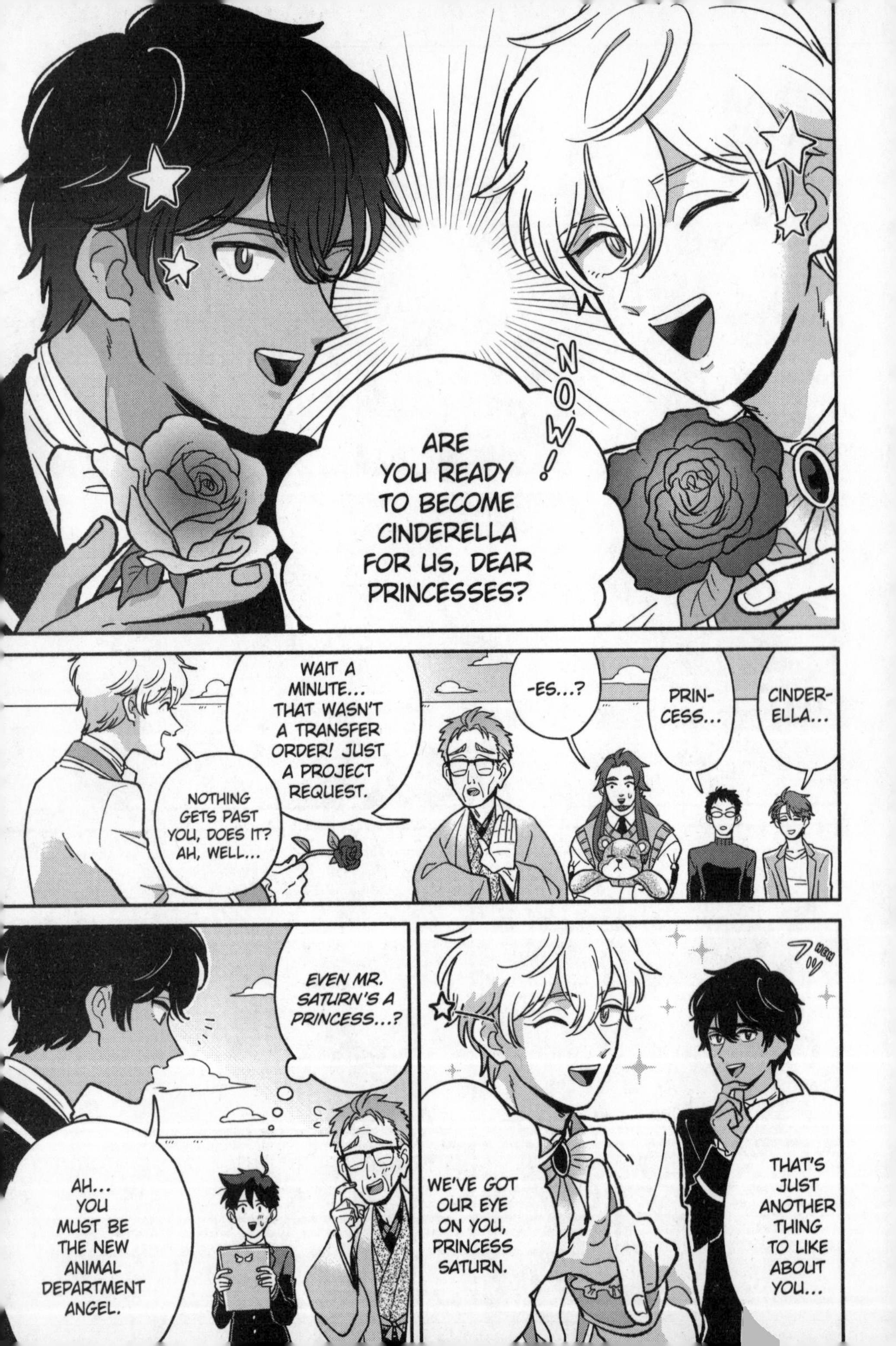
NOW!
ARE YOU READY TO BECOME CINDERELLA FOR US, DEAR PRINCESSES?
CINDER-ELLA...
PRIN-CESS...
-ES...?
WAIT A MINUTE... THAT WASN'T A TRANSFER ORDER! JUST A PROJECT REQUEST.
NOTHING GETS PAST YOU, DOES IT? AH, WELL...
HEH
THAT'S JUST ANOTHER THING TO LIKE ABOUT YOU...
WE'VE GOT OUR EYE ON YOU, PRINCESS SATURN.
EVEN MR. SATURN'S A PRINCESS...?
AH... YOU MUST BE THE NEW ANIMAL DEPARTMENT ANGEL.

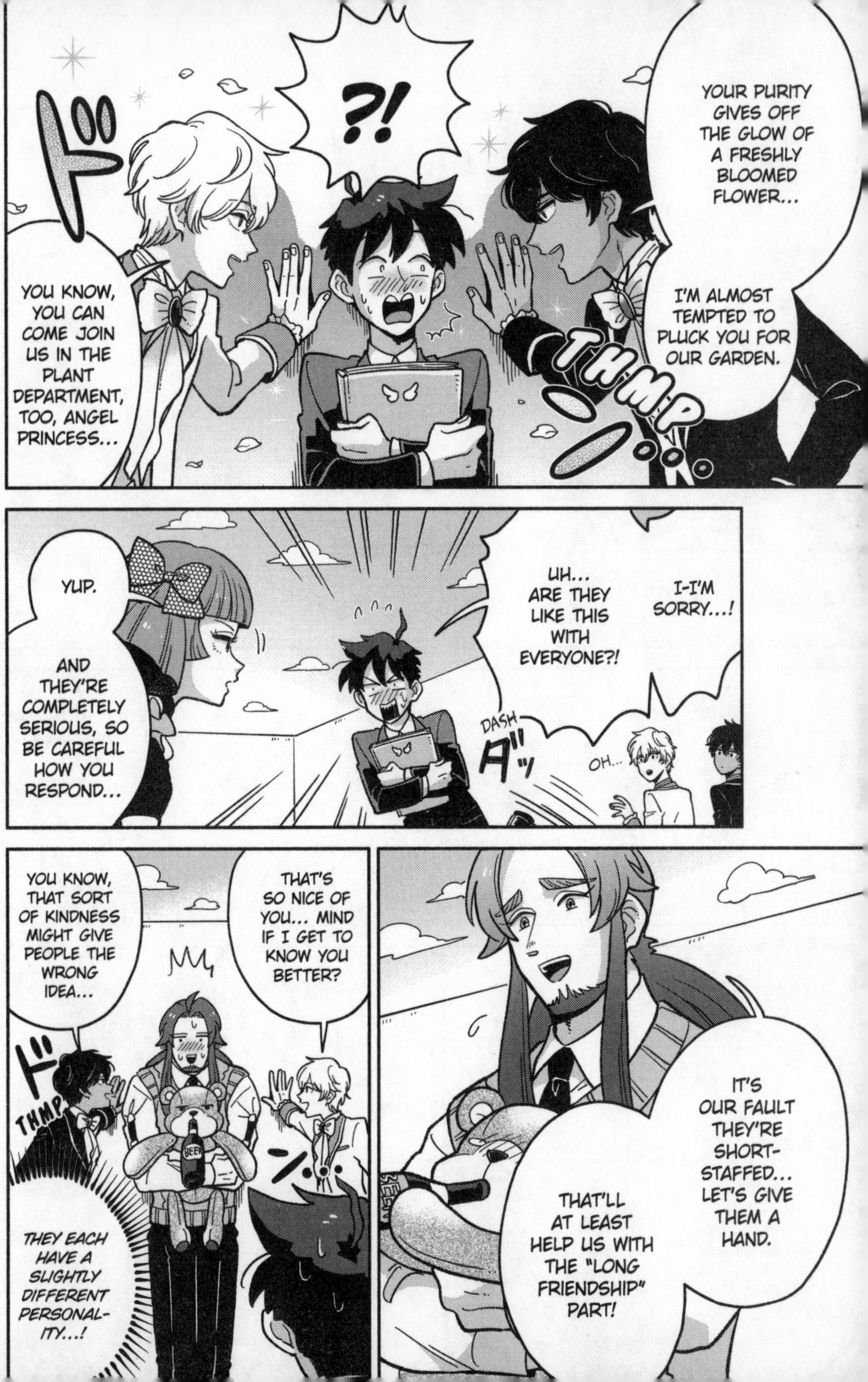
YOUR PURITY GIVES OFF THE GLOW OF A FRESHLY BLOOMED FLOWER...
I'M ALMOST TEMPTED TO PLUCK YOU FOR OUR GARDEN.
THMP
?!
ドッ
YOU KNOW, YOU CAN COME JOIN US IN THE PLANT DEPARTMENT, TOO, ANGEL PRINCESS...
I-I'M SORRY...!
UH... ARE THEY LIKE THIS WITH EVERYONE?!
OH...
DASH ダッ
YUP.
AND THEY'RE COMPLETELY SERIOUS, SO BE CAREFUL HOW YOU RESPOND...
IT'S OUR FAULT THEY'RE SHORT-STAFFED... LET'S GIVE THEM A HAND.
THAT'LL AT LEAST HELP US WITH THE "LONG FRIENDSHIP" PART!
THAT'S SO NICE OF YOU... MIND IF I GET TO KNOW YOU BETTER?
YOU KNOW, THAT SORT OF KINDNESS MIGHT GIVE PEOPLE THE WRONG IDEA...
THMP
BEER
THEY EACH HAVE A SLIGHTLY DIFFERENT PERSONALITY...!

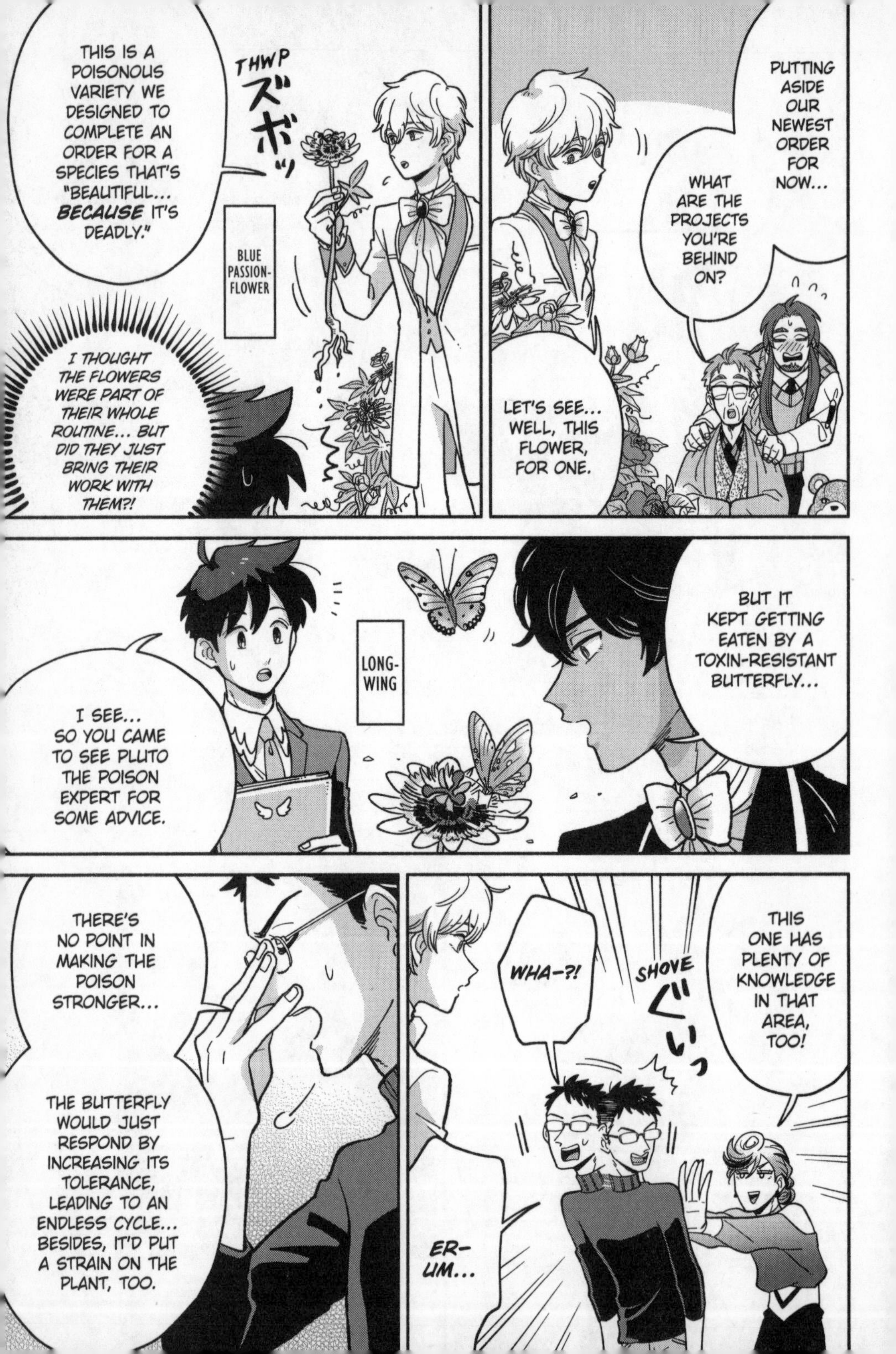
PUTTING ASIDE OUR NEWEST ORDER FOR NOW...
WHAT ARE THE PROJECTS YOU'RE BEHIND ON?
LET'S SEE... WELL, THIS FLOWER, FOR ONE.
THIS IS A POISONOUS VARIETY WE DESIGNED TO COMPLETE AN ORDER FOR A SPECIES THAT'S "BEAUTIFUL... **BECAUSE** IT'S DEADLY."
THWP
ズボッ
BLUE PASSION-FLOWER
I THOUGHT THE FLOWERS WERE PART OF THEIR WHOLE ROUTINE... BUT DID THEY JUST BRING THEIR WORK WITH THEM?!
BUT IT KEPT GETTING EATEN BY A TOXIN-RESISTANT BUTTERFLY...
LONG-WING
I SEE... SO YOU CAME TO SEE PLUTO THE POISON EXPERT FOR SOME ADVICE.
THIS ONE HAS PLENTY OF KNOWLEDGE IN THAT AREA, TOO!
SHOVE
ぐいっ
WHA-?!
ER-UM...
THERE'S NO POINT IN MAKING THE POISON STRONGER...
THE BUTTERFLY WOULD JUST RESPOND BY INCREASING ITS TOLERANCE, LEADING TO AN ENDLESS CYCLE... BESIDES, IT'D PUT A STRAIN ON THE PLANT, TOO.

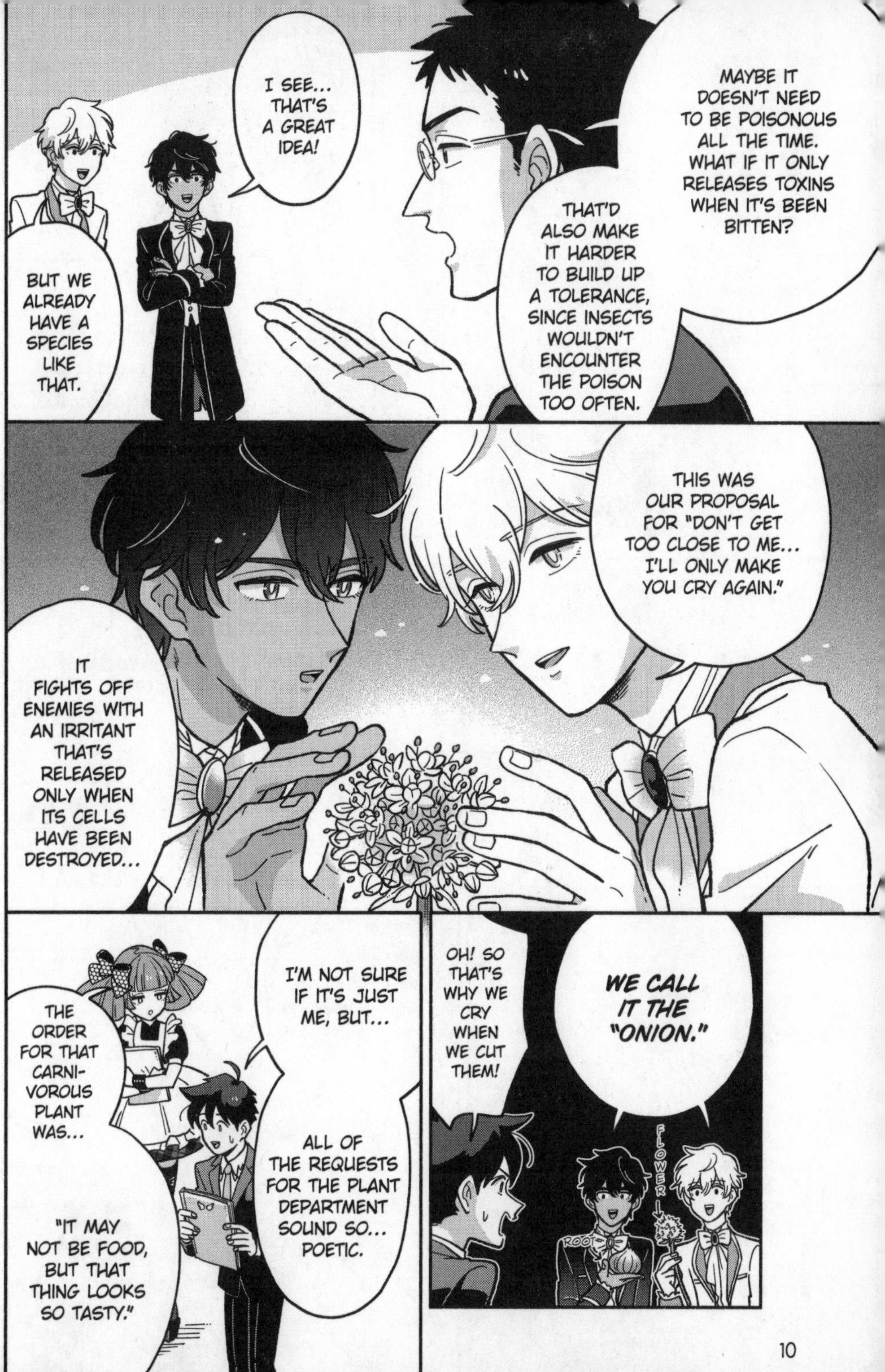
MAYBE IT DOESN'T NEED TO BE POISONOUS ALL THE TIME. WHAT IF IT ONLY RELEASES TOXINS WHEN IT'S BEEN BITTEN?
THAT'D ALSO MAKE IT HARDER TO BUILD UP A TOLERANCE, SINCE INSECTS WOULDN'T ENCOUNTER THE POISON TOO OFTEN.
I SEE... THAT'S A GREAT IDEA!
BUT WE ALREADY HAVE A SPECIES LIKE THAT.
THIS WAS OUR PROPOSAL FOR "DON'T GET TOO CLOSE TO ME... I'LL ONLY MAKE YOU CRY AGAIN."
IT FIGHTS OFF ENEMIES WITH AN IRRITANT THAT'S RELEASED ONLY WHEN ITS CELLS HAVE BEEN DESTROYED...
WE CALL IT THE "ONION."
OH! SO THAT'S WHY WE CRY WHEN WE CUT THEM!
FLOWER
ROOT
I'M NOT SURE IF IT'S JUST ME, BUT...
ALL OF THE REQUESTS FOR THE PLANT DEPARTMENT SOUND SO... POETIC.
THE ORDER FOR THAT CARNI-VOROUS PLANT WAS...
"IT MAY NOT BE FOOD, BUT THAT THING LOOKS SO TASTY."

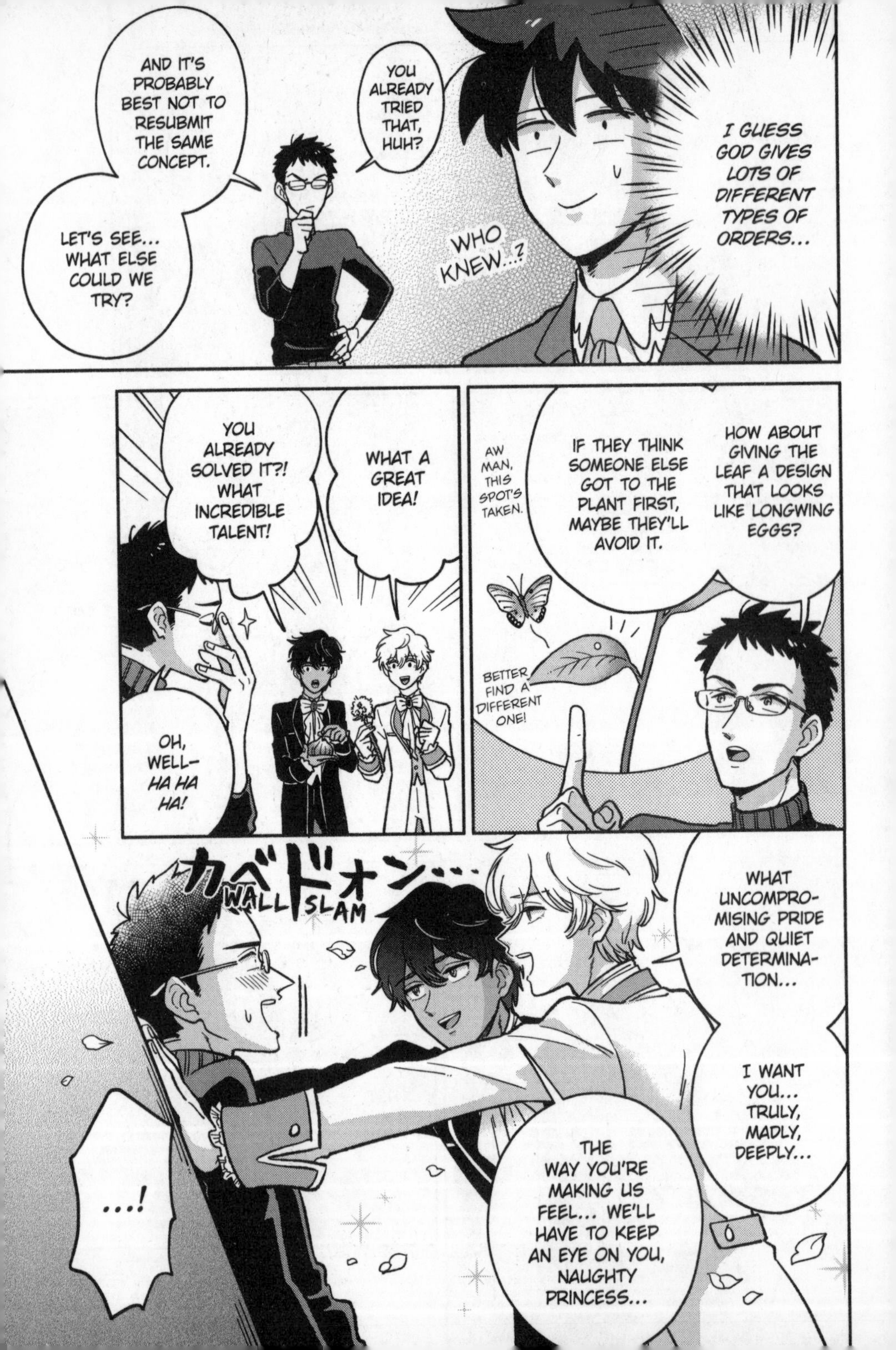
I GUESS GOD GIVES LOTS OF DIFFERENT TYPES OF ORDERS...
WHO KNEW...?
YOU ALREADY TRIED THAT, HUH?
AND IT'S PROBABLY BEST NOT TO RESUBMIT THE SAME CONCEPT.
LET'S SEE... WHAT ELSE COULD WE TRY?
HOW ABOUT GIVING THE LEAF A DESIGN THAT LOOKS LIKE LONGWING EGGS?
IF THEY THINK SOMEONE ELSE GOT TO THE PLANT FIRST, MAYBE THEY'LL AVOID IT.
AW MAN, THIS SPOT'S TAKEN.
BETTER FIND A DIFFERENT ONE!
WHAT A GREAT IDEA!
YOU ALREADY SOLVED IT?! WHAT INCREDIBLE TALENT!
OH, WELL— HA HA HA!
WHAT UNCOMPROMISING PRIDE AND QUIET DETERMINATION...
カベドオン…
WALL SLAM
I WANT YOU... TRULY, MADLY, DEEPLY...
THE WAY YOU'RE MAKING US FEEL... WE'LL HAVE TO KEEP AN EYE ON YOU, NAUGHTY PRINCESS...
...!

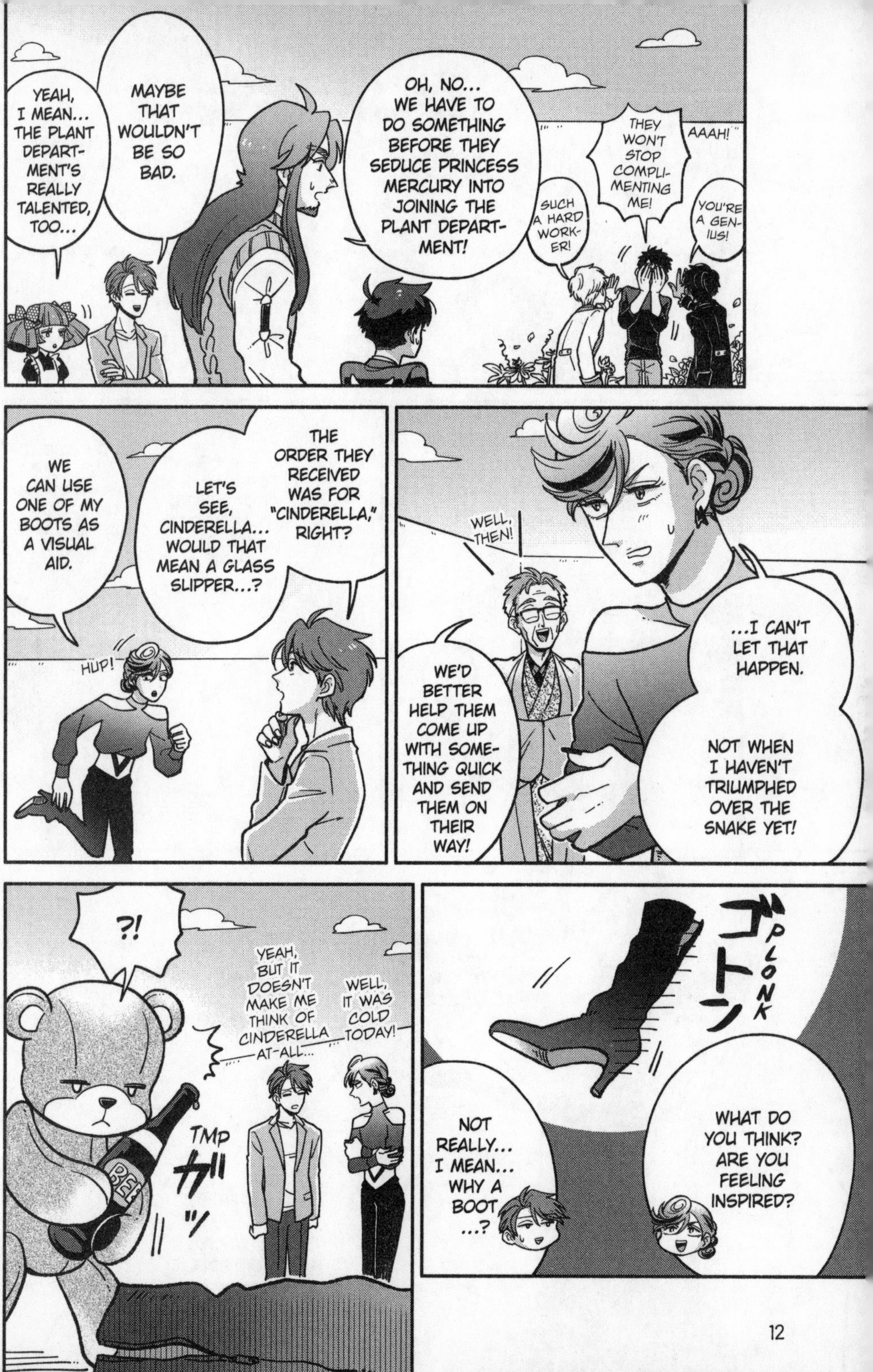
AAAH!
THEY WON'T STOP COMPLIMENTING ME!
YOU'RE A GENIUS!
SUCH A HARD WORKER!
OH, NO... WE HAVE TO DO SOMETHING BEFORE THEY SEDUCE PRINCESS MERCURY INTO JOINING THE PLANT DEPARTMENT!
MAYBE THAT WOULDN'T BE SO BAD.
YEAH, I MEAN... THE PLANT DEPARTMENT'S REALLY TALENTED, TOO...
...I CAN'T LET THAT HAPPEN.
NOT WHEN I HAVEN'T TRIUMPHED OVER THE SNAKE YET!
WELL, THEN!
WE'D BETTER HELP THEM COME UP WITH SOMETHING QUICK AND SEND THEM ON THEIR WAY!
THE ORDER THEY RECEIVED WAS FOR "CINDERELLA," RIGHT?
LET'S SEE, CINDERELLA... WOULD THAT MEAN A GLASS SLIPPER...?
WE CAN USE ONE OF MY BOOTS AS A VISUAL AID.
HUP!
ゴトン
PLONK
WHAT DO YOU THINK? ARE YOU FEELING INSPIRED?
NOT REALLY... I MEAN... WHY A BOOT...?
WELL, IT WAS COLD TODAY!
YEAH, BUT IT DOESN'T MAKE ME THINK OF CINDERELLA AT ALL...
?!
TMP
ガッ

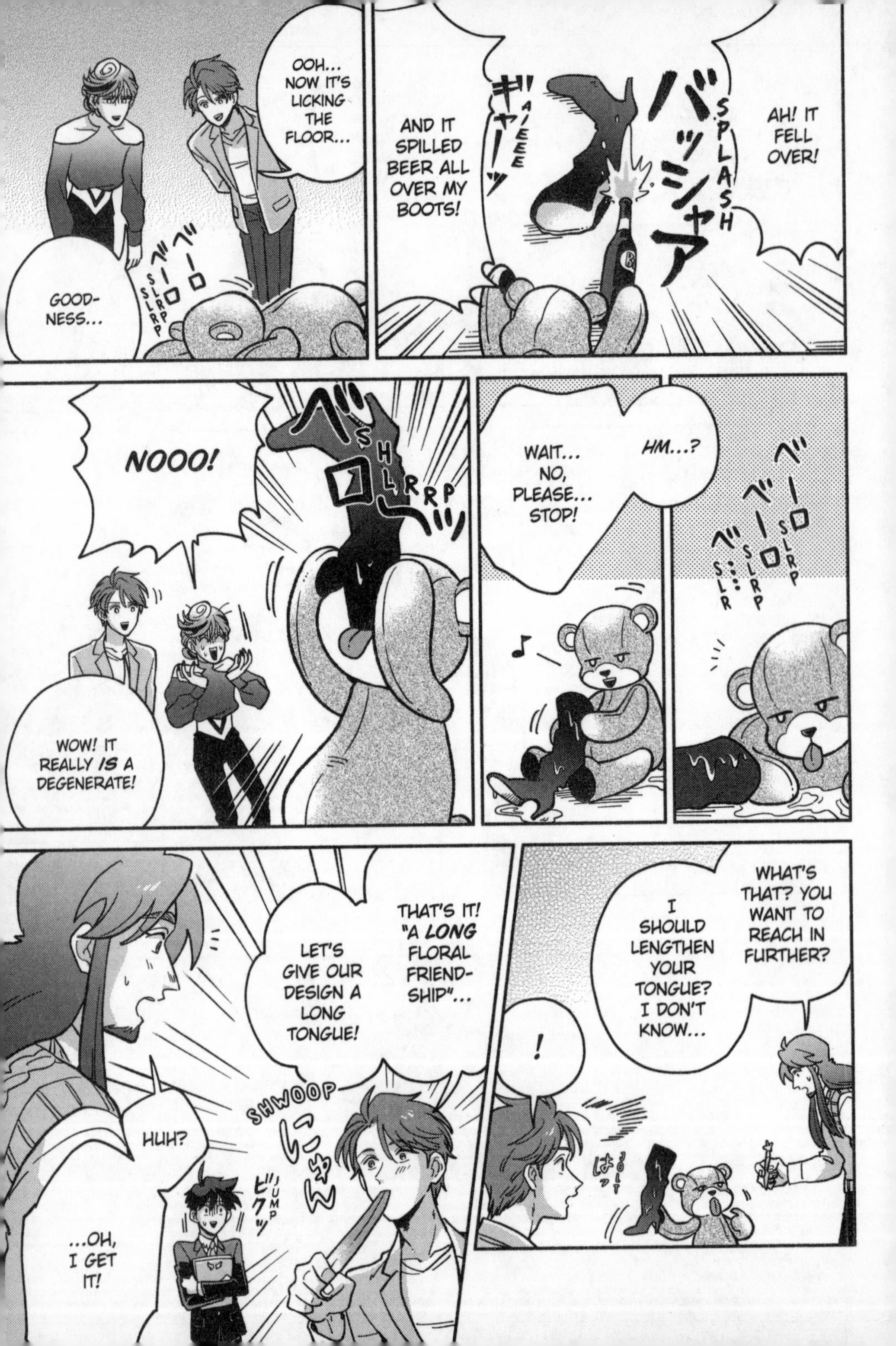
AH! IT FELL OVER!
バッシャア
SPLASH
AND IT SPILLED BEER ALL OVER MY BOOTS!
ギャーッ
AIEEE
OOH... NOW IT'S LICKING THE FLOOR...
ベーロベーロ
SLRP SLRP
GOODNESS...
ベーロ ベーロ ベ…
SLRP SLRP SLR
HM...?
WAIT... NO, PLEASE... STOP!
ベロー
SHLRRRP
NOOO!
WOW! IT REALLY *IS* A DEGENERATE!
WHAT'S THAT? YOU WANT TO REACH IN FURTHER?
I SHOULD LENGTHEN YOUR TONGUE? I DON'T KNOW...
!
はっ
JOLT
THAT'S IT! "A *LONG* FLORAL FRIENDSHIP"...
LET'S GIVE OUR DESIGN A LONG TONGUE!
にゅん
SHWOOP
HUH?
ビクッ
JUMP
...OH, I GET IT!

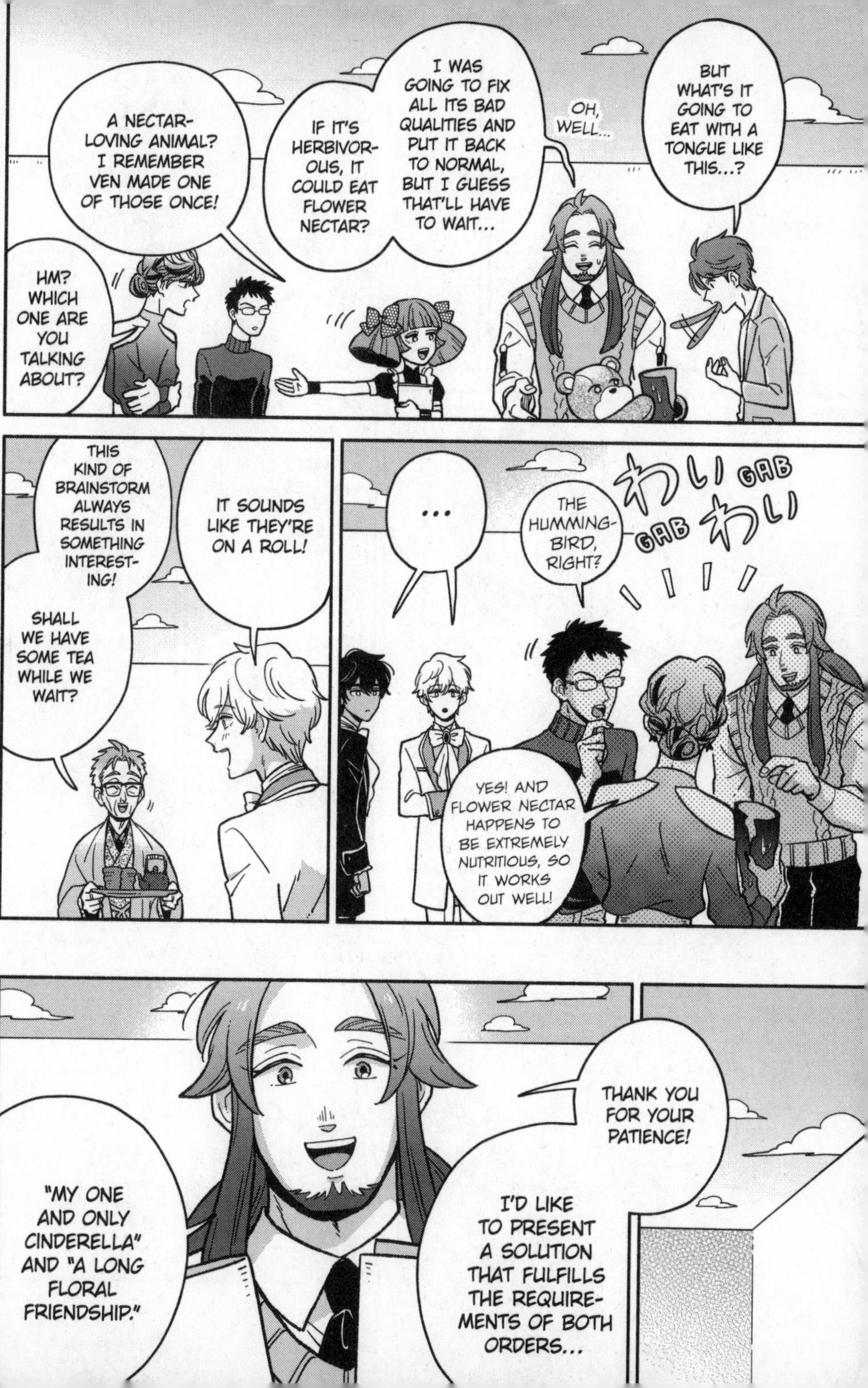
BUT WHAT'S IT GOING TO EAT WITH A TONGUE LIKE THIS...?
OH, WELL...
I WAS GOING TO FIX ALL ITS BAD QUALITIES AND PUT IT BACK TO NORMAL, BUT I GUESS THAT'LL HAVE TO WAIT...
IF IT'S HERBIVOR-OUS, IT COULD EAT FLOWER NECTAR?
A NECTAR-LOVING ANIMAL? I REMEMBER VEN MADE ONE OF THOSE ONCE!
HM? WHICH ONE ARE YOU TALKING ABOUT?
わい GAB
GAB わい
THE HUMMING-BIRD, RIGHT?
...
YES! AND FLOWER NECTAR HAPPENS TO BE EXTREMELY NUTRITIOUS, SO IT WORKS OUT WELL!
IT SOUNDS LIKE THEY'RE ON A ROLL!
THIS KIND OF BRAINSTORM ALWAYS RESULTS IN SOMETHING INTEREST-ING!
SHALL WE HAVE SOME TEA WHILE WE WAIT?
THANK YOU FOR YOUR PATIENCE!
I'D LIKE TO PRESENT A SOLUTION THAT FULFILLS THE REQUIRE-MENTS OF BOTH ORDERS...
"MY ONE AND ONLY CINDERELLA" AND "A LONG FLORAL FRIENDSHIP."

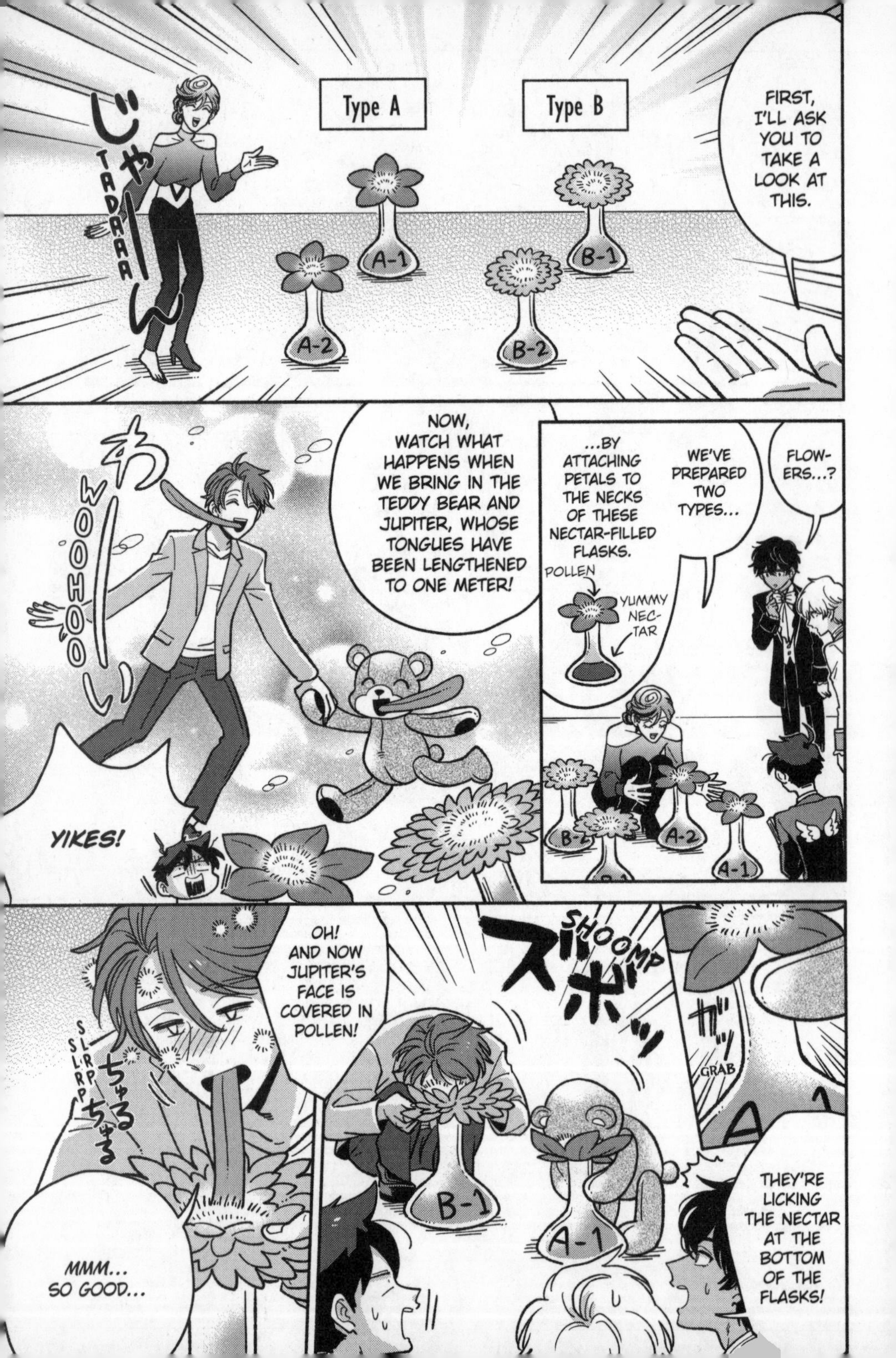
FIRST, I'LL ASK YOU TO TAKE A LOOK AT THIS.
Type B
Type A
B-1
B-2
A-1
A-2
じゃーん
TADAAAA
FLOW-ERS...?
WE'VE PREPARED TWO TYPES...
...BY ATTACHING PETALS TO THE NECKS OF THESE NECTAR-FILLED FLASKS.
POLLEN
YUMMY NEC-TAR
B-2
A-2
A-1
NOW, WATCH WHAT HAPPENS WHEN WE BRING IN THE TEDDY BEAR AND JUPITER, WHOSE TONGUES HAVE BEEN LENGTHENED TO ONE METER!
わーい
WOOHOOO
YIKES!
ガッ
GRAB
THEY'RE LICKING THE NECTAR AT THE BOTTOM OF THE FLASKS!
スポッ
SHOOMP
A-1
B-1
OH! AND NOW JUPITER'S FACE IS COVERED IN POLLEN!
ちゅるちゅる
SLRP SLRP
MMM... SO GOOD...

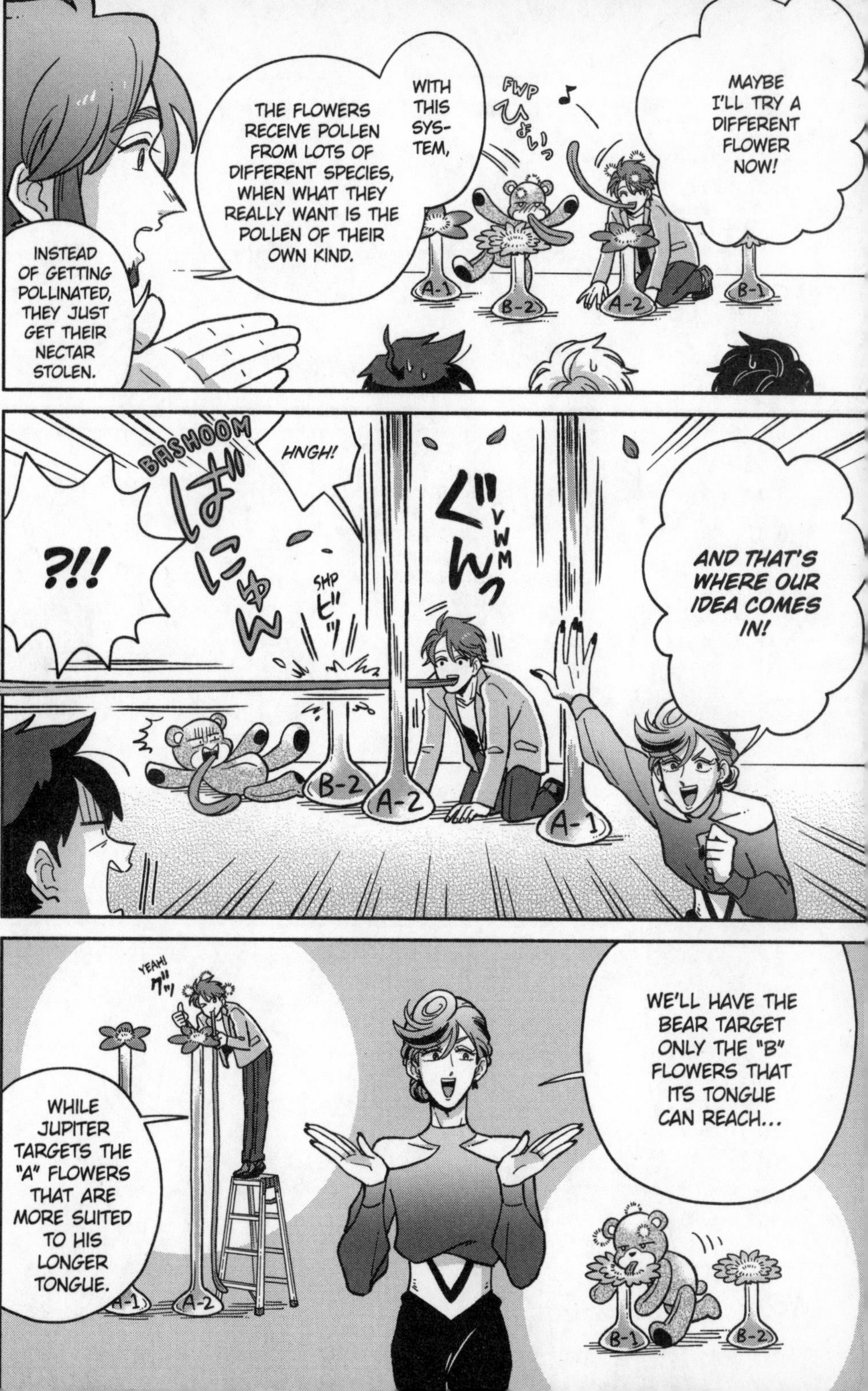
MAYBE I'LL TRY A DIFFERENT FLOWER NOW!
FWP ひょいっ
WITH THIS SYS-TEM,
THE FLOWERS RECEIVE POLLEN FROM LOTS OF DIFFERENT SPECIES, WHEN WHAT THEY REALLY WANT IS THE POLLEN OF THEIR OWN KIND.
INSTEAD OF GETTING POLLINATED, THEY JUST GET THEIR NECTAR STOLEN.
B-1
A-2
B-2
A-1
AND THAT'S WHERE OUR IDEA COMES IN!
VWM ぐいんっ
SHP ビッ
HNGH!
BASHOOM ばにゅん
?!!
A-1
A-2
B-2
WE'LL HAVE THE BEAR TARGET ONLY THE "B" FLOWERS THAT ITS TONGUE CAN REACH...
YEAH! グッ
WHILE JUPITER TARGETS THE "A" FLOWERS THAT ARE MORE SUITED TO HIS LONGER TONGUE.
A-1
A-2
B-1
B-2

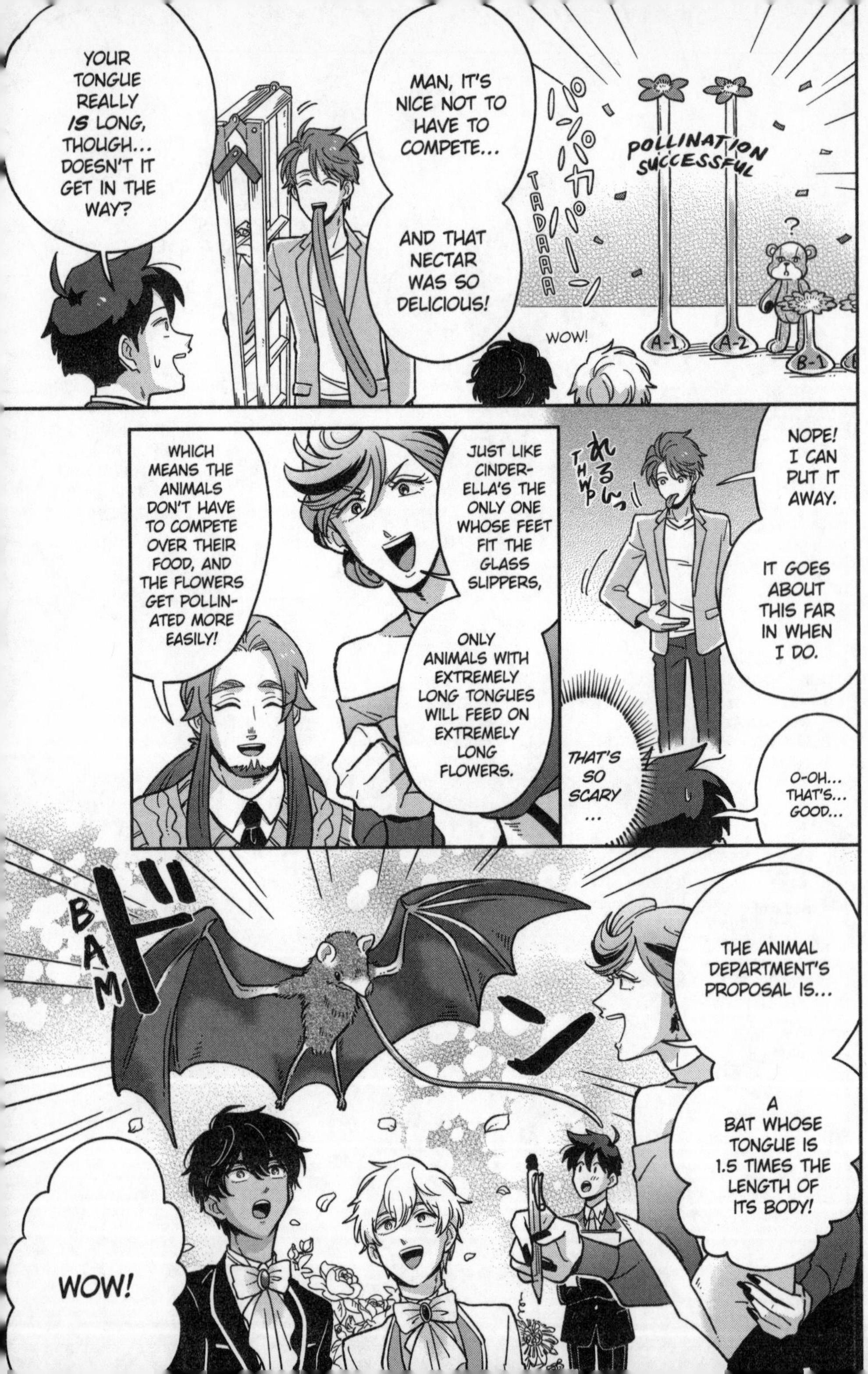
POLLINATION SUCCESSFUL
TADAAAA
WOW!
?
A-1
A-2
B-1
MAN, IT'S NICE NOT TO HAVE TO COMPETE...
AND THAT NECTAR WAS SO DELICIOUS!
YOUR TONGUE REALLY *IS* LONG, THOUGH... DOESN'T IT GET IN THE WAY?
NOPE! I CAN PUT IT AWAY.
IT GOES ABOUT THIS FAR IN WHEN I DO.
THWP
THAT'S SO SCARY...
O-OH... THAT'S... GOOD...
JUST LIKE CINDERELLA'S THE ONLY ONE WHOSE FEET FIT THE GLASS SLIPPERS,
ONLY ANIMALS WITH EXTREMELY LONG TONGUES WILL FEED ON EXTREMELY LONG FLOWERS.
WHICH MEANS THE ANIMALS DON'T HAVE TO COMPETE OVER THEIR FOOD, AND THE FLOWERS GET POLLINATED MORE EASILY!
THE ANIMAL DEPARTMENT'S PROPOSAL IS...
A BAT WHOSE TONGUE IS 1.5 TIMES THE LENGTH OF ITS BODY!
BAM
WOW!

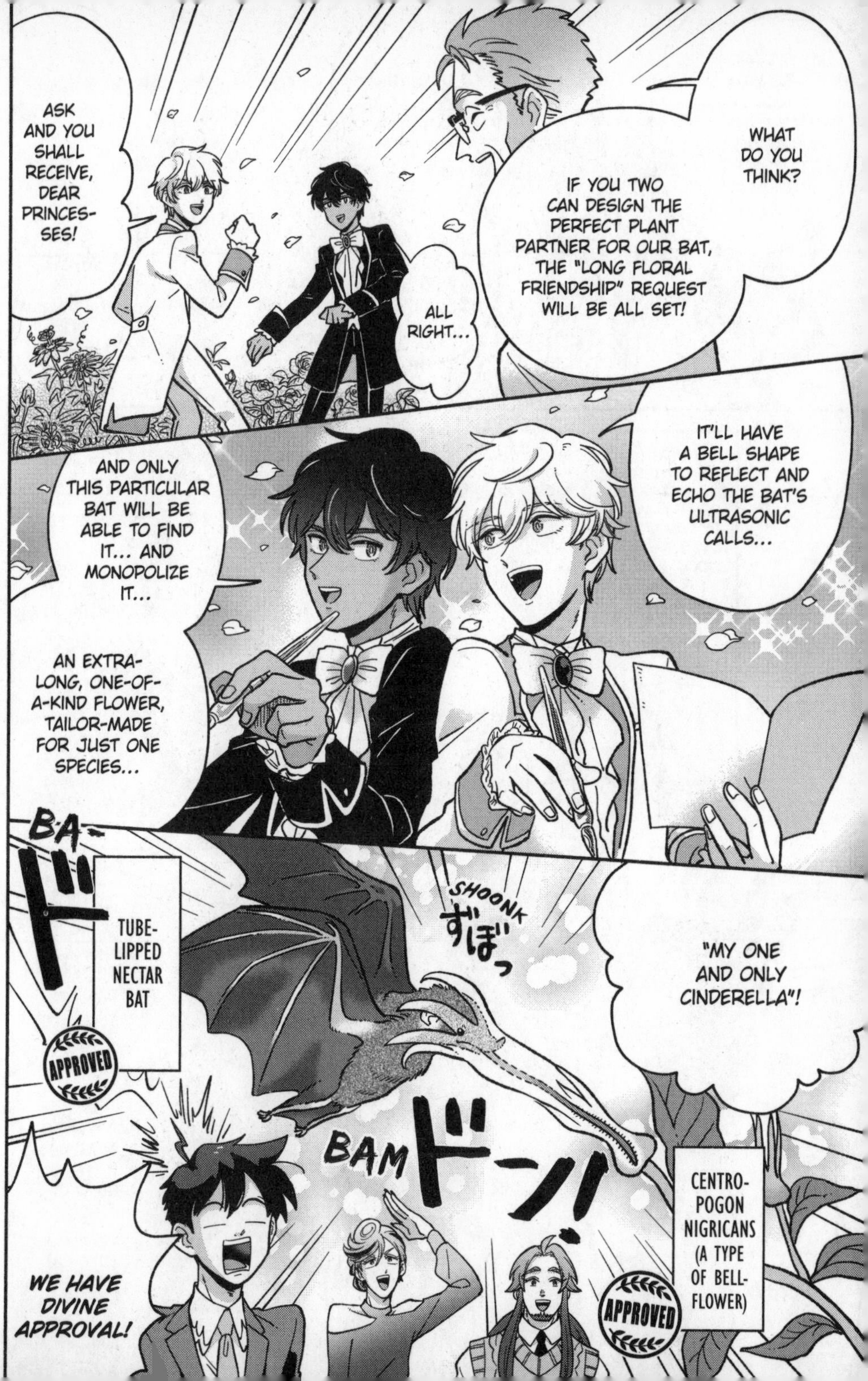
WHAT DO YOU THINK?
IF YOU TWO CAN DESIGN THE PERFECT PLANT PARTNER FOR OUR BAT, THE "LONG FLORAL FRIENDSHIP" REQUEST WILL BE ALL SET!
ALL RIGHT...
ASK AND YOU SHALL RECEIVE, DEAR PRINCES-SES!
IT'LL HAVE A BELL SHAPE TO REFLECT AND ECHO THE BAT'S ULTRASONIC CALLS...
AND ONLY THIS PARTICULAR BAT WILL BE ABLE TO FIND IT... AND MONOPOLIZE IT...
AN EXTRA-LONG, ONE-OF-A-KIND FLOWER, TAILOR-MADE FOR JUST ONE SPECIES...
"MY ONE AND ONLY CINDERELLA"!
SHOONK
ずぼっ
BA-
ド
TUBE-LIPPED NECTAR BAT
APPROVED
BAM
ドーン
CENTRO-POGON NIGRICANS (A TYPE OF BELL-FLOWER)
APPROVED
WE HAVE DIVINE APPROVAL!

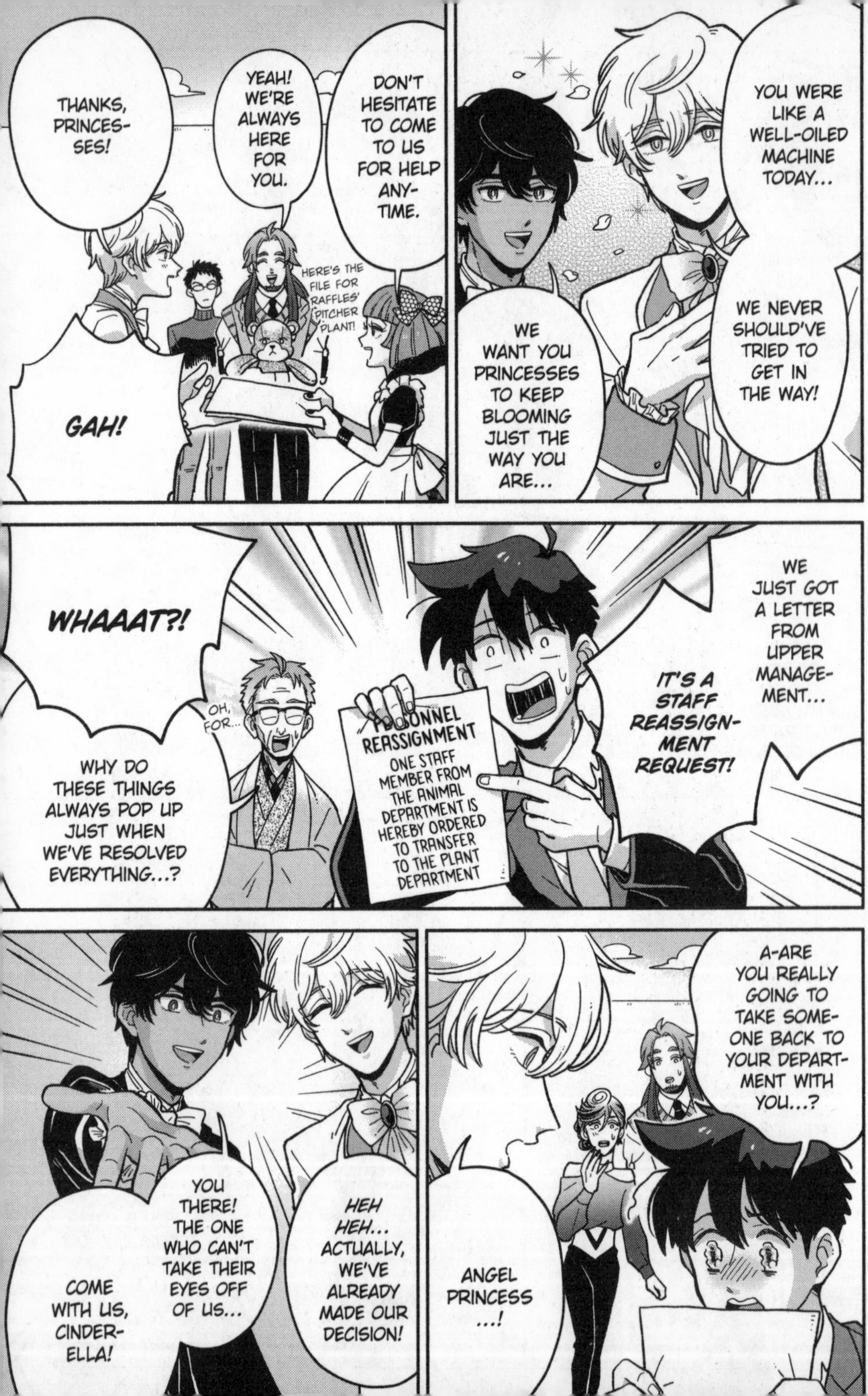
YOU WERE LIKE A WELL-OILED MACHINE TODAY...
WE NEVER SHOULD'VE TRIED TO GET IN THE WAY!
WE WANT YOU PRINCESSES TO KEEP BLOOMING JUST THE WAY YOU ARE...
DON'T HESITATE TO COME TO US FOR HELP ANY-TIME.
YEAH! WE'RE ALWAYS HERE FOR YOU.
THANKS, PRINCESSES!
HERE'S THE FILE FOR RAFFLES' PITCHER PLANT!
GAH!
WE JUST GOT A LETTER FROM UPPER MANAGE-MENT...
IT'S A STAFF REASSIGN-MENT REQUEST!
REASSIGNMENT
ONE STAFF MEMBER FROM THE ANIMAL DEPARTMENT IS HEREBY ORDERED TO TRANSFER TO THE PLANT DEPARTMENT
OH, FOR...
WHAAAT?!
WHY DO THESE THINGS ALWAYS POP UP JUST WHEN WE'VE RESOLVED EVERYTHING...?
A-ARE YOU REALLY GOING TO TAKE SOME-ONE BACK TO YOUR DEPART-MENT WITH YOU...?
ANGEL PRINCESS ...!
HEH HEH... ACTUALLY, WE'VE ALREADY MADE OUR DECISION!
YOU THERE! THE ONE WHO CAN'T TAKE THEIR EYES OFF OF US...
COME WITH US, CINDER-ELLA!

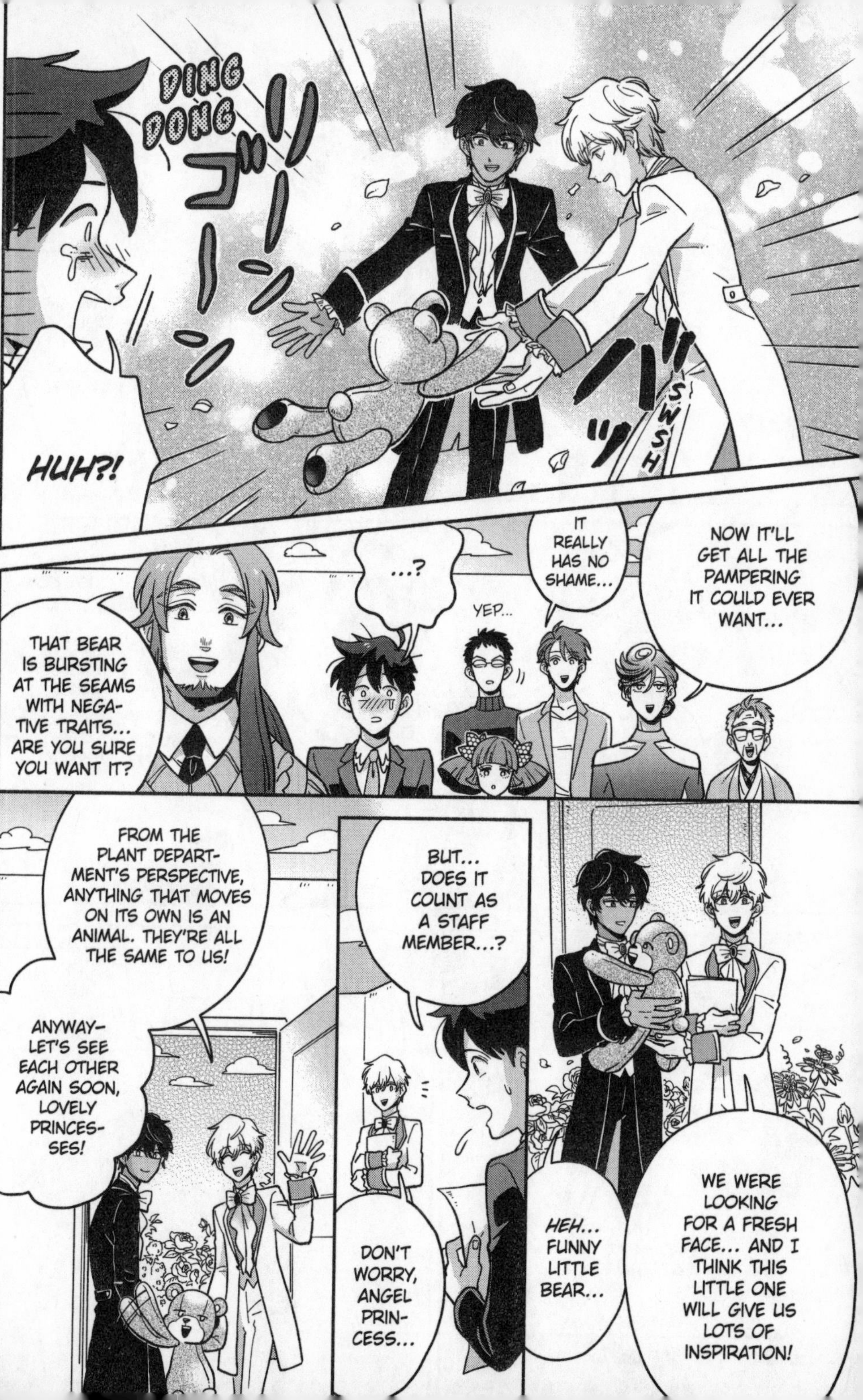
DING DONG
SWSH
HUH?!
NOW IT'LL GET ALL THE PAMPERING IT COULD EVER WANT...
IT REALLY HAS NO SHAME...
YEP...
...?
THAT BEAR IS BURSTING AT THE SEAMS WITH NEGATIVE TRAITS... ARE YOU SURE YOU WANT IT?
WE WERE LOOKING FOR A FRESH FACE... AND I THINK THIS LITTLE ONE WILL GIVE US LOTS OF INSPIRATION!
HEH... FUNNY LITTLE BEAR...
BUT... DOES IT COUNT AS A STAFF MEMBER...?
DON'T WORRY, ANGEL PRINCESS...
FROM THE PLANT DEPARTMENT'S PERSPECTIVE, ANYTHING THAT MOVES ON ITS OWN IS AN ANIMAL. THEY'RE ALL THE SAME TO US!
ANYWAY— LET'S SEE EACH OTHER AGAIN SOON, LOVELY PRINCESSES!

THE ENCYCLOPEDIA OF REAL ANIMALS 36

ANIMAL 85 TUBE-LIPPED NECTAR BAT

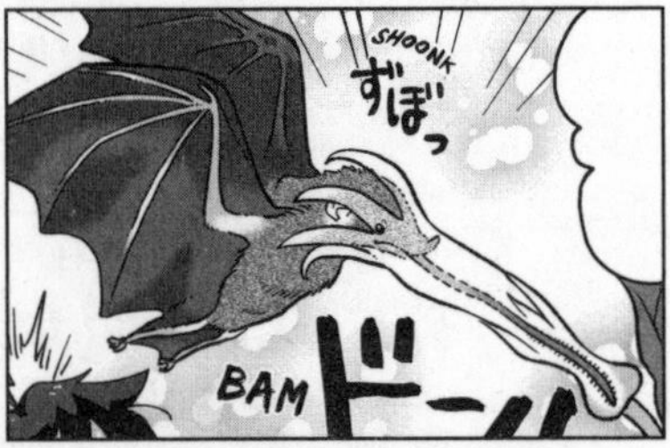
SHOONK
ずぼっ
BAM

THE REAL THING

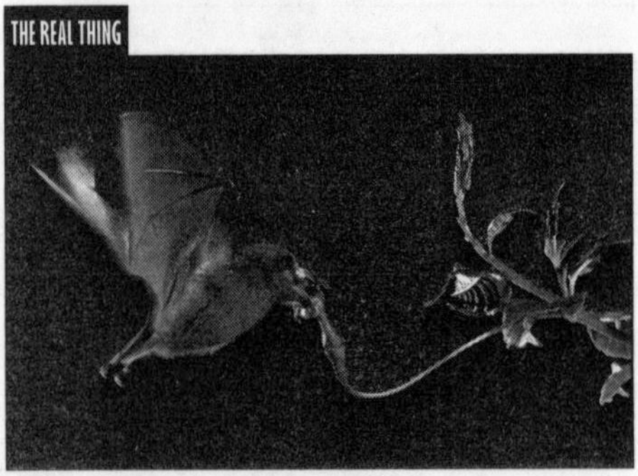

The bat flaps its wings to stay aloft while using its long tongue to lap up the flower's nectar.

Photo: Minden Pictures/Aflo

[Name] *Anoura fistulata*
[Classification] Class: Mammalia
Order: Chiroptera
Family: Phyllostomidae
Genus: *Anoura*
[Habitat] Ecuador
[Length] Approximately 6 cm (2.4 in)

The tube-lipped nectar bat was first discovered in 2005, and is known to have a tongue 1.5 times longer than their body. Its body length only measures approximately six centimeters (2.4 inches), while its tongue can be up to nine centimeters (3.5 inches) long.

Its substantial tongue allows this bat to feed on nectar from *Centropogon nigricans* flowers, which are a type of bellflower that can grow up to eight or nine centimeters (3.1-3.5 inches) long. The tongue is far too large to fit inside the bat's mouth, and must be stored in the rib cage instead.

Like hummingbirds or certain insects, the tube-lipped nectar bat hovers in midair and extends its tongue deep inside the flower to feed. Once it reaches the nectary at the bottom, the bat uses the short growths on the tip of its tongue to efficiently scrape up the nectar. It is believed that *Centropogon nigricans* is pollinated exclusively by this species.

ANIMAL 86 | BLUE PASSIONFLOWER

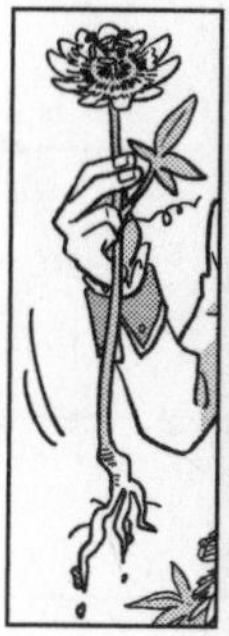

THE REAL THING

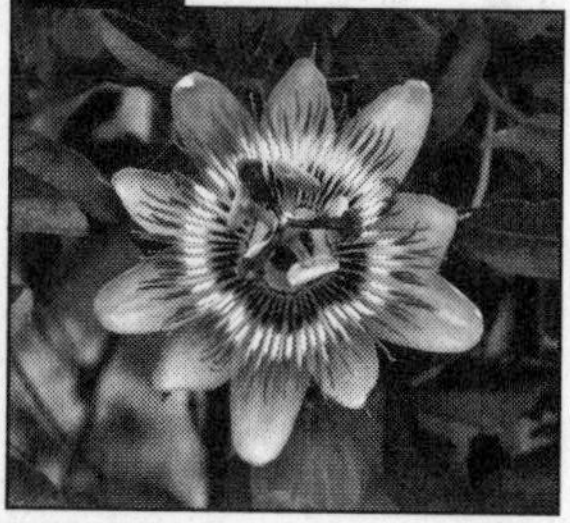

Photo: Aflo

The leaves and stems contain cyanogenic compounds and other toxins.

The blue passionflower has a prominent stamen that juts high above the rest of the plant so that it can sneakily smear its pollen onto the backs of unsuspecting insects. As mentioned in this chapter, certain species of the same family grow leaves with small yellow protrusions at their base that look similar to butterfly eggs. This ingenious defense tactic is meant to trick passing longwings into believing another butterfly has already laid claim to the plant, and thus protects the plant from the insect's larvae, which are immune to the effects of the plant's toxins.

[Name]	*Passiflora caerulea*
[Classification]	Clade: Angiosperms Order: Malpighiales Family: Passifloraceae Genus: *Passiflora*
[Habitat]	Mainly South America
[Height]	More than 3 m (9.8 ft)

SPECIAL FEATURE | THE COEVOLUTION OF PLANTS AND NECTAR-EATING ANIMALS

Animals want to feed on nectar, and plants want their pollen distributed. The animals extend their tongues or proboscises as far as they can to try to feed with minimum effort, but since the plants would prefer the animals to get coated in their pollen, they evolve with their nectaries positioned deep within their flowers. In response, the animals' tongues and proboscises grow even longer… This repeated cycle of reciprocal dependence and rivalry between two species is known as coevolution.

MORGAN'S SPHINX MOTH

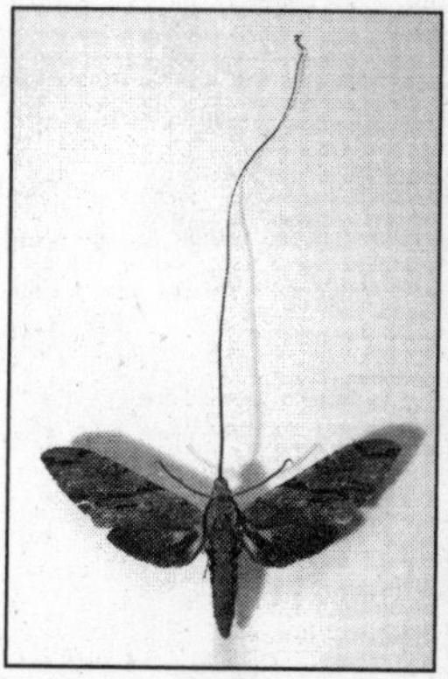

DARWIN'S ORCHID

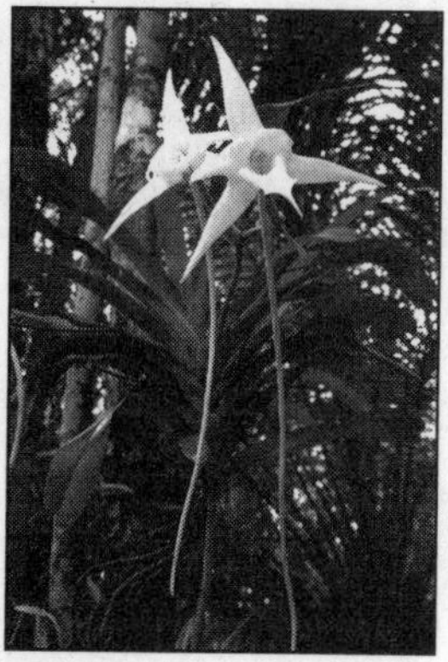

A moth with an extra-long proboscis and an orchid with an extra-long spur.

Photo: Aflo

BEAR'S ORIGINAL FORM

HEAVEN'S DESIGN TEAM

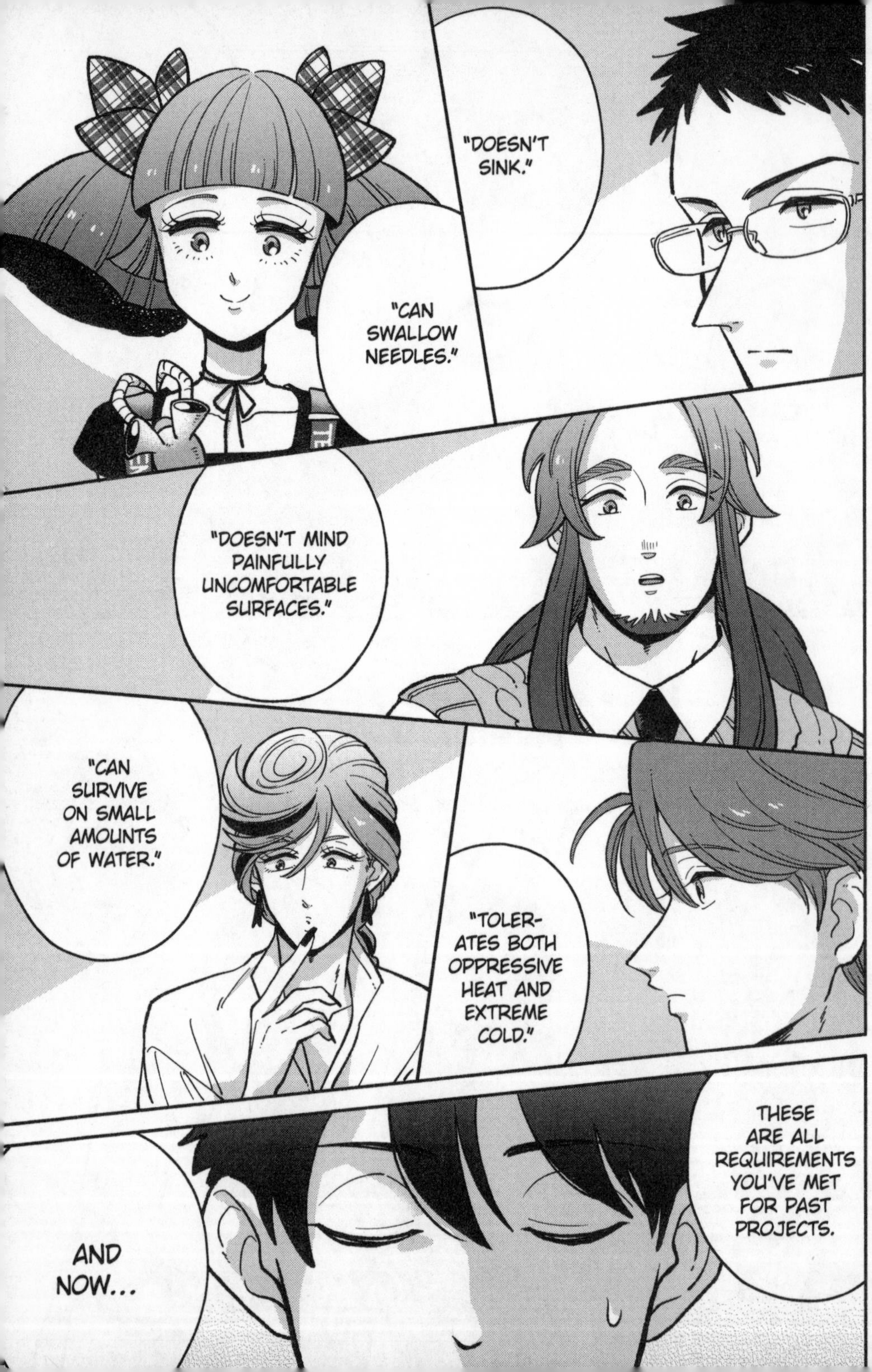
"DOESN'T SINK."
"CAN SWALLOW NEEDLES."
"DOESN'T MIND PAINFULLY UNCOMFORTABLE SURFACES."
"TOLER-ATES BOTH OPPRESSIVE HEAT AND EXTREME COLD."
"CAN SURVIVE ON SMALL AMOUNTS OF WATER."
THESE ARE ALL REQUIREMENTS YOU'VE MET FOR PAST PROJECTS.
AND NOW...

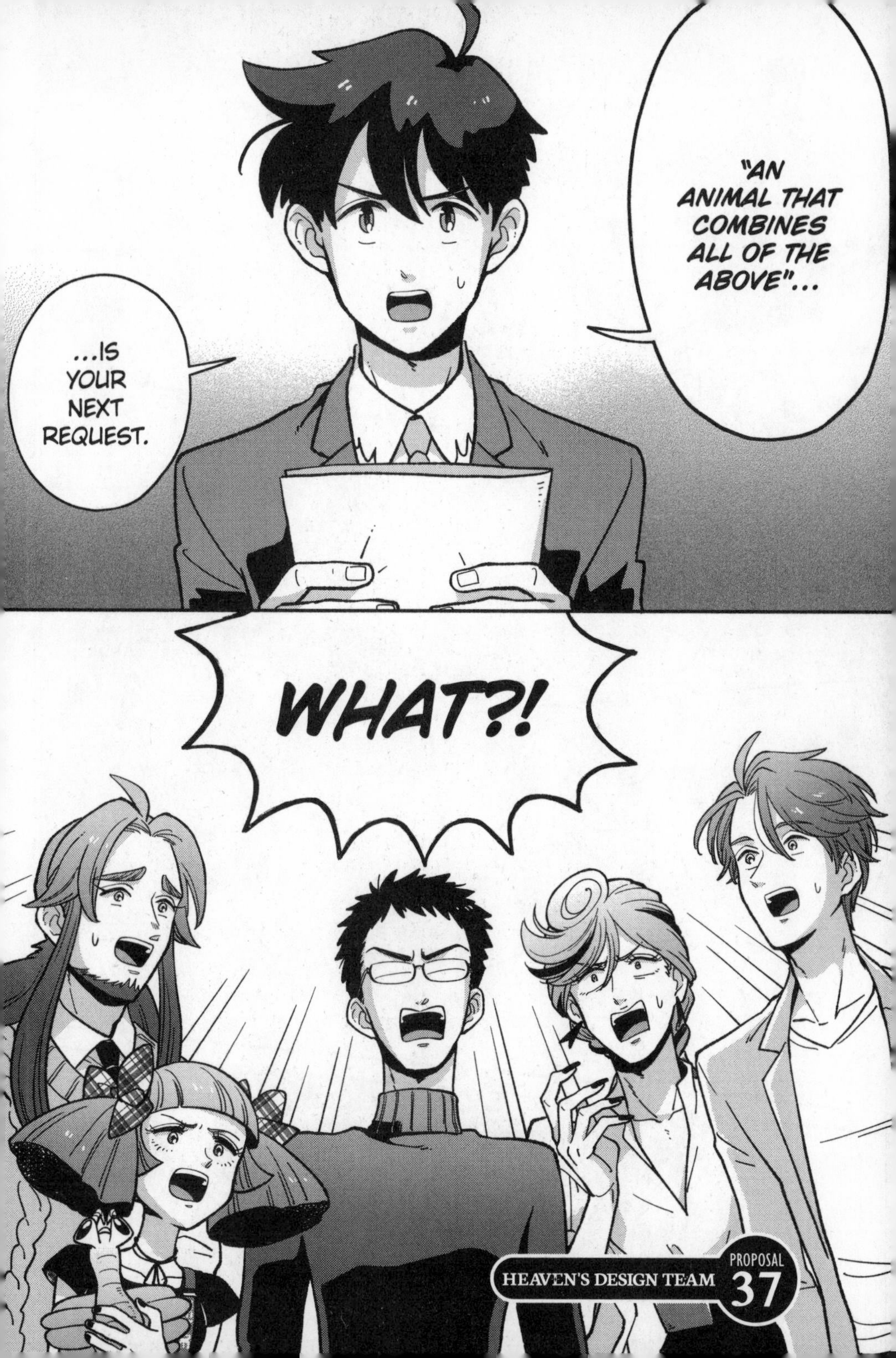
"AN ANIMAL THAT COMBINES ALL OF THE ABOVE"...
...IS YOUR NEXT REQUEST.
WHAT?!
HEAVEN'S DESIGN TEAM
PROPOSAL 37

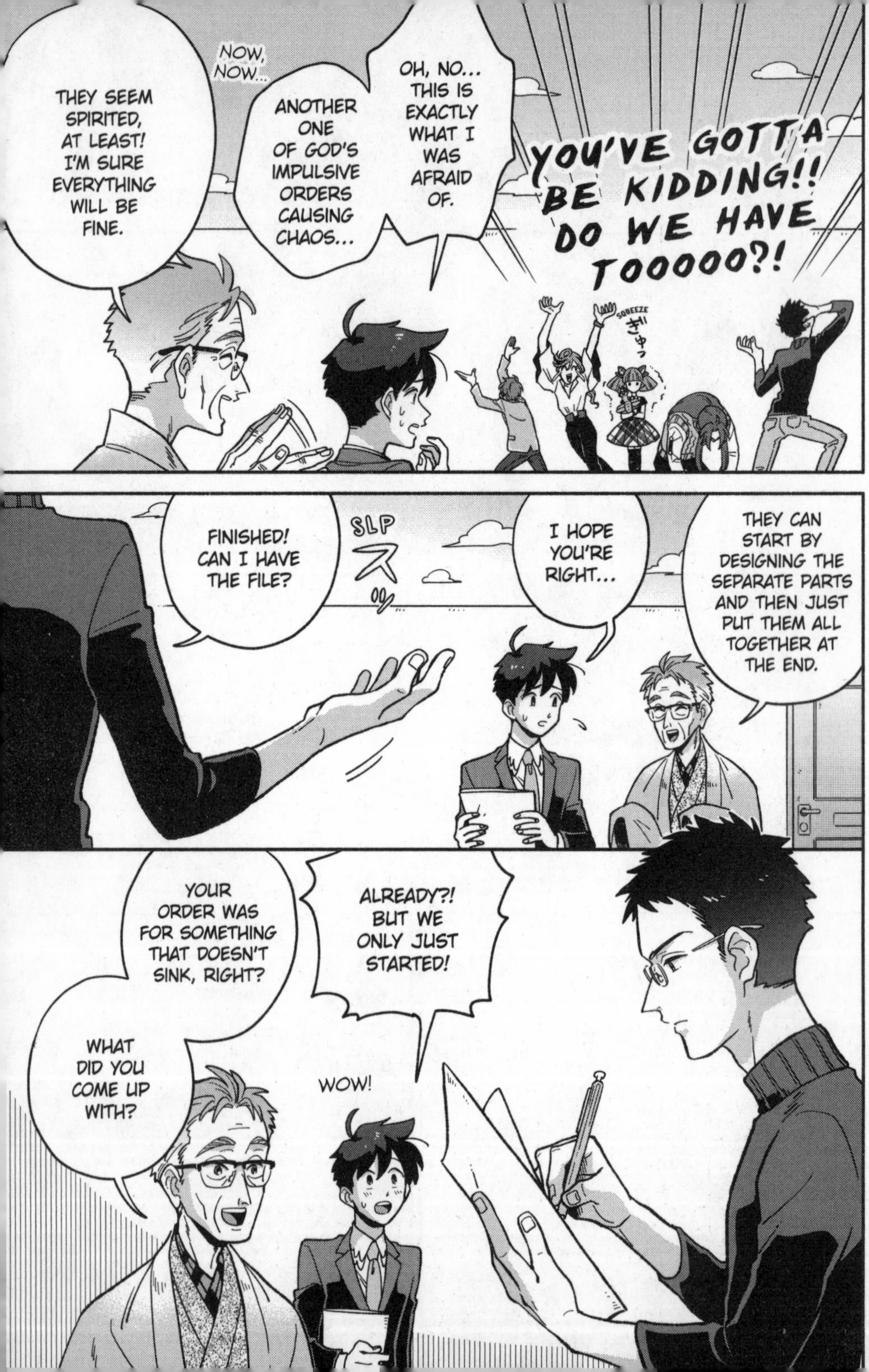
YOU'VE GOTTA BE KIDDING!! DO WE HAVE TOOOOO?!
SQUEEZE
ぎゅっ
OH, NO... THIS IS EXACTLY WHAT I WAS AFRAID OF.
ANOTHER ONE OF GOD'S IMPULSIVE ORDERS CAUSING CHAOS...
NOW, NOW...
THEY SEEM SPIRITED, AT LEAST! I'M SURE EVERYTHING WILL BE FINE.
THEY CAN START BY DESIGNING THE SEPARATE PARTS AND THEN JUST PUT THEM ALL TOGETHER AT THE END.
I HOPE YOU'RE RIGHT...
SLP
ス
FINISHED! CAN I HAVE THE FILE?
ALREADY?! BUT WE ONLY JUST STARTED!
YOUR ORDER WAS FOR SOMETHING THAT DOESN'T SINK, RIGHT?
WOW!
WHAT DID YOU COME UP WITH?

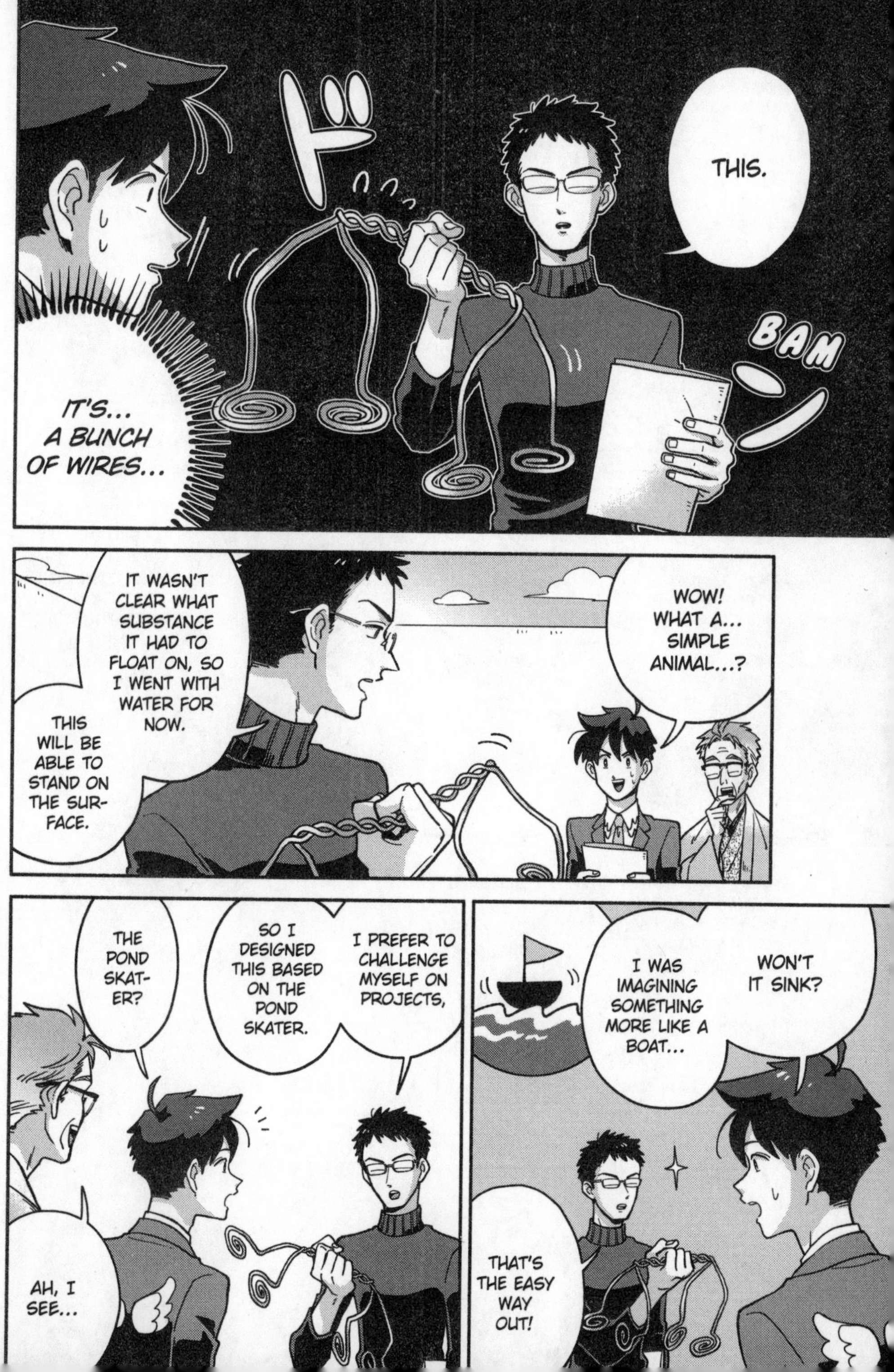
THIS.
BAM
ド
IT'S... A BUNCH OF WIRES...
WOW! WHAT A... SIMPLE ANIMAL...?
IT WASN'T CLEAR WHAT SUBSTANCE IT HAD TO FLOAT ON, SO I WENT WITH WATER FOR NOW.
THIS WILL BE ABLE TO STAND ON THE SURFACE.
WON'T IT SINK?
I WAS IMAGINING SOMETHING MORE LIKE A BOAT...
THAT'S THE EASY WAY OUT!
I PREFER TO CHALLENGE MYSELF ON PROJECTS,
SO I DESIGNED THIS BASED ON THE POND SKATER.
THE POND SKATER?
AH, I SEE...

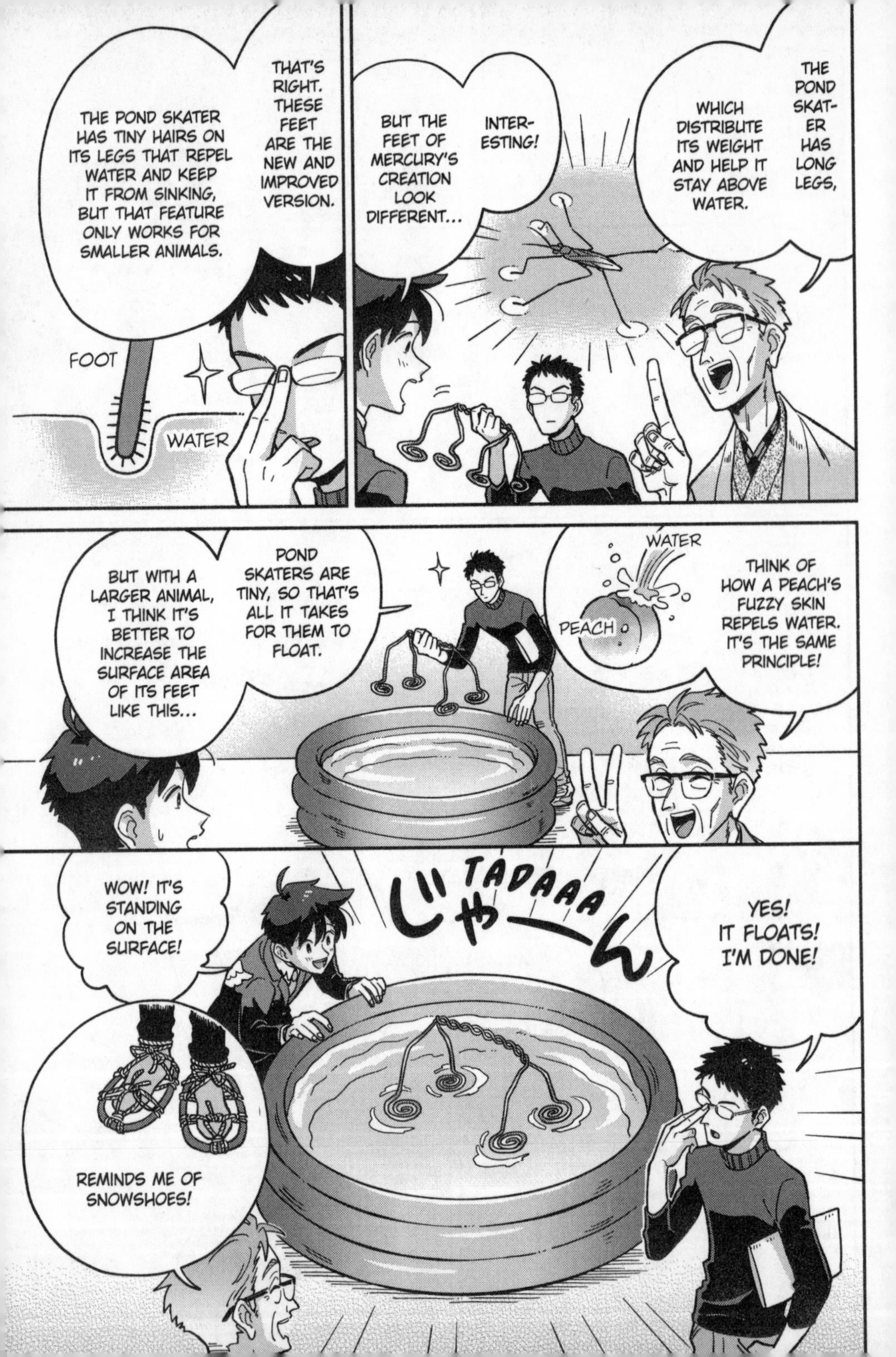
THE POND SKATER HAS LONG LEGS,
WHICH DISTRIBUTE ITS WEIGHT AND HELP IT STAY ABOVE WATER.
INTERESTING!
BUT THE FEET OF MERCURY'S CREATION LOOK DIFFERENT...
THAT'S RIGHT. THESE FEET ARE THE NEW AND IMPROVED VERSION.
THE POND SKATER HAS TINY HAIRS ON ITS LEGS THAT REPEL WATER AND KEEP IT FROM SINKING, BUT THAT FEATURE ONLY WORKS FOR SMALLER ANIMALS.
FOOT
WATER
WATER
PEACH
THINK OF HOW A PEACH'S FUZZY SKIN REPELS WATER. IT'S THE SAME PRINCIPLE!
POND SKATERS ARE TINY, SO THAT'S ALL IT TAKES FOR THEM TO FLOAT.
BUT WITH A LARGER ANIMAL, I THINK IT'S BETTER TO INCREASE THE SURFACE AREA OF ITS FEET LIKE THIS...
YES! IT FLOATS! I'M DONE!
じゃーん
TADAAAA
WOW! IT'S STANDING ON THE SURFACE!
REMINDS ME OF SNOWSHOES!

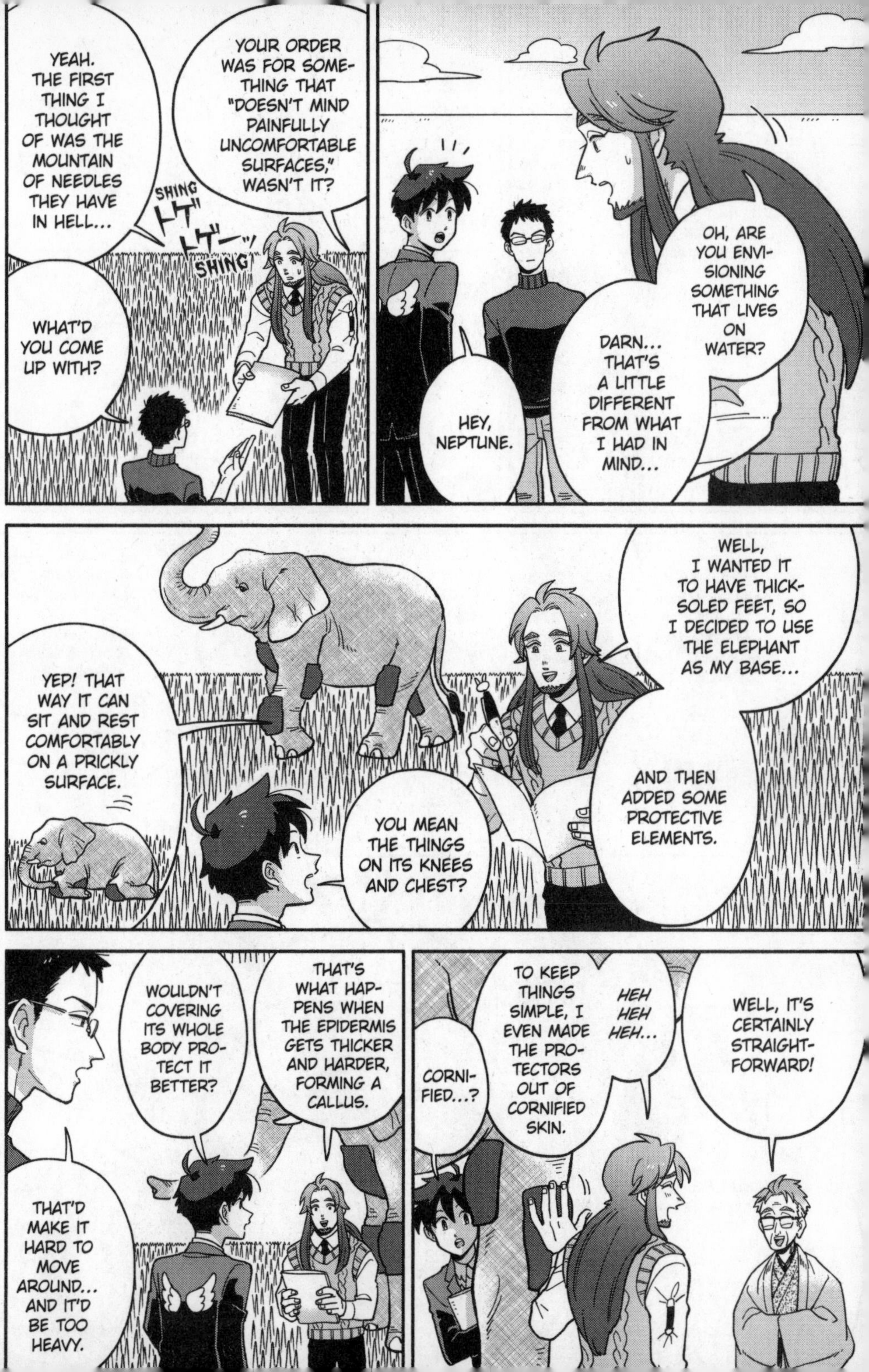
OH, ARE YOU ENVISIONING SOMETHING THAT LIVES ON WATER?
DARN... THAT'S A LITTLE DIFFERENT FROM WHAT I HAD IN MIND...
HEY, NEPTUNE.
YOUR ORDER WAS FOR SOMETHING THAT "DOESN'T MIND PAINFULLY UNCOMFORTABLE SURFACES," WASN'T IT?
YEAH. THE FIRST THING I THOUGHT OF WAS THE MOUNTAIN OF NEEDLES THEY HAVE IN HELL...
SHING トゲ
トゲーッ SHING
WHAT'D YOU COME UP WITH?
WELL, I WANTED IT TO HAVE THICK-SOLED FEET, SO I DECIDED TO USE THE ELEPHANT AS MY BASE...
AND THEN ADDED SOME PROTECTIVE ELEMENTS.
YOU MEAN THE THINGS ON ITS KNEES AND CHEST?
YEP! THAT WAY IT CAN SIT AND REST COMFORTABLY ON A PRICKLY SURFACE.
WELL, IT'S CERTAINLY STRAIGHTFORWARD!
HEH HEH HEH...
TO KEEP THINGS SIMPLE, I EVEN MADE THE PROTECTORS OUT OF CORNIFIED SKIN.
CORNIFIED...?
THAT'S WHAT HAPPENS WHEN THE EPIDERMIS GETS THICKER AND HARDER, FORMING A CALLUS.
WOULDN'T COVERING ITS WHOLE BODY PROTECT IT BETTER?
THAT'D MAKE IT HARD TO MOVE AROUND... AND IT'D BE TOO HEAVY.

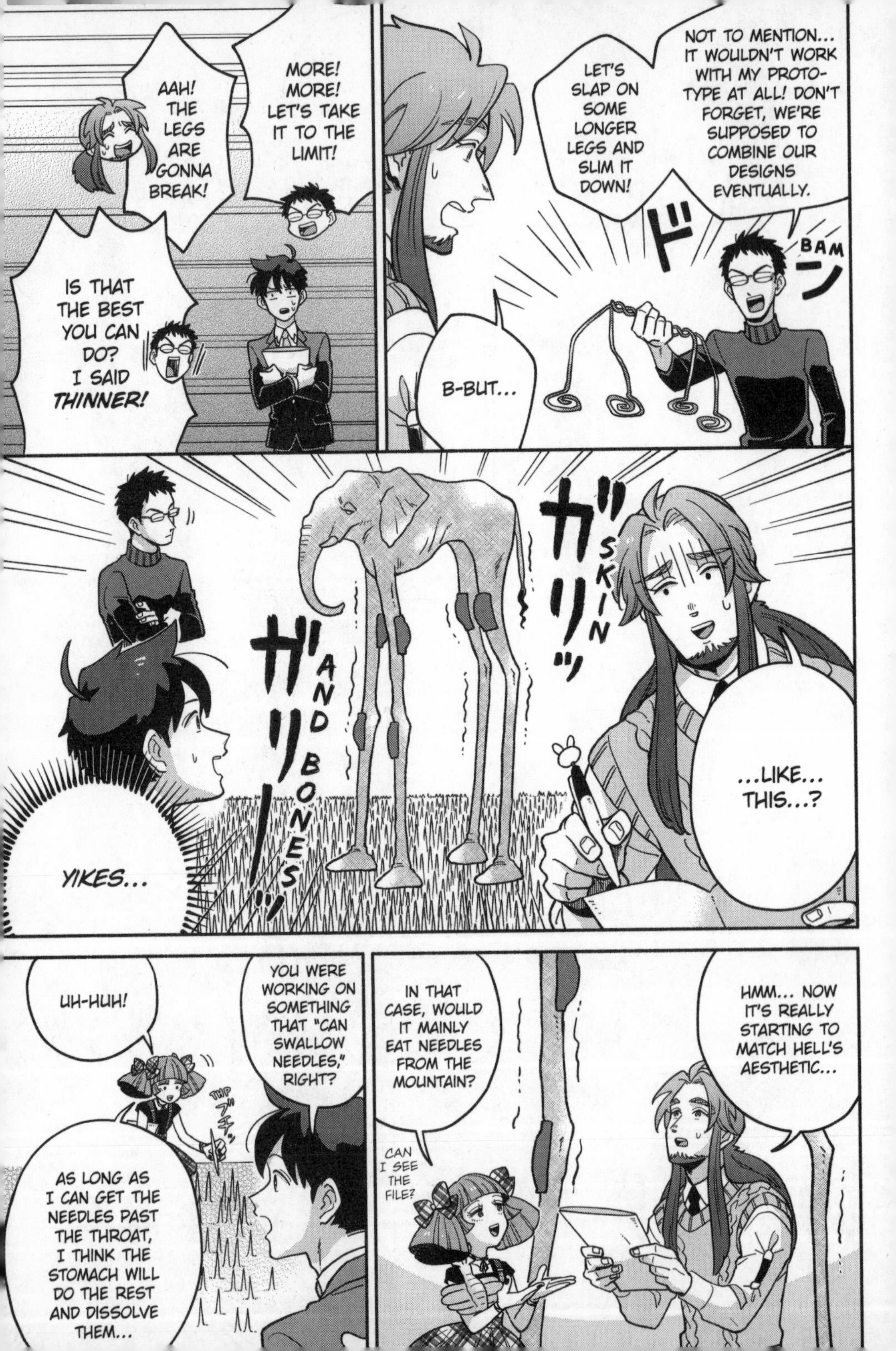

NOT TO MENTION... IT WOULDN'T WORK WITH MY PROTO-TYPE AT ALL! DON'T FORGET, WE'RE SUPPOSED TO COMBINE OUR DESIGNS EVENTUALLY.
LET'S SLAP ON SOME LONGER LEGS AND SLIM IT DOWN!
ドン
BAM
B-BUT...
MORE! MORE! LET'S TAKE IT TO THE LIMIT!
AAH! THE LEGS ARE GONNA BREAK!
IS THAT THE BEST YOU CAN DO? I SAID THINNER!
...LIKE... THIS...?
ガリッ
SKIN
ガリ
AND BONES
YIKES...
HMM... NOW IT'S REALLY STARTING TO MATCH HELL'S AESTHETIC...
IN THAT CASE, WOULD IT MAINLY EAT NEEDLES FROM THE MOUNTAIN?
CAN I SEE THE FILE?
YOU WERE WORKING ON SOMETHING THAT "CAN SWALLOW NEEDLES," RIGHT?
UH-HUH!
THP
AS LONG AS I CAN GET THE NEEDLES PAST THE THROAT, I THINK THE STOMACH WILL DO THE REST AND DISSOLVE THEM...

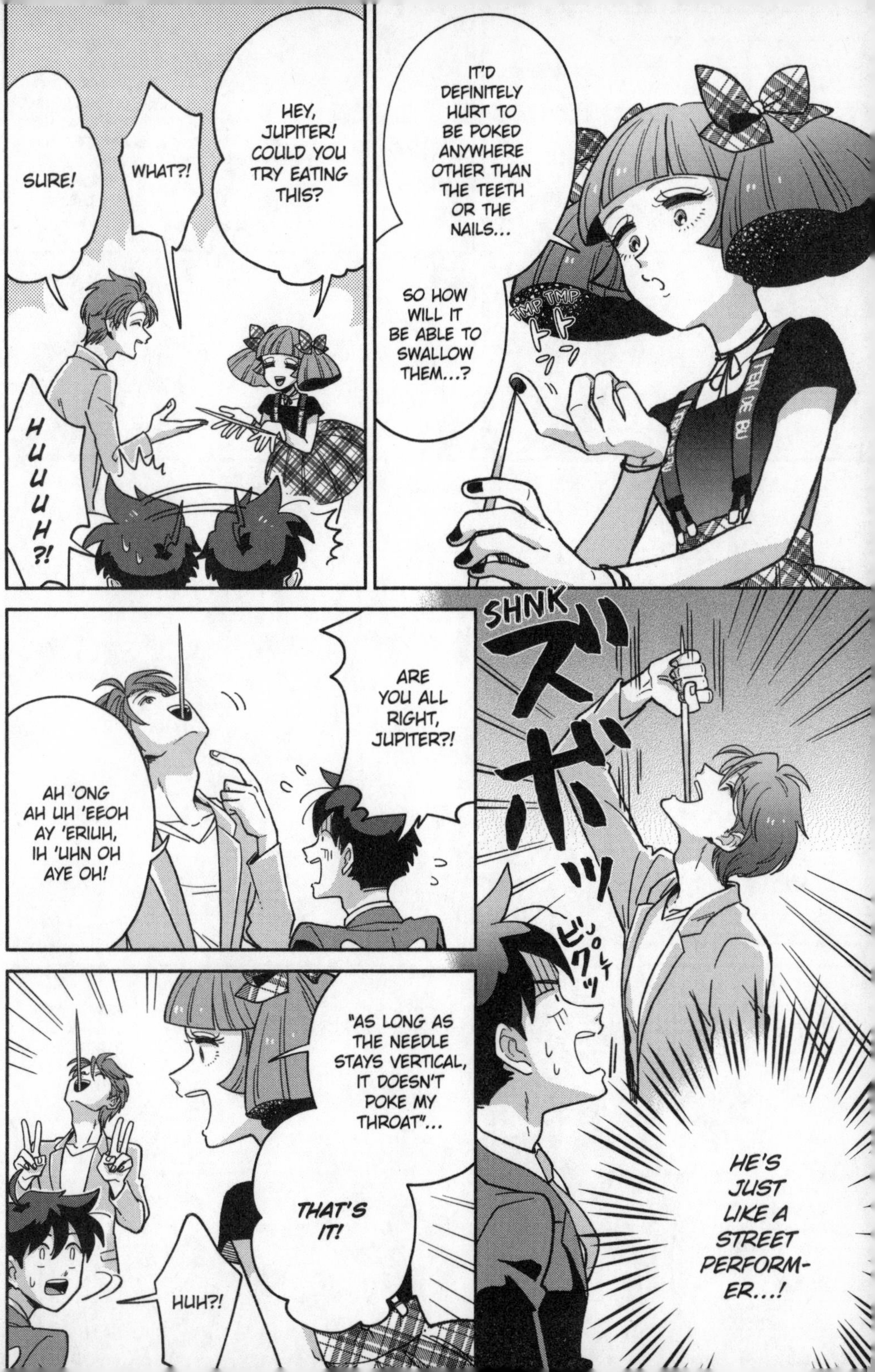
IT'D DEFINITELY HURT TO BE POKED ANYWHERE OTHER THAN THE TEETH OR THE NAILS...
TMP TMP
SO HOW WILL IT BE ABLE TO SWALLOW THEM...?
HEY, JUPITER! COULD YOU TRY EATING THIS?
WHAT?!
SURE!
HUUUUH?!
SHNK
JOLT
HE'S JUST LIKE A STREET PERFORMER...!
ARE YOU ALL RIGHT, JUPITER?!
AH 'ONG AH UH 'EEOH AY 'ERIUH, IH 'UHN OH AYE OH!
"AS LONG AS THE NEEDLE STAYS VERTICAL, IT DOESN'T POKE MY THROAT"...
THAT'S IT!
HUH?!

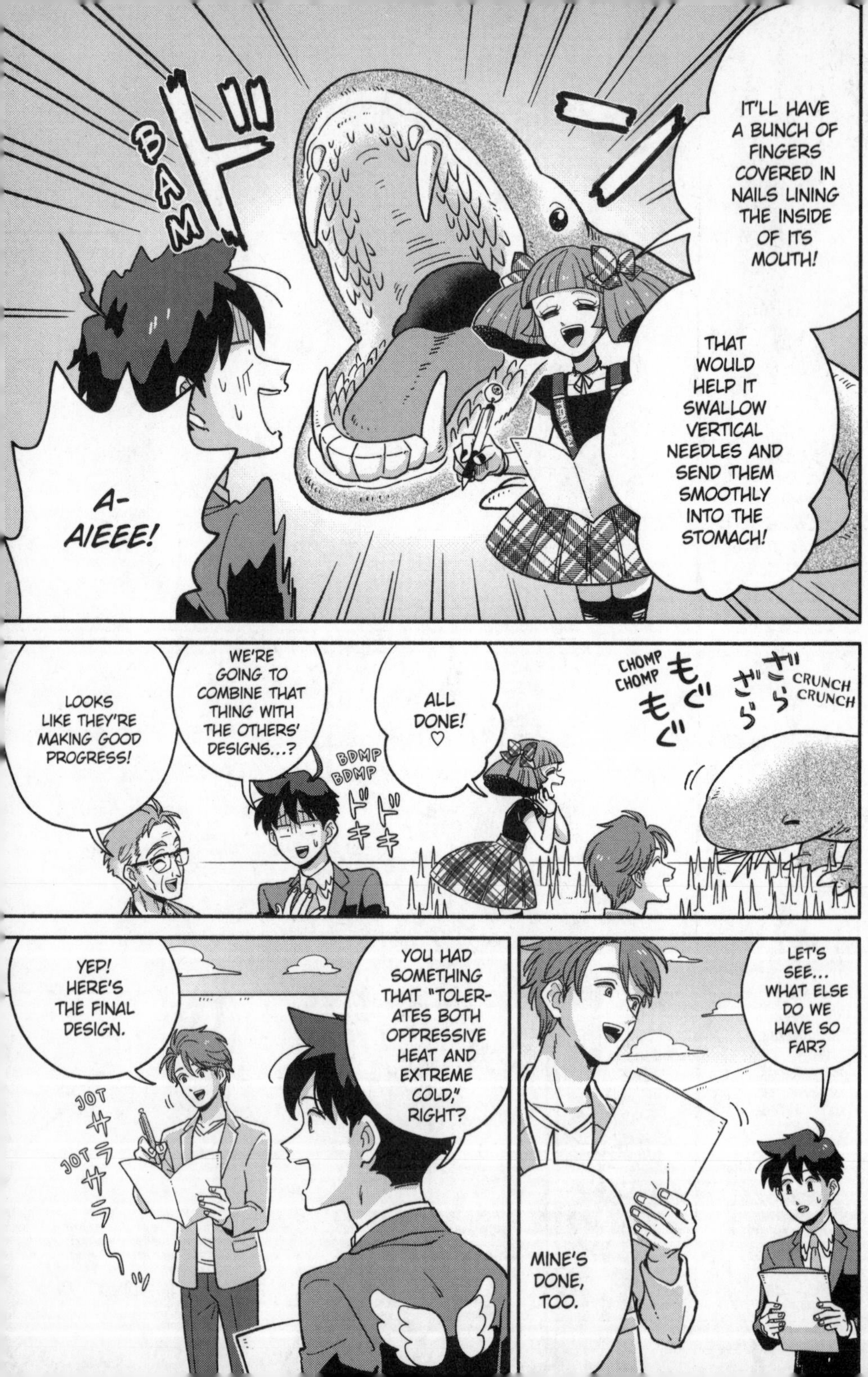
IT'LL HAVE A BUNCH OF FINGERS COVERED IN NAILS LINING THE INSIDE OF ITS MOUTH!
THAT WOULD HELP IT SWALLOW VERTICAL NEEDLES AND SEND THEM SMOOTHLY INTO THE STOMACH!
BAM
A-AIEEE!
CRUNCH CRUNCH
ざらざら
CHOMP CHOMP
もぐもぐ
ALL DONE! ♡
BDMP BDMP
ドキドキ
WE'RE GOING TO COMBINE THAT THING WITH THE OTHERS' DESIGNS...?
LOOKS LIKE THEY'RE MAKING GOOD PROGRESS!
LET'S SEE... WHAT ELSE DO WE HAVE SO FAR?
MINE'S DONE, TOO.
YOU HAD SOMETHING THAT "TOLERATES BOTH OPPRESSIVE HEAT AND EXTREME COLD," RIGHT?
YEP! HERE'S THE FINAL DESIGN.
JOT JOT
サラサラ〜ッ

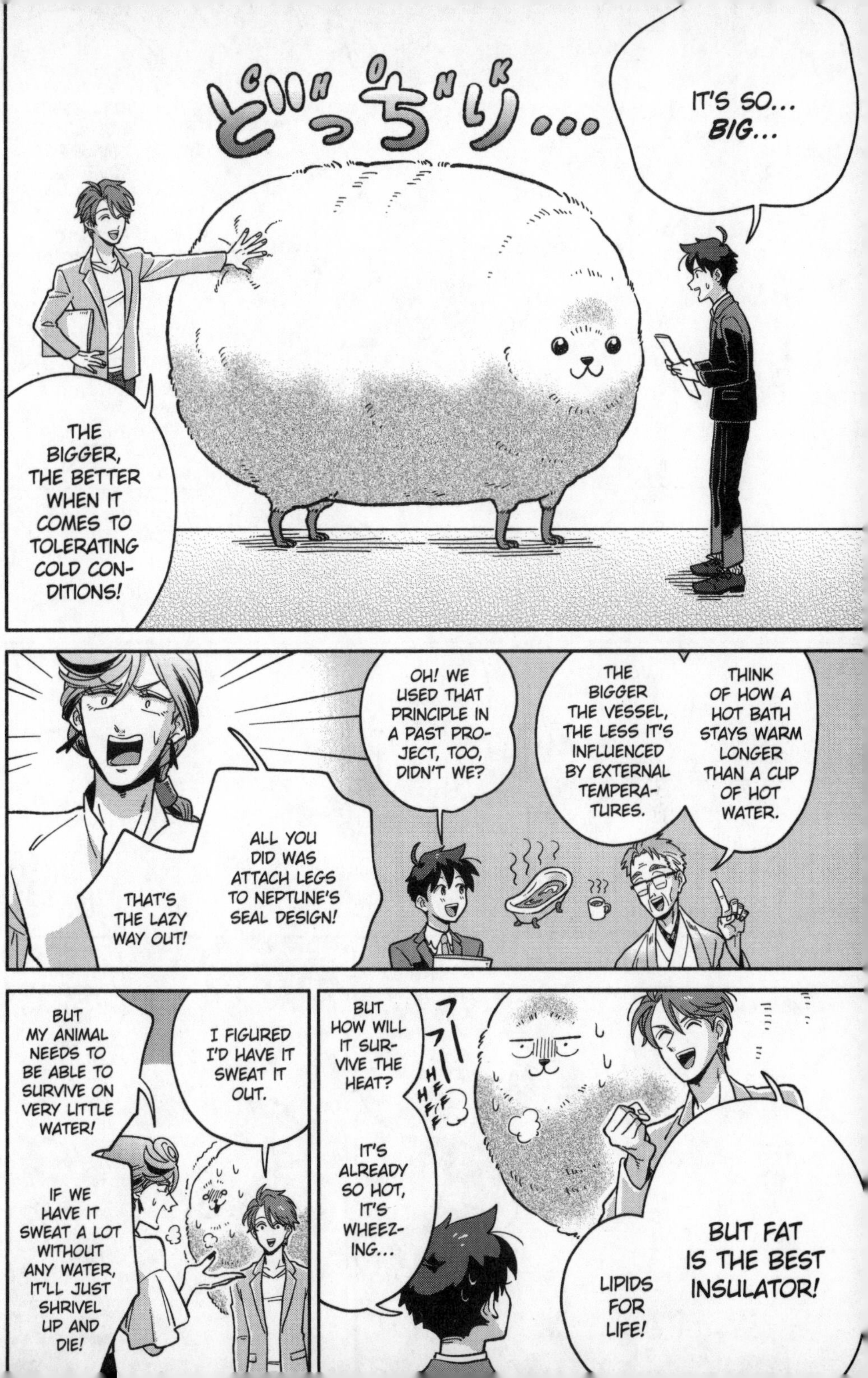
CHONK...
IT'S SO... *BIG*...
THE BIGGER, THE BETTER WHEN IT COMES TO TOLERATING COLD CON-DITIONS!
THINK OF HOW A HOT BATH STAYS WARM LONGER THAN A CUP OF HOT WATER.
THE BIGGER THE VESSEL, THE LESS IT'S INFLUENCED BY EXTERNAL TEMPERA-TURES.
OH! WE USED THAT PRINCIPLE IN A PAST PRO-JECT, TOO, DIDN'T WE?
ALL YOU DID WAS ATTACH LEGS TO NEPTUNE'S SEAL DESIGN!
THAT'S THE LAZY WAY OUT!
HFF HFF
BUT HOW WILL IT SUR-VIVE THE HEAT?
IT'S ALREADY SO HOT, IT'S WHEEZ-ING...
BUT FAT IS THE BEST INSULATOR!
LIPIDS FOR LIFE!
I FIGURED I'D HAVE IT SWEAT IT OUT.
BUT MY ANIMAL NEEDS TO BE ABLE TO SURVIVE ON VERY LITTLE WATER!
IF WE HAVE IT SWEAT A LOT WITHOUT ANY WATER, IT'LL JUST SHRIVEL UP AND DIE!

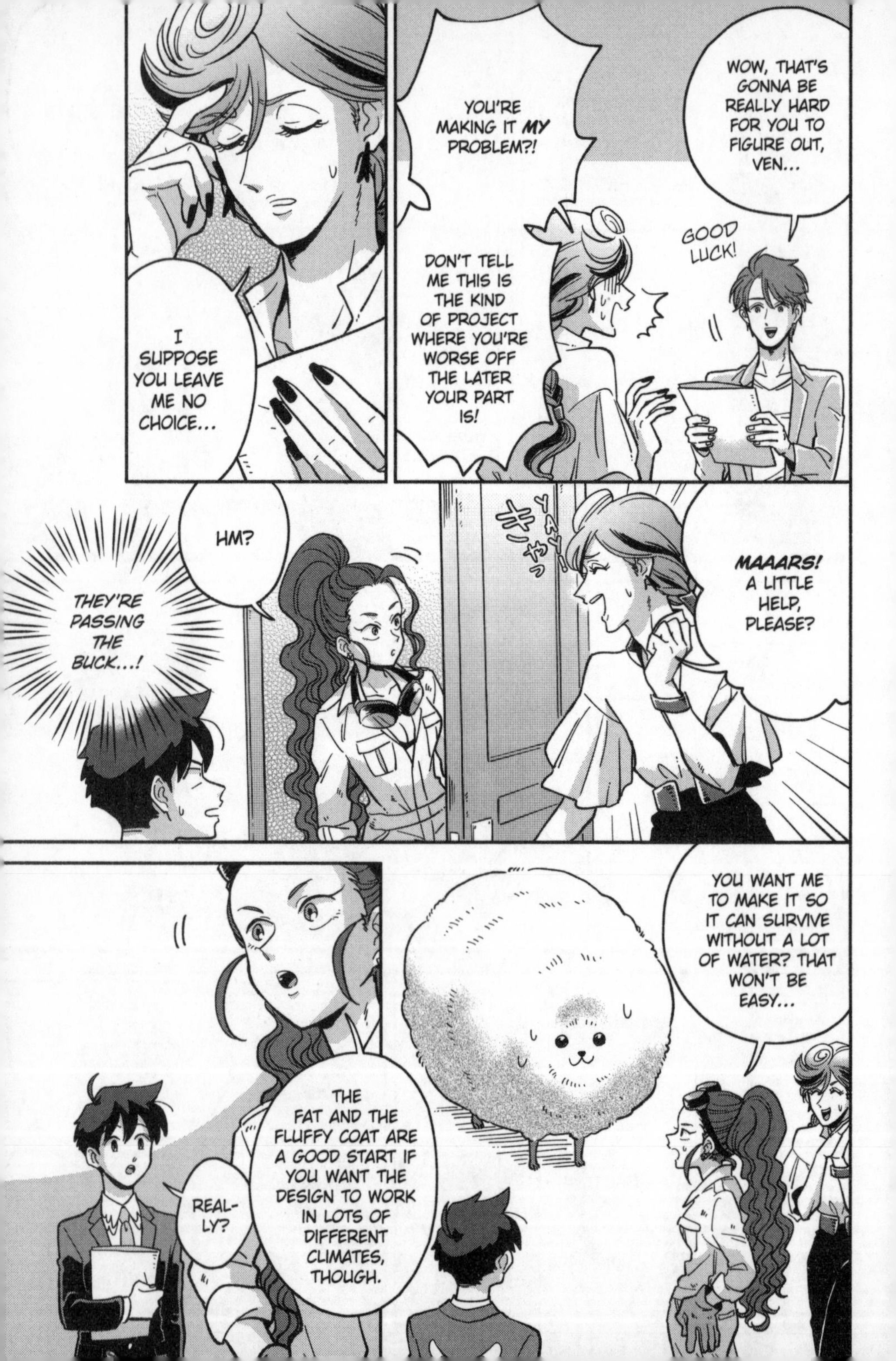
WOW, THAT'S GONNA BE REALLY HARD FOR YOU TO FIGURE OUT, VEN...
GOOD LUCK!
YOU'RE MAKING IT **MY** PROBLEM?!
DON'T TELL ME THIS IS THE KIND OF PROJECT WHERE YOU'RE WORSE OFF THE LATER YOUR PART IS!
I SUPPOSE YOU LEAVE ME NO CHOICE...
MAAARS! A LITTLE HELP, PLEASE?
YAY!
HM?
THEY'RE PASSING THE BUCK...!
YOU WANT ME TO MAKE IT SO IT CAN SURVIVE WITHOUT A LOT OF WATER? THAT WON'T BE EASY...
THE FAT AND THE FLUFFY COAT ARE A GOOD START IF YOU WANT THE DESIGN TO WORK IN LOTS OF DIFFERENT CLIMATES, THOUGH.
REAL-LY?

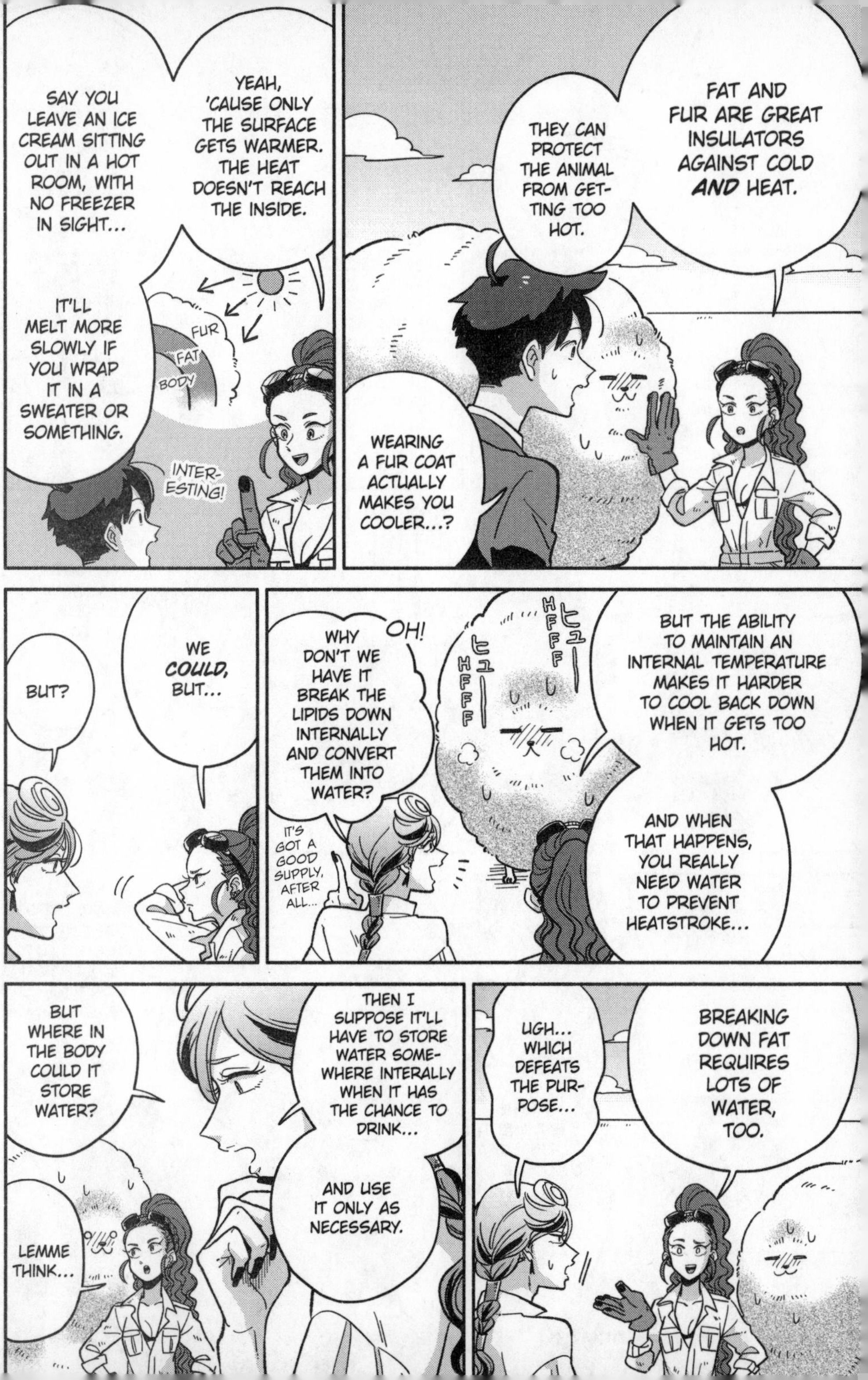
FAT AND FUR ARE GREAT INSULATORS AGAINST COLD AND HEAT.
THEY CAN PROTECT THE ANIMAL FROM GET-TING TOO HOT.
WEARING A FUR COAT ACTUALLY MAKES YOU COOLER...?
YEAH, 'CAUSE ONLY THE SURFACE GETS WARMER. THE HEAT DOESN'T REACH THE INSIDE.
SAY YOU LEAVE AN ICE CREAM SITTING OUT IN A HOT ROOM, WITH NO FREEZER IN SIGHT...
FUR
FAT
BODY
IT'LL MELT MORE SLOWLY IF YOU WRAP IT IN A SWEATER OR SOMETHING.
INTER-ESTING!
BUT THE ABILITY TO MAINTAIN AN INTERNAL TEMPERATURE MAKES IT HARDER TO COOL BACK DOWN WHEN IT GETS TOO HOT.
ヒュー HFFF
ヒュー HFFF
AND WHEN THAT HAPPENS, YOU REALLY NEED WATER TO PREVENT HEATSTROKE...
OH!
WHY DON'T WE HAVE IT BREAK THE LIPIDS DOWN INTERNALLY AND CONVERT THEM INTO WATER?
IT'S GOT A GOOD SUPPLY, AFTER ALL...
WE COULD, BUT...
BUT?
BREAKING DOWN FAT REQUIRES LOTS OF WATER, TOO.
UGH... WHICH DEFEATS THE PUR-POSE...
THEN I SUPPOSE IT'LL HAVE TO STORE WATER SOME-WHERE INTERALLY WHEN IT HAS THE CHANCE TO DRINK...
AND USE IT ONLY AS NECESSARY.
BUT WHERE IN THE BODY COULD IT STORE WATER?
LEMME THINK...

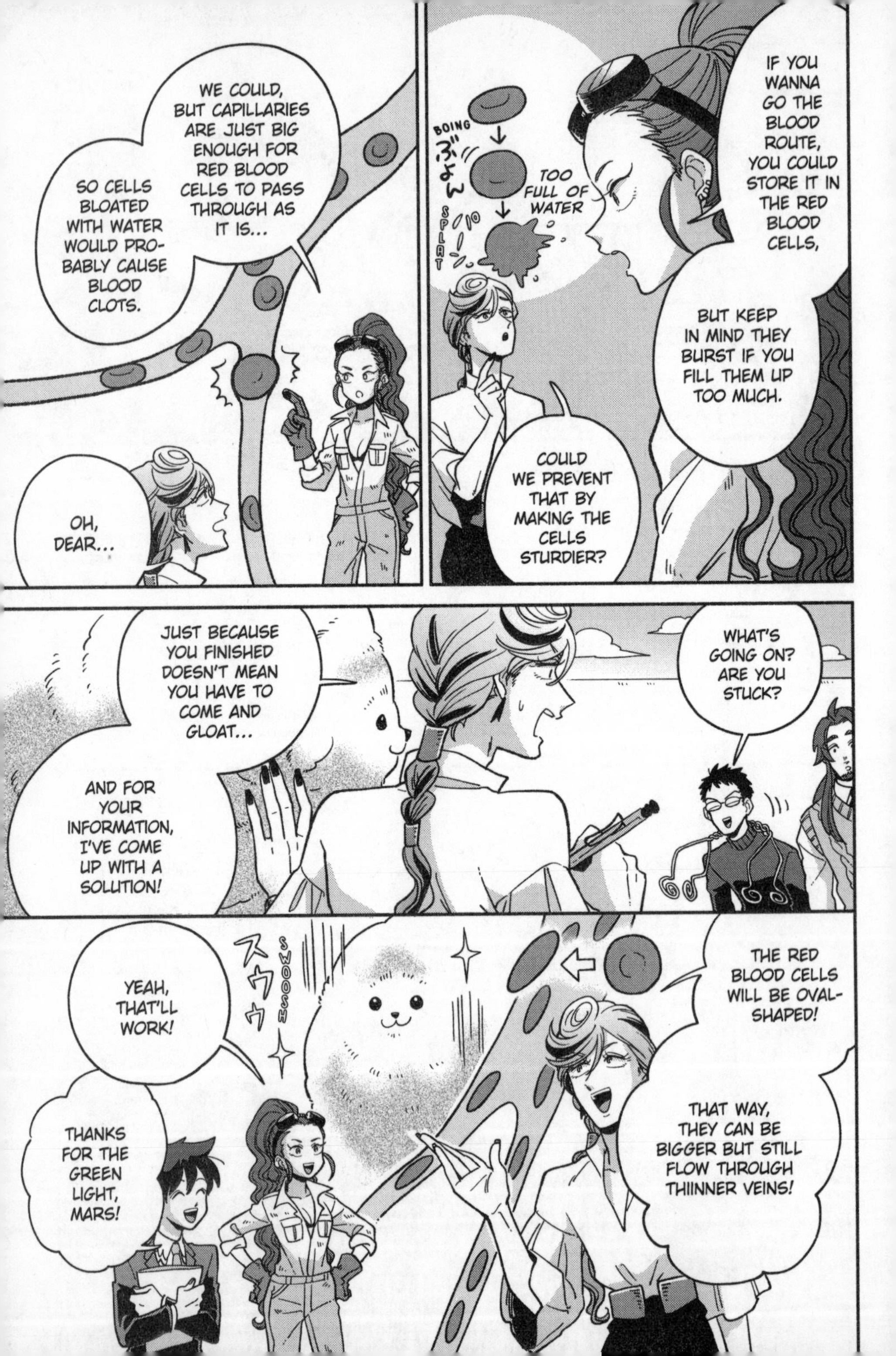
IF YOU WANNA GO THE BLOOD ROUTE, YOU COULD STORE IT IN THE RED BLOOD CELLS,
BOING
ぶよん
TOO FULL OF WATER
SPLAT
BUT KEEP IN MIND THEY BURST IF YOU FILL THEM UP TOO MUCH.
COULD WE PREVENT THAT BY MAKING THE CELLS STURDIER?
WE COULD, BUT CAPILLARIES ARE JUST BIG ENOUGH FOR RED BLOOD CELLS TO PASS THROUGH AS IT IS...
SO CELLS BLOATED WITH WATER WOULD PROBABLY CAUSE BLOOD CLOTS.
OH, DEAR...
WHAT'S GOING ON? ARE YOU STUCK?
JUST BECAUSE YOU FINISHED DOESN'T MEAN YOU HAVE TO COME AND GLOAT...
AND FOR YOUR INFORMATION, I'VE COME UP WITH A SOLUTION!
THE RED BLOOD CELLS WILL BE OVAL-SHAPED!
THAT WAY, THEY CAN BE BIGGER BUT STILL FLOW THROUGH THIINNER VEINS!
スウゥ
SWOOSH
YEAH, THAT'LL WORK!
THANKS FOR THE GREEN LIGHT, MARS!

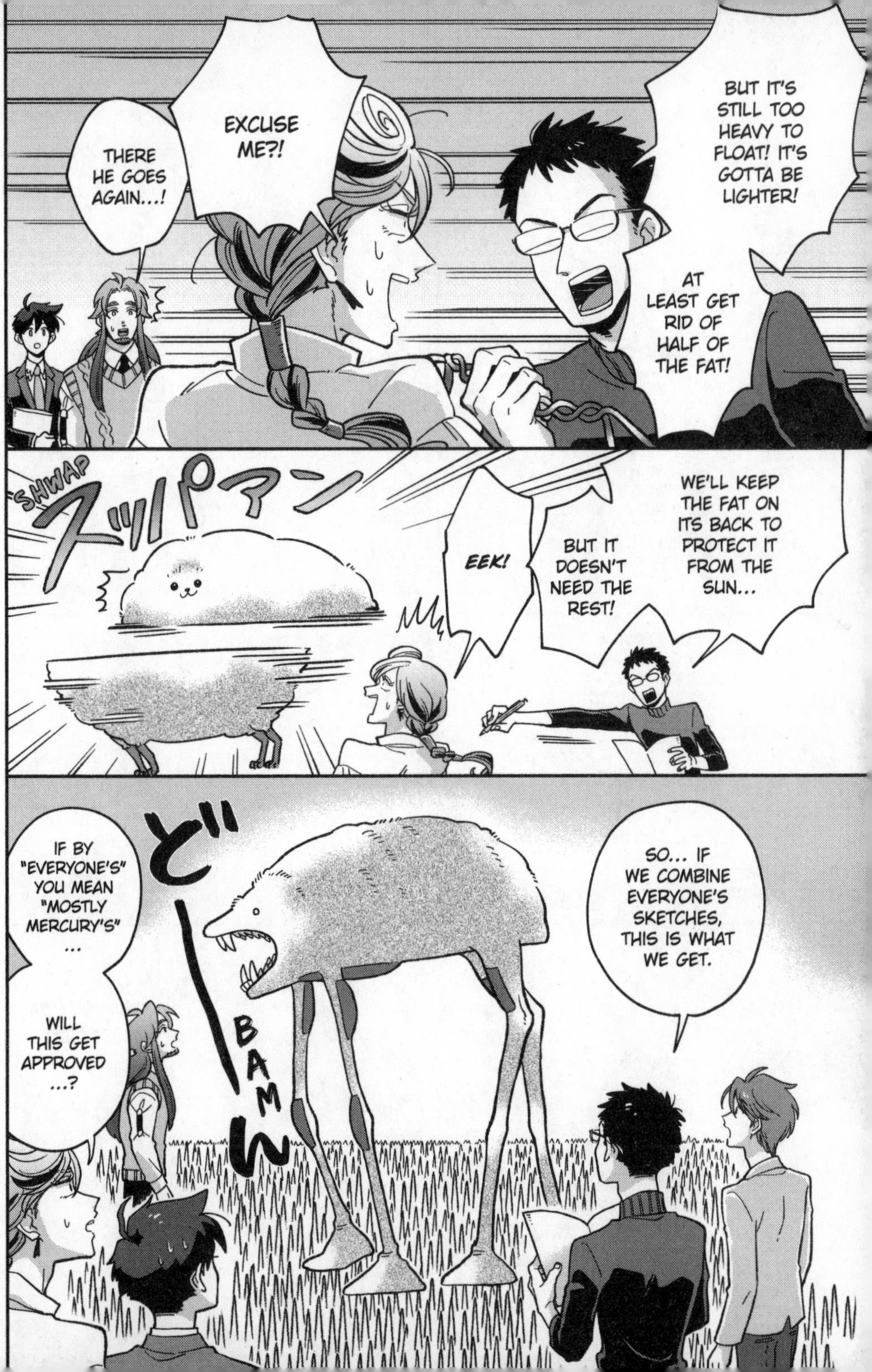
BUT IT'S STILL TOO HEAVY TO FLOAT! IT'S GOTTA BE LIGHTER!
AT LEAST GET RID OF HALF OF THE FAT!
EXCUSE ME?!
THERE HE GOES AGAIN...!
WE'LL KEEP THE FAT ON ITS BACK TO PROTECT IT FROM THE SUN...
BUT IT DOESN'T NEED THE REST!
EEK!
SHWAP
SO... IF WE COMBINE EVERYONE'S SKETCHES, THIS IS WHAT WE GET.
BAM
IF BY "EVERYONE'S" YOU MEAN "MOSTLY MERCURY'S" ...
WILL THIS GET APPROVED ...?

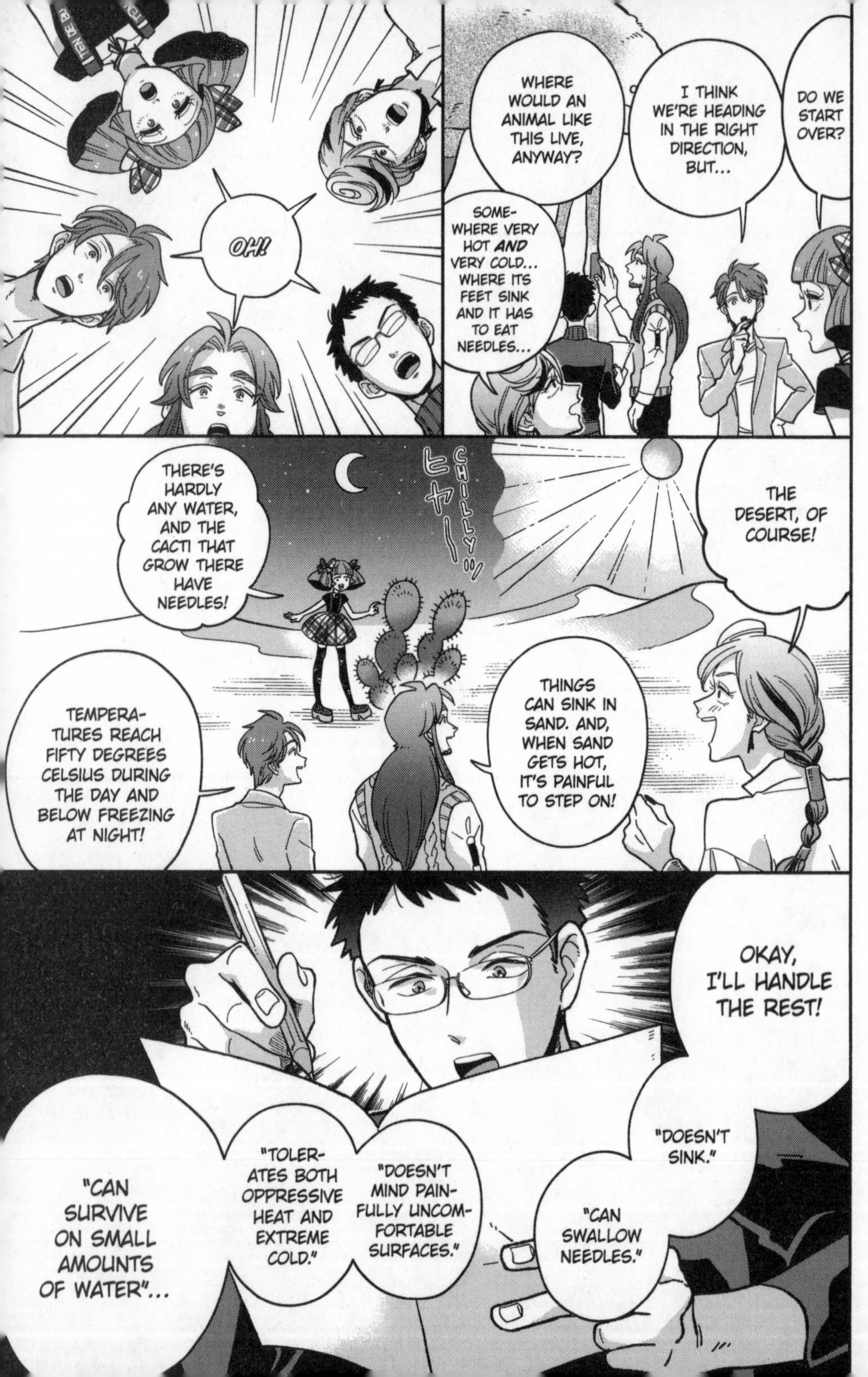
DO WE START OVER?
I THINK WE'RE HEADING IN THE RIGHT DIRECTION, BUT...
WHERE WOULD AN ANIMAL LIKE THIS LIVE, ANYWAY?
SOME-WHERE VERY HOT **AND** VERY COLD... WHERE ITS FEET SINK AND IT HAS TO EAT NEEDLES...
OH!
THE DESERT, OF COURSE!
ヒャー CHILLY
THERE'S HARDLY ANY WATER, AND THE CACTI THAT GROW THERE HAVE NEEDLES!
THINGS CAN SINK IN SAND. AND, WHEN SAND GETS HOT, IT'S PAINFUL TO STEP ON!
TEMPERA-TURES REACH FIFTY DEGREES CELSIUS DURING THE DAY AND BELOW FREEZING AT NIGHT!
OKAY, I'LL HANDLE THE REST!
"DOESN'T SINK."
"CAN SWALLOW NEEDLES."
"DOESN'T MIND PAIN-FULLY UNCOM-FORTABLE SURFACES."
"TOLER-ATES BOTH OPPRESSIVE HEAT AND EXTREME COLD."
"CAN SURVIVE ON SMALL AMOUNTS OF WATER"...

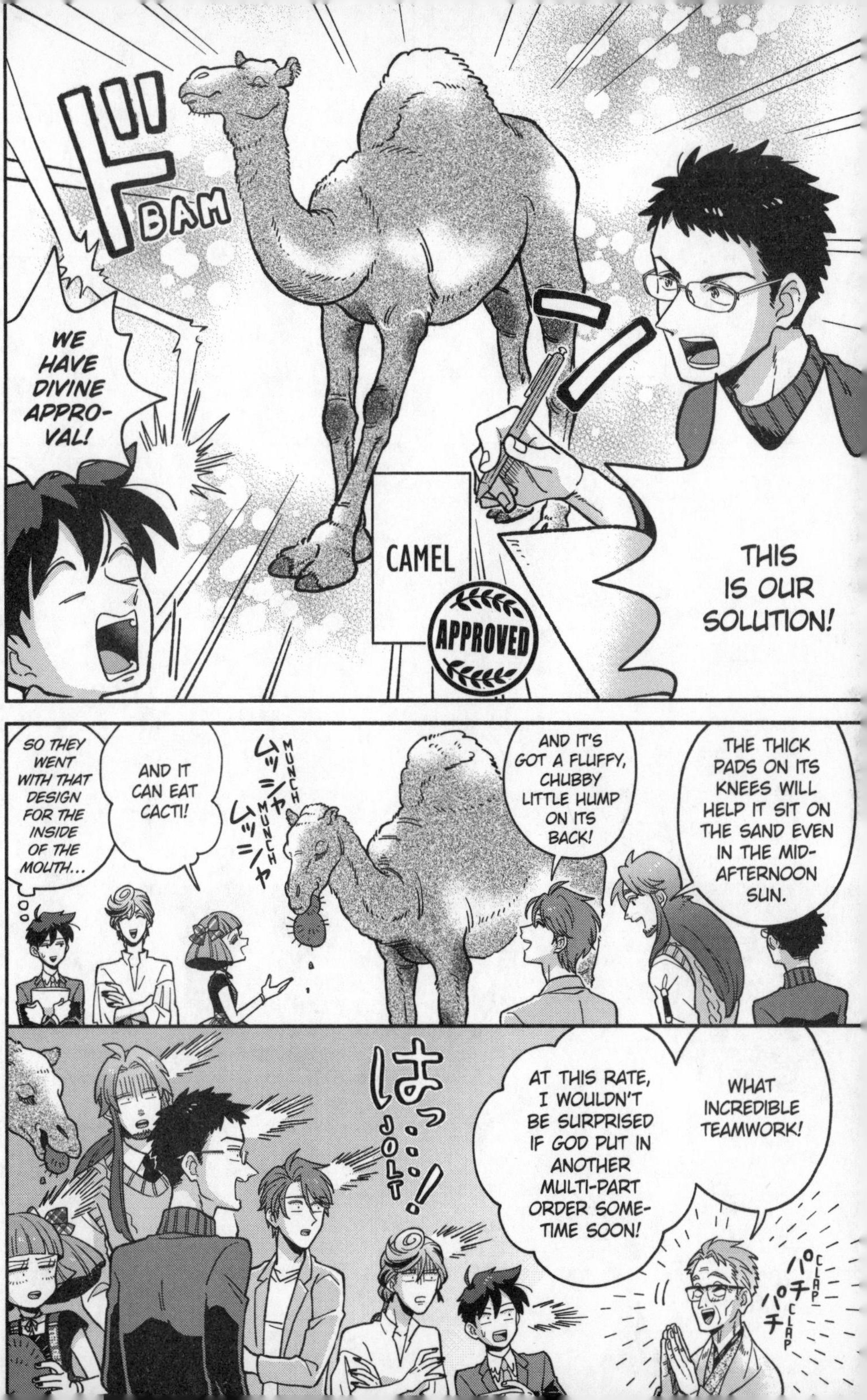
THIS IS OUR SOLUTION!
ー
ド BAM
WE HAVE DIVINE APPROVAL!
CAMEL
APPROVED
THE THICK PADS ON ITS KNEES WILL HELP IT SIT ON THE SAND EVEN IN THE MID-AFTERNOON SUN.
AND IT'S GOT A FLUFFY, CHUBBY LITTLE HUMP ON ITS BACK!
ムッシャ MUNCH ムッシャ MUNCH
AND IT CAN EAT CACTI!
SO THEY WENT WITH THAT DESIGN FOR THE INSIDE OF THE MOUTH...
WHAT INCREDIBLE TEAMWORK!
AT THIS RATE, I WOULDN'T BE SURPRISED IF GOD PUT IN ANOTHER MULTI-PART ORDER SOME-TIME SOON!
パチ CLAP パチ CLAP
はっ JOLT

THE ENCYCLOPEDIA OF REAL ANIMALS 37

ANIMAL 87 | CAMEL

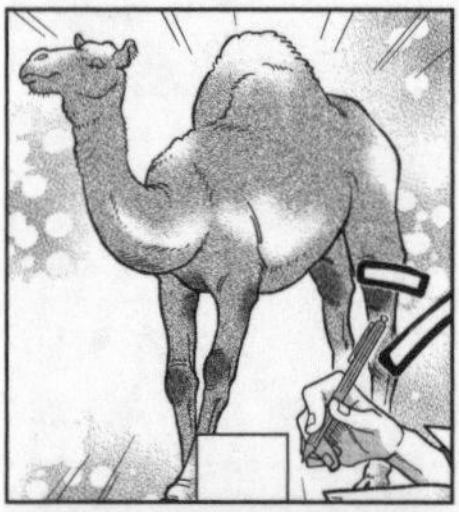

THE REAL THING

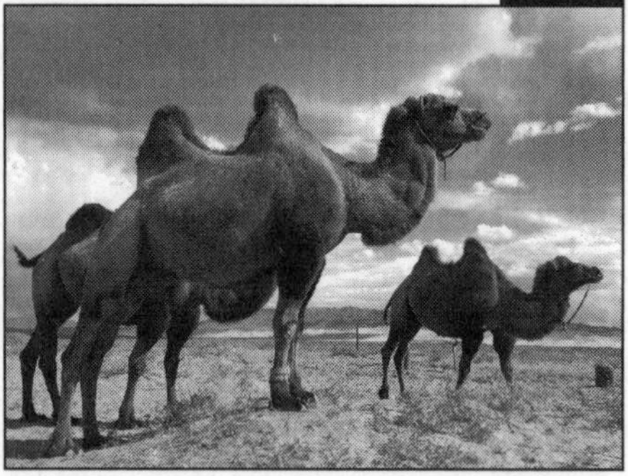

Domesticated Bactrian camels. Fewer than 1,000 remain in the wild.

Photo: Aflo

[Name]	*Camelus*
[Classification]	Class: Mammalia Order: Artiodactyla Family: Camelidae Genus: *Camelus*
[Habitat]	N. Africa to W. Asia (Dromedary) and the steppes of Central Asia (Bactrian camel)
[Height]	200-350 cm (6.6-11.5 ft)

The camel is specially adapted to life in extreme climates like deserts. Long eyelashes and a full nictitating membrane, in addition to nostrils that can close, create a protective barrier against dust. Its wide, flat feet distribute the camel's weight to prevent it from sinking into the sand, while its long legs keep its body far from the ground and away from the sand's heat. The camel has thick, leathery pads on the upper parts of its front legs, the knees of its back legs, and its chest. These patches allow the ungulate to kick back and relax even on hot sand. The camel can also go without drinking water for extended periods, and survives body temperatures that would be fatal to most other mammals.

Because of the scarcity of water in arid climates, the camel traps vapor in its nostrils and reabsorbs it when it exhales. To conserve moisture, the camel rarely sweats.

The humps on the camel's back are filled not with water, but with fat. They serve as sources of energy and also provide extra protection against increased body temperatures caused by the sun's heat. The concentration of subcutaneous fat on the back allows heat to escape from other areas of the body. The camel's thick fur also acts as further insulation against the heat. The camel can drink more than 80 liters (21 gallons) of water at once, and stores the moisture in its blood. In other mammals, this process would cause the cells to burst from the change in osmotic pressure; however, because the camel's red blood cells are flat and oval-shaped, they are sturdier than their round counterparts. The cells' shape also helps with circulation when the camel is dehydrated and its blood is more highly concentrated than usual.

A camel's mouth is covered in papillae.
Photo: Minden Pictures/Aflo

Camels eat grass, the leaves of low-lying trees, and prickly cacti. When eating cacti, the camel expertly rotates each piece and aligns the needles to point in the same direction by using the papillae lining its mouth. This prevents the camel from being injured by the needles when swallowing.

HEAVEN'S DESIGN TEAM

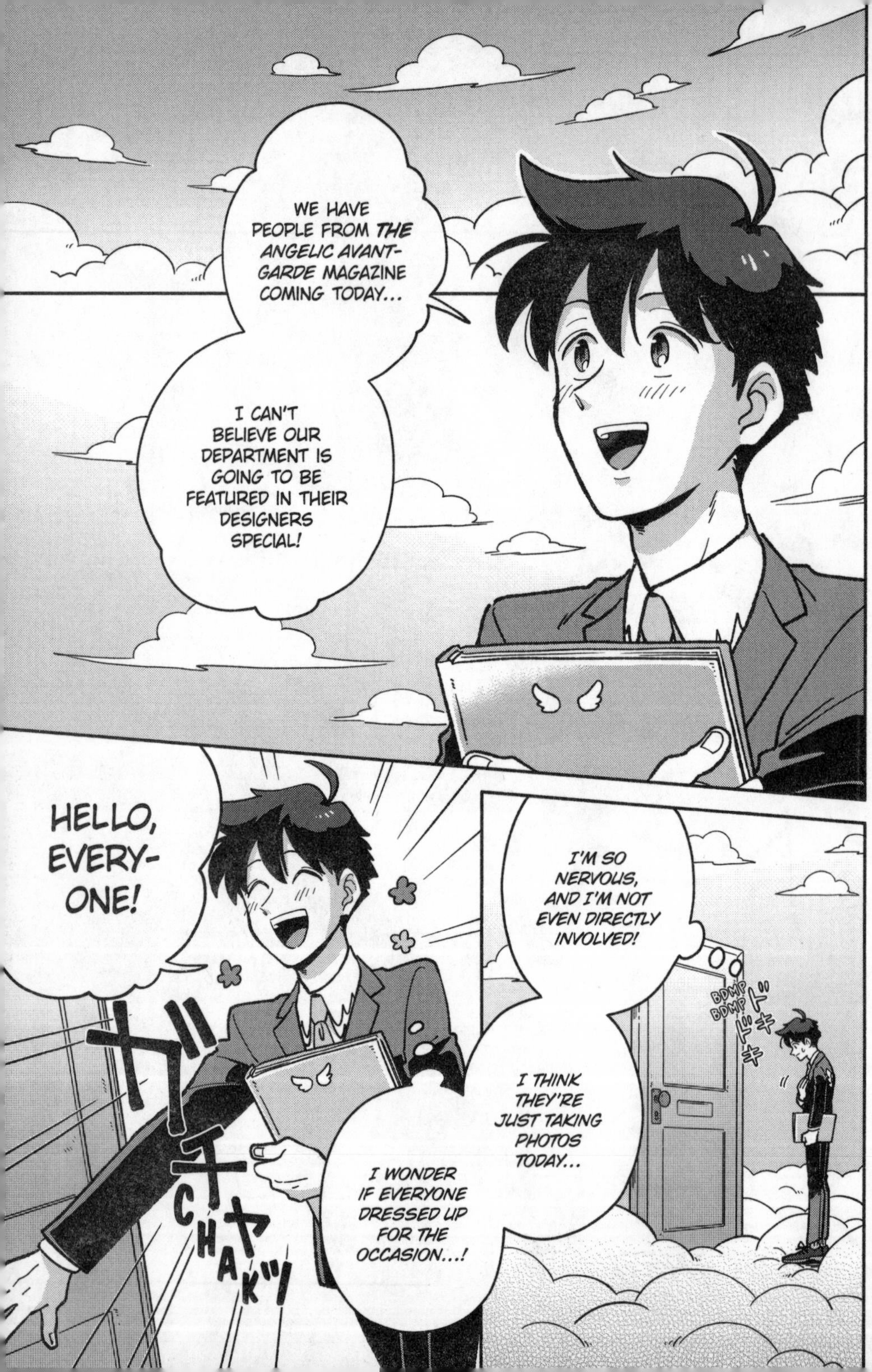
WE HAVE PEOPLE FROM *THE ANGELIC AVANT-GARDE* MAGAZINE COMING TODAY...
I CAN'T BELIEVE OUR DEPARTMENT IS GOING TO BE FEATURED IN THEIR DESIGNERS SPECIAL!
I'M SO NERVOUS, AND I'M NOT EVEN DIRECTLY INVOLVED!
BDMP BDMP
I THINK THEY'RE JUST TAKING PHOTOS TODAY...
I WONDER IF EVERYONE DRESSED UP FOR THE OCCASION...!
HELLO, EVERY-ONE!
CHAK

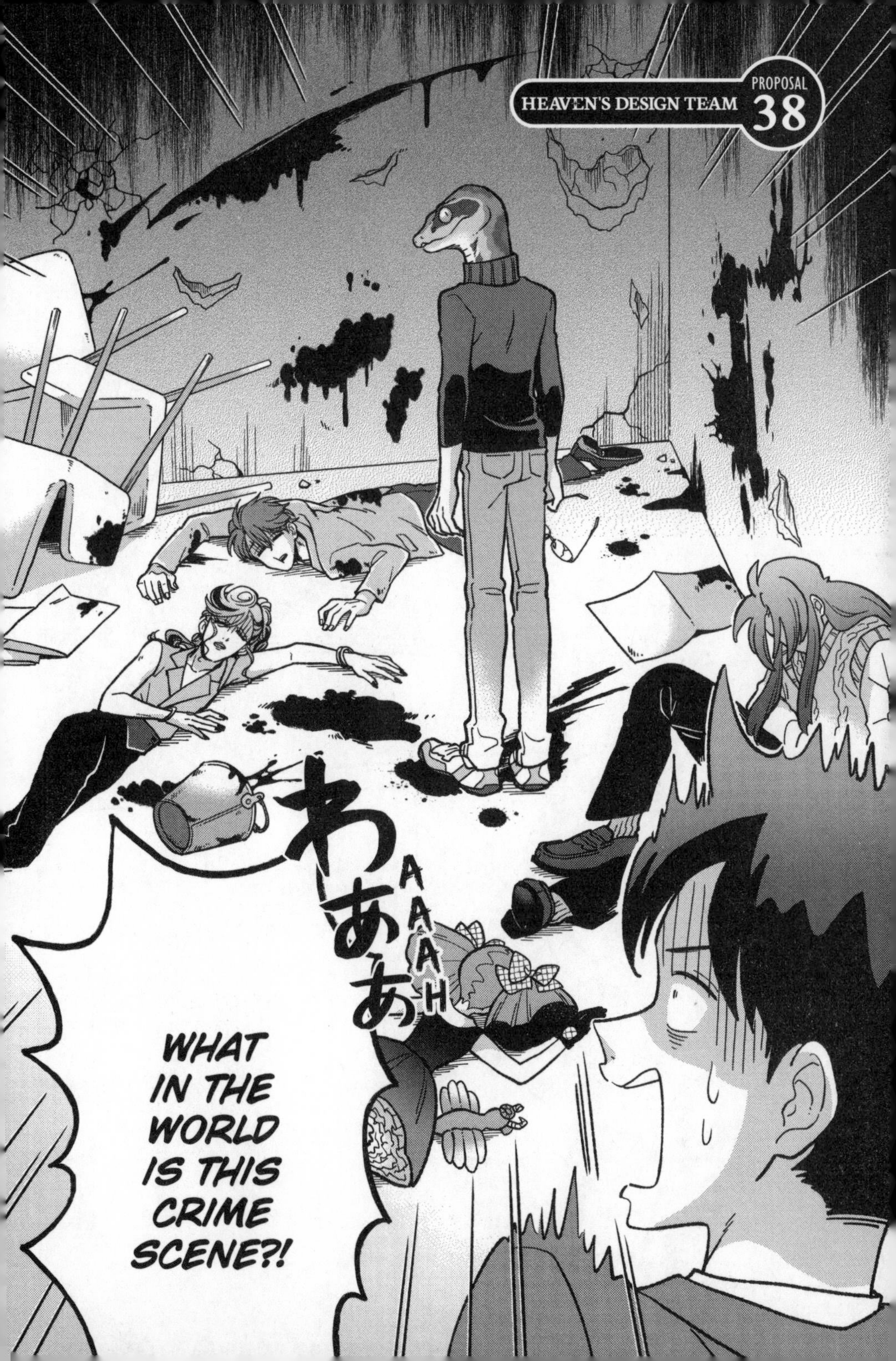
HEAVEN'S DESIGN TEAM
PROPOSAL
38
わああ
AAAAH
WHAT IN THE WORLD IS THIS CRIME SCENE?!

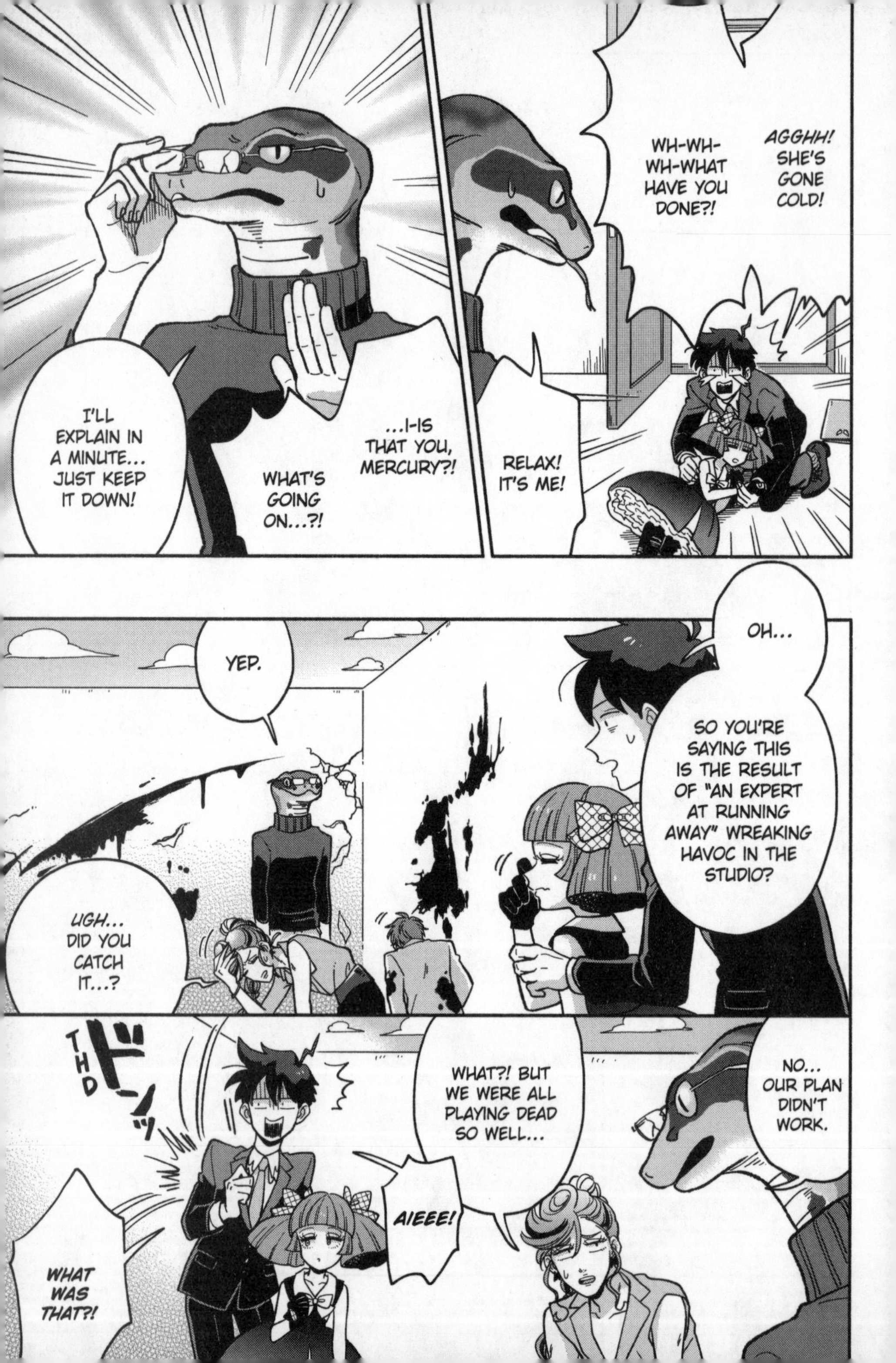
AGGHH! SHE'S GONE COLD!
WH-WH-WH-WHAT HAVE YOU DONE?!
RELAX! IT'S ME!
...I-IS THAT YOU, MERCURY?!
WHAT'S GOING ON...?!
I'LL EXPLAIN IN A MINUTE... JUST KEEP IT DOWN!
OH...
SO YOU'RE SAYING THIS IS THE RESULT OF "AN EXPERT AT RUNNING AWAY" WREAKING HAVOC IN THE STUDIO?
YEP.
UGH... DID YOU CATCH IT...?
NO... OUR PLAN DIDN'T WORK.
WHAT?! BUT WE WERE ALL PLAYING DEAD SO WELL...
AIEEE!
THD
WHAT WAS THAT?!

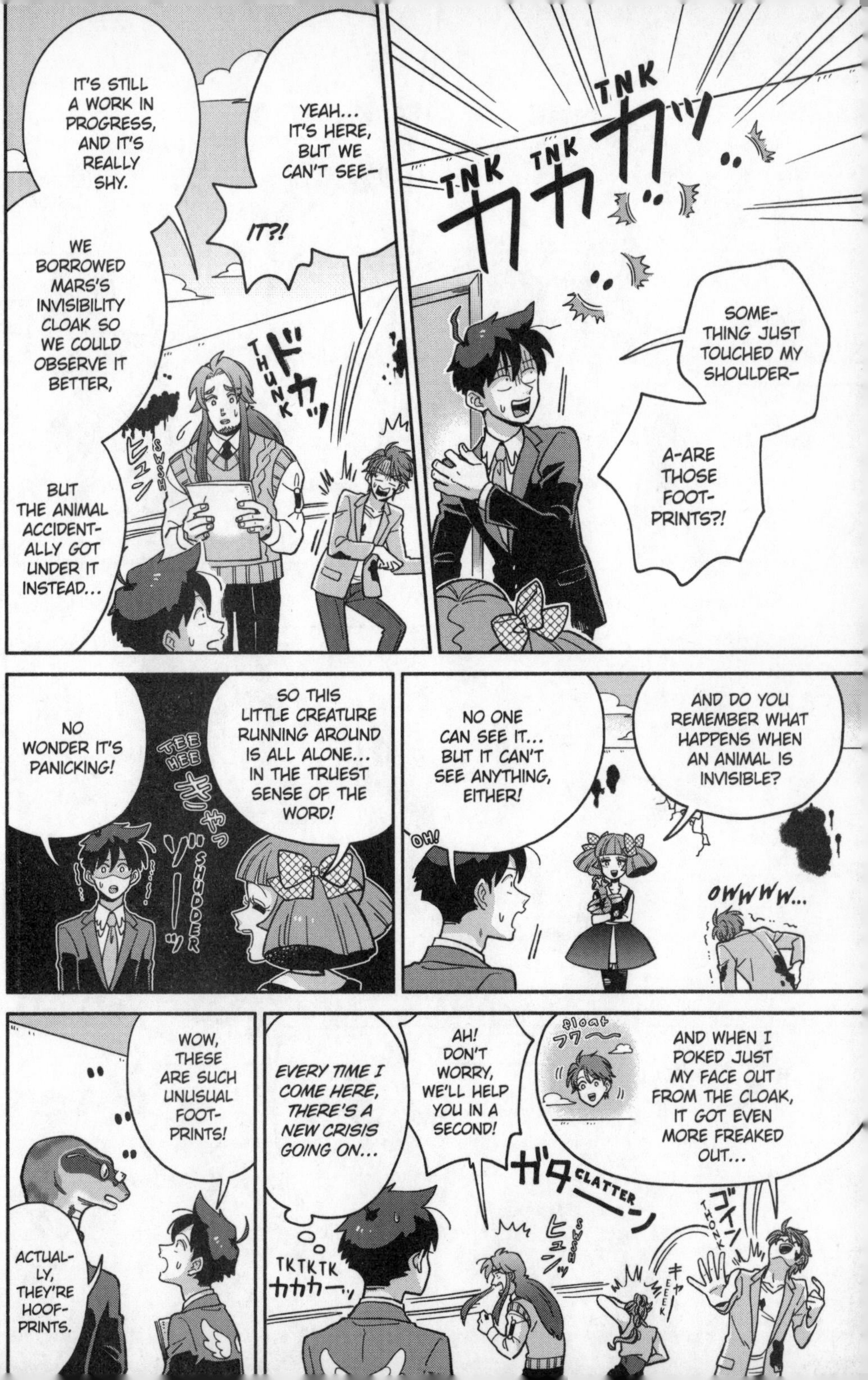
TNK TNK TNK
SOMETHING JUST TOUCHED MY SHOULDER-
A-ARE THOSE FOOTPRINTS?!
YEAH... IT'S HERE, BUT WE CAN'T SEE-
IT'S STILL A WORK IN PROGRESS, AND IT'S REALLY SHY.
IT?!
THUNK
WE BORROWED MARS'S INVISIBILITY CLOAK SO WE COULD OBSERVE IT BETTER,
SWSH
BUT THE ANIMAL ACCIDENTALLY GOT UNDER IT INSTEAD...
AND DO YOU REMEMBER WHAT HAPPENS WHEN AN ANIMAL IS INVISIBLE?
NO ONE CAN SEE IT... BUT IT CAN'T SEE ANYTHING, EITHER!
OH!
OWWWW...
SO THIS LITTLE CREATURE RUNNING AROUND IS ALL ALONE... IN THE TRUEST SENSE OF THE WORD!
NO WONDER IT'S PANICKING!
TEE HEE
SHUDDER
AND WHEN I POKED JUST MY FACE OUT FROM THE CLOAK, IT GOT EVEN MORE FREAKED OUT...
float
AH! DON'T WORRY, WE'LL HELP YOU IN A SECOND!
CLATTER
THONK
EEEEK
SWSH
EVERY TIME I COME HERE, THERE'S A NEW CRISIS GOING ON...
TKTKTK
WOW, THESE ARE SUCH UNUSUAL FOOTPRINTS!
ACTUALLY, THEY'RE HOOFPRINTS.

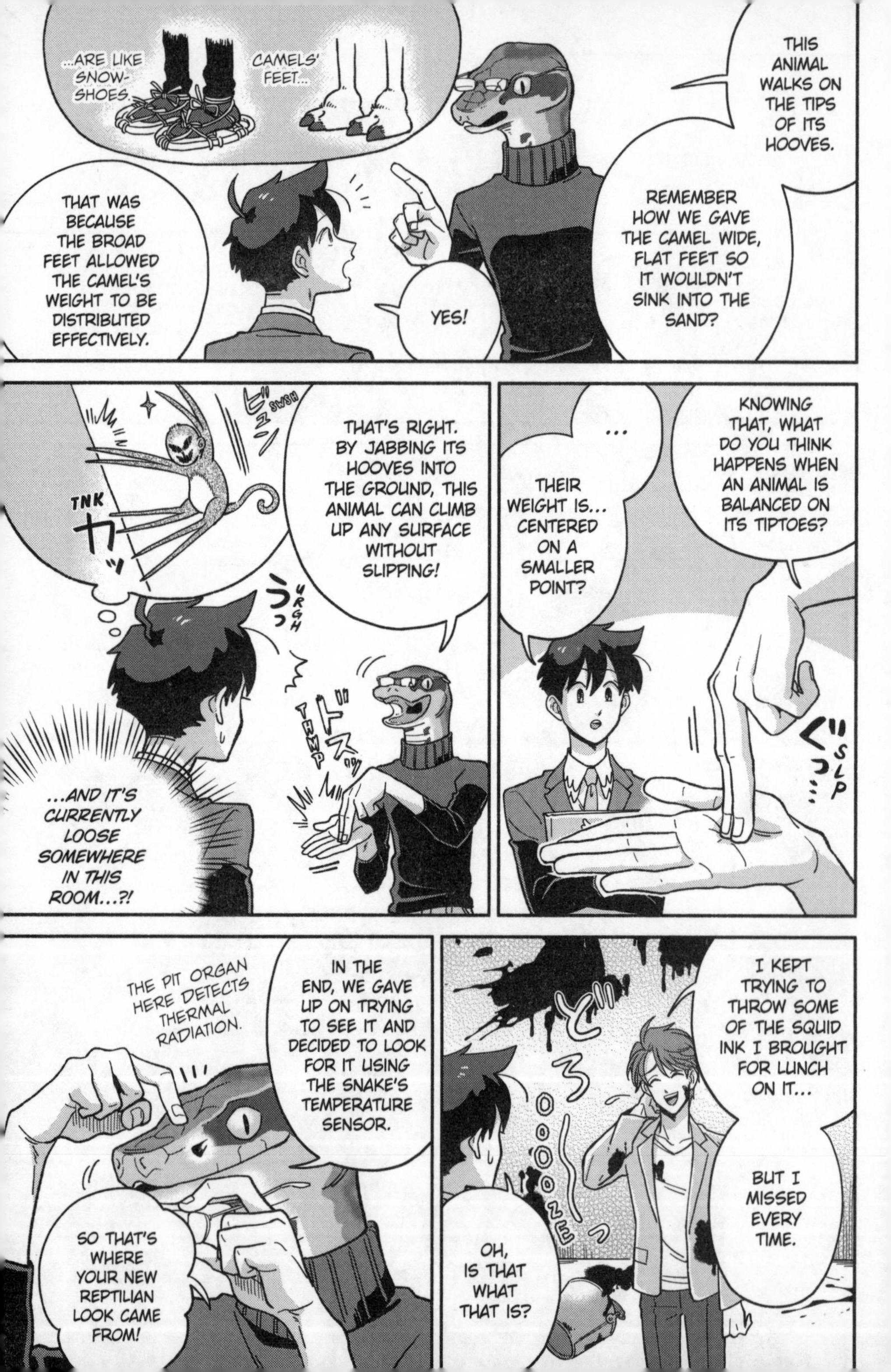
THIS ANIMAL WALKS ON THE TIPS OF ITS HOOVES.
REMEMBER HOW WE GAVE THE CAMEL WIDE, FLAT FEET SO IT WOULDN'T SINK INTO THE SAND?
YES!
CAMELS' FEET...
...ARE LIKE SNOW-SHOES.
THAT WAS BECAUSE THE BROAD FEET ALLOWED THE CAMEL'S WEIGHT TO BE DISTRIBUTED EFFECTIVELY.
KNOWING THAT, WHAT DO YOU THINK HAPPENS WHEN AN ANIMAL IS BALANCED ON ITS TIPTOES?
...
THEIR WEIGHT IS... CENTERED ON A SMALLER POINT?
SLP
THAT'S RIGHT. BY JABBING ITS HOOVES INTO THE GROUND, THIS ANIMAL CAN CLIMB UP ANY SURFACE WITHOUT SLIPPING!
SWSH
TNK
URGH
THMP
...AND IT'S CURRENTLY LOOSE SOMEWHERE IN THIS ROOM...?!
I KEPT TRYING TO THROW SOME OF THE SQUID INK I BROUGHT FOR LUNCH ON IT...
BUT I MISSED EVERY TIME.
OOZE
OH, IS THAT WHAT THAT IS?
IN THE END, WE GAVE UP ON TRYING TO SEE IT AND DECIDED TO LOOK FOR IT USING THE SNAKE'S TEMPERATURE SENSOR.
THE PIT ORGAN HERE DETECTS THERMAL RADIATION.
SO THAT'S WHERE YOUR NEW REPTILIAN LOOK CAME FROM!

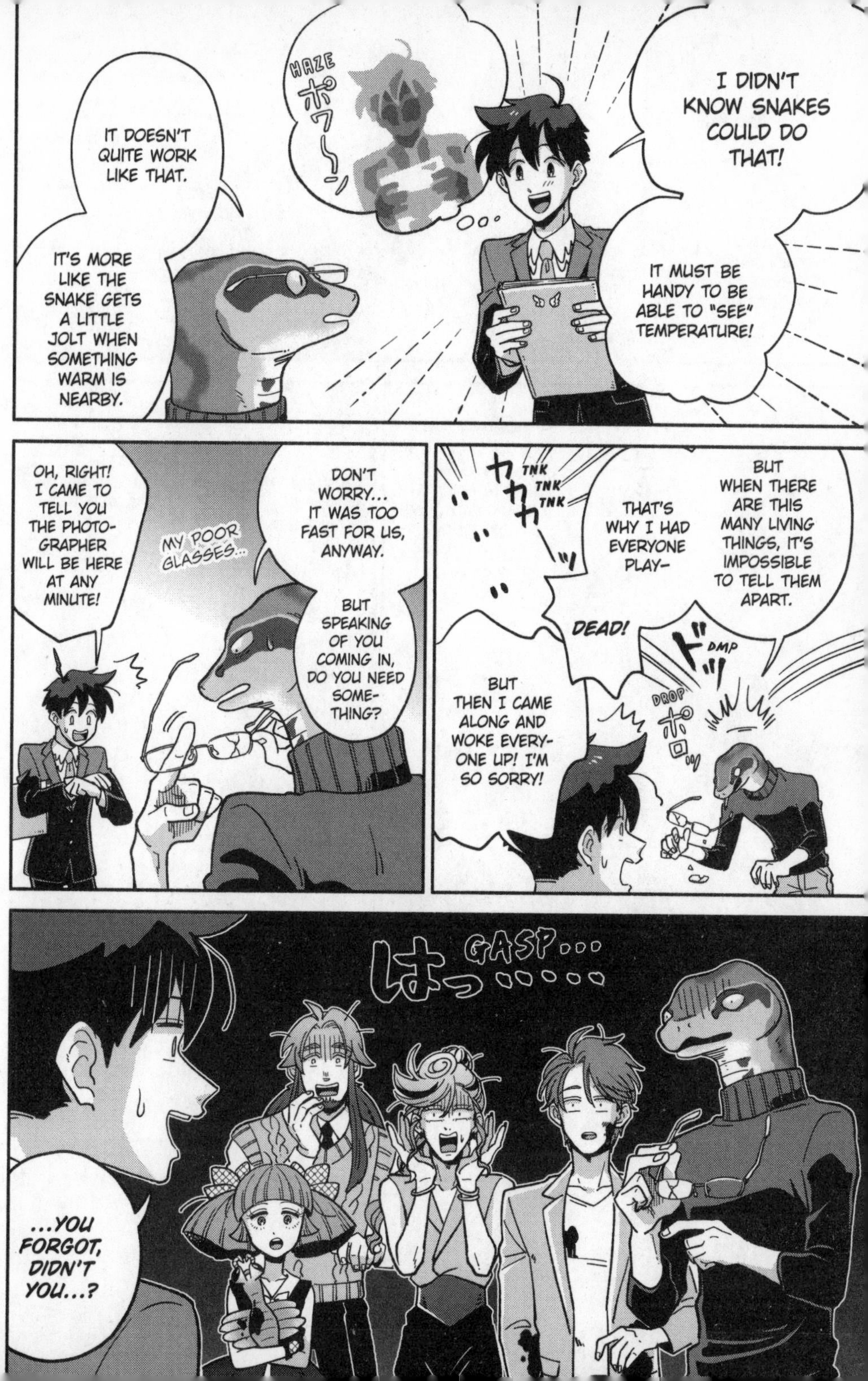
I DIDN'T KNOW SNAKES COULD DO THAT!
IT MUST BE HANDY TO BE ABLE TO "SEE" TEMPERATURE!
HAZE
IT DOESN'T QUITE WORK LIKE THAT.
IT'S MORE LIKE THE SNAKE GETS A LITTLE JOLT WHEN SOMETHING WARM IS NEARBY.
BUT WHEN THERE ARE THIS MANY LIVING THINGS, IT'S IMPOSSIBLE TO TELL THEM APART.
THAT'S WHY I HAD EVERYONE PLAY-
TNK TNK TNK
DEAD!
DMP
DROP
BUT THEN I CAME ALONG AND WOKE EVERY-ONE UP! I'M SO SORRY!
DON'T WORRY... IT WAS TOO FAST FOR US, ANYWAY.
BUT SPEAKING OF YOU COMING IN, DO YOU NEED SOME-THING?
MY POOR GLASSES...
OH, RIGHT! I CAME TO TELL YOU THE PHOTO-GRAPHER WILL BE HERE AT ANY MINUTE!
GASP...
...YOU FORGOT, DIDN'T YOU...?

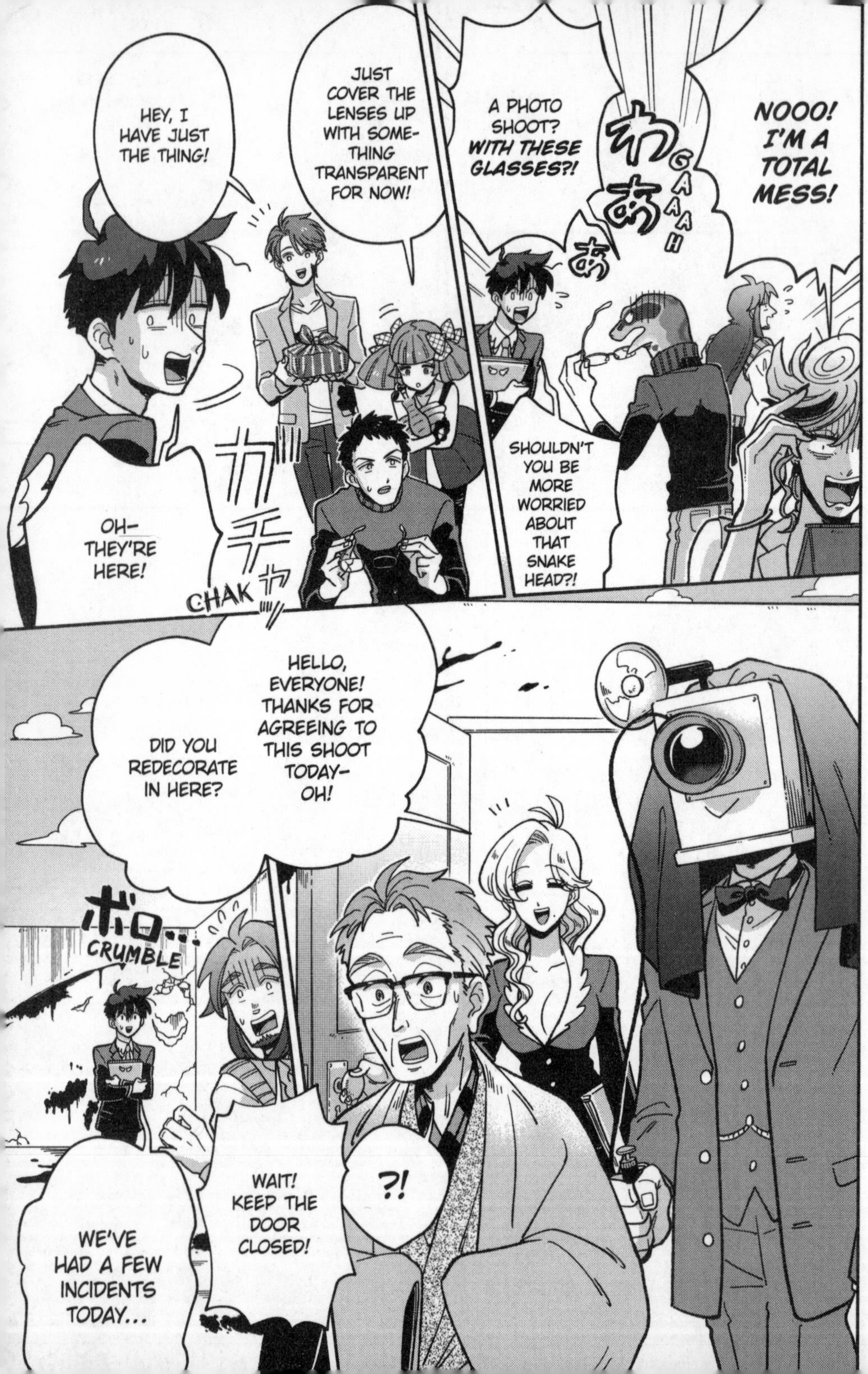
NOOO! I'M A TOTAL MESS!
わああ GAAAAH
A PHOTO SHOOT? WITH THESE GLASSES?!
SHOULDN'T YOU BE MORE WORRIED ABOUT THAT SNAKE HEAD?!
JUST COVER THE LENSES UP WITH SOME-THING TRANSPARENT FOR NOW!
HEY, I HAVE JUST THE THING!
カチャ CHAK
OH— THEY'RE HERE!
HELLO, EVERYONE! THANKS FOR AGREEING TO THIS SHOOT TODAY— OH!
DID YOU REDECORATE IN HERE?
ボロ… CRUMBLE
?!
WAIT! KEEP THE DOOR CLOSED!
WE'VE HAD A FEW INCIDENTS TODAY...

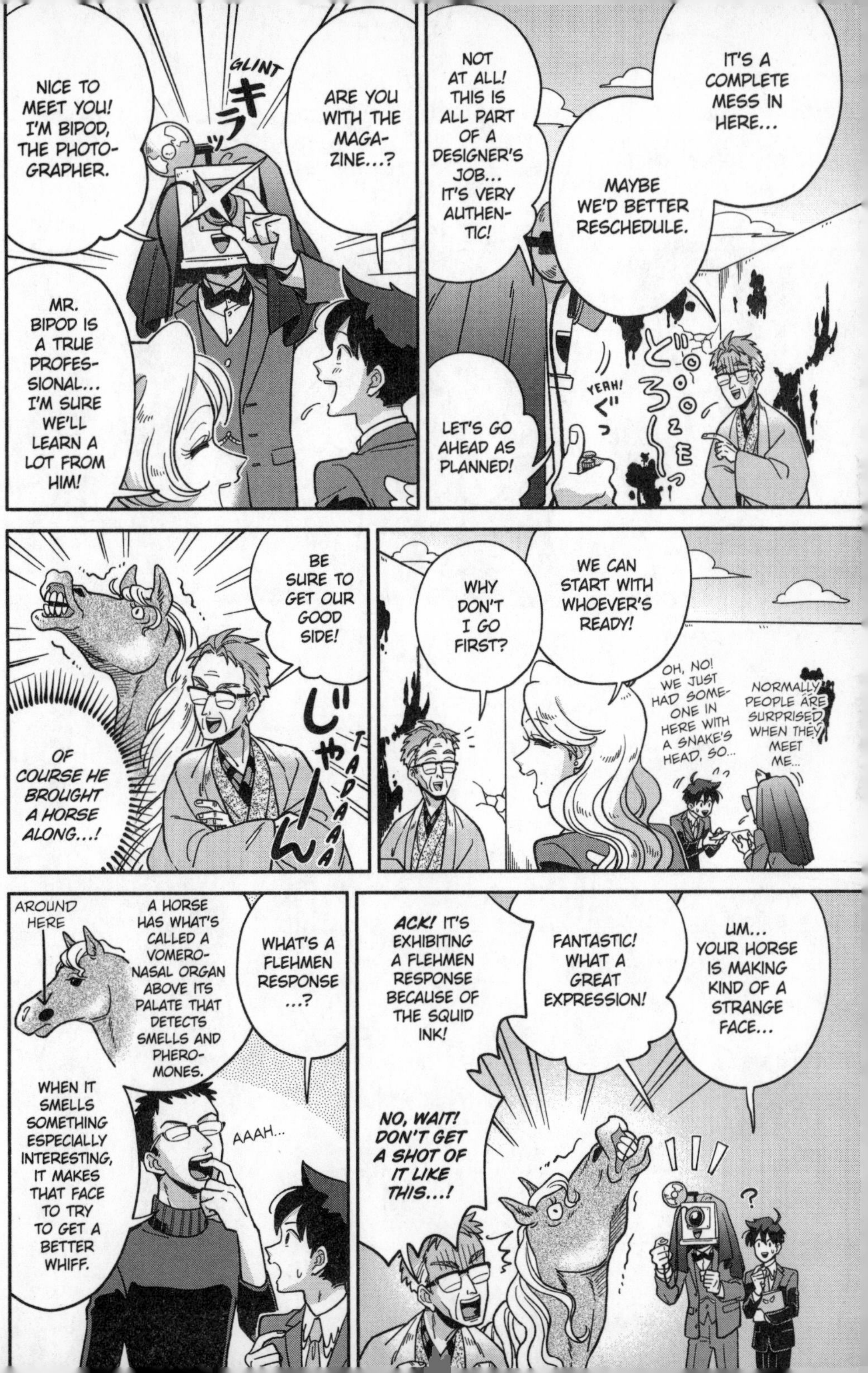
IT'S A COMPLETE MESS IN HERE...
MAYBE WE'D BETTER RESCHEDULE.
NOT AT ALL! THIS IS ALL PART OF A DESIGNER'S JOB... IT'S VERY AUTHENTIC!
LET'S GO AHEAD AS PLANNED!
YEAH!
ARE YOU WITH THE MAGAZINE...?
GLINT
NICE TO MEET YOU! I'M BIPOD, THE PHOTOGRAPHER.
MR. BIPOD IS A TRUE PROFESSIONAL... I'M SURE WE'LL LEARN A LOT FROM HIM!
WE CAN START WITH WHOEVER'S READY!
WHY DON'T I GO FIRST?
NORMALLY PEOPLE ARE SURPRISED WHEN THEY MEET ME...
OH, NO! WE JUST HAD SOMEONE IN HERE WITH A SNAKE'S HEAD, SO...
BE SURE TO GET OUR GOOD SIDE!
TADAAAA
OF COURSE HE BROUGHT A HORSE ALONG...!
UM... YOUR HORSE IS MAKING KIND OF A STRANGE FACE...
FANTASTIC! WHAT A GREAT EXPRESSION!
ACK! IT'S EXHIBITING A FLEHMEN RESPONSE BECAUSE OF THE SQUID INK!
NO, WAIT! DON'T GET A SHOT OF IT LIKE THIS...!
!!!
?
WHAT'S A FLEHMEN RESPONSE...?
A HORSE HAS WHAT'S CALLED A VOMERONASAL ORGAN ABOVE ITS PALATE THAT DETECTS SMELLS AND PHEROMONES.
AROUND HERE
WHEN IT SMELLS SOMETHING ESPECIALLY INTERESTING, IT MAKES THAT FACE TO TRY TO GET A BETTER WHIFF.
AAAH...

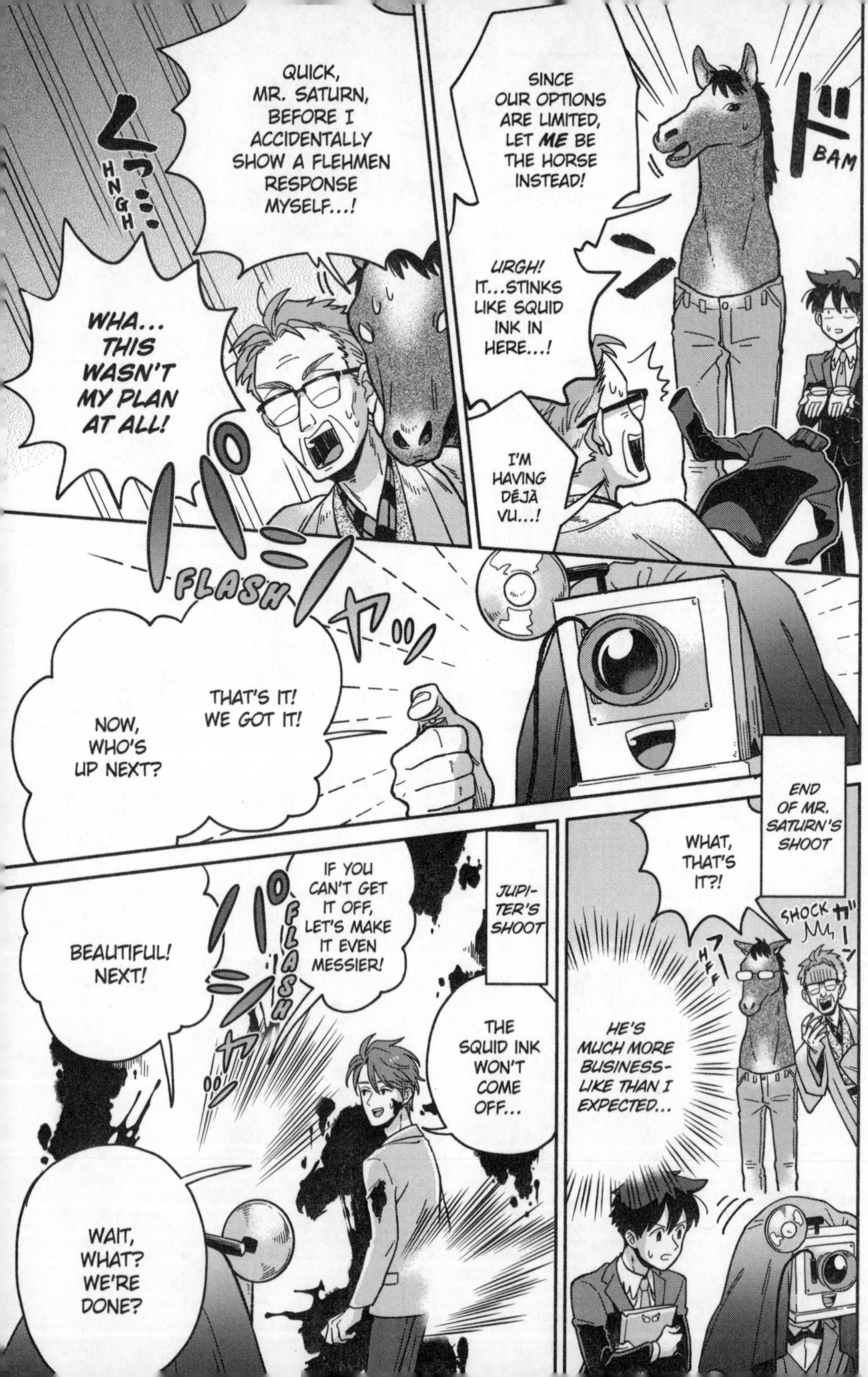

SINCE OUR OPTIONS ARE LIMITED, LET *ME* BE THE HORSE INSTEAD!
BAM
URGH! IT...STINKS LIKE SQUID INK IN HERE...!
I'M HAVING DÉJÀ VU...!
QUICK, MR. SATURN, BEFORE I ACCIDENTALLY SHOW A FLEHMEN RESPONSE MYSELF...!
HNGH
WHA... THIS WASN'T MY PLAN AT ALL!
FLASH
THAT'S IT! WE GOT IT!
NOW, WHO'S UP NEXT?
END OF MR. SATURN'S SHOOT
WHAT, THAT'S IT?!
SHOCK
HFF
HE'S MUCH MORE BUSINESS-LIKE THAN I EXPECTED...
JUPITER'S SHOOT
IF YOU CAN'T GET IT OFF, LET'S MAKE IT EVEN MESSIER!
FLASH
BEAUTIFUL! NEXT!
THE SQUID INK WON'T COME OFF...
WAIT, WHAT? WE'RE DONE?

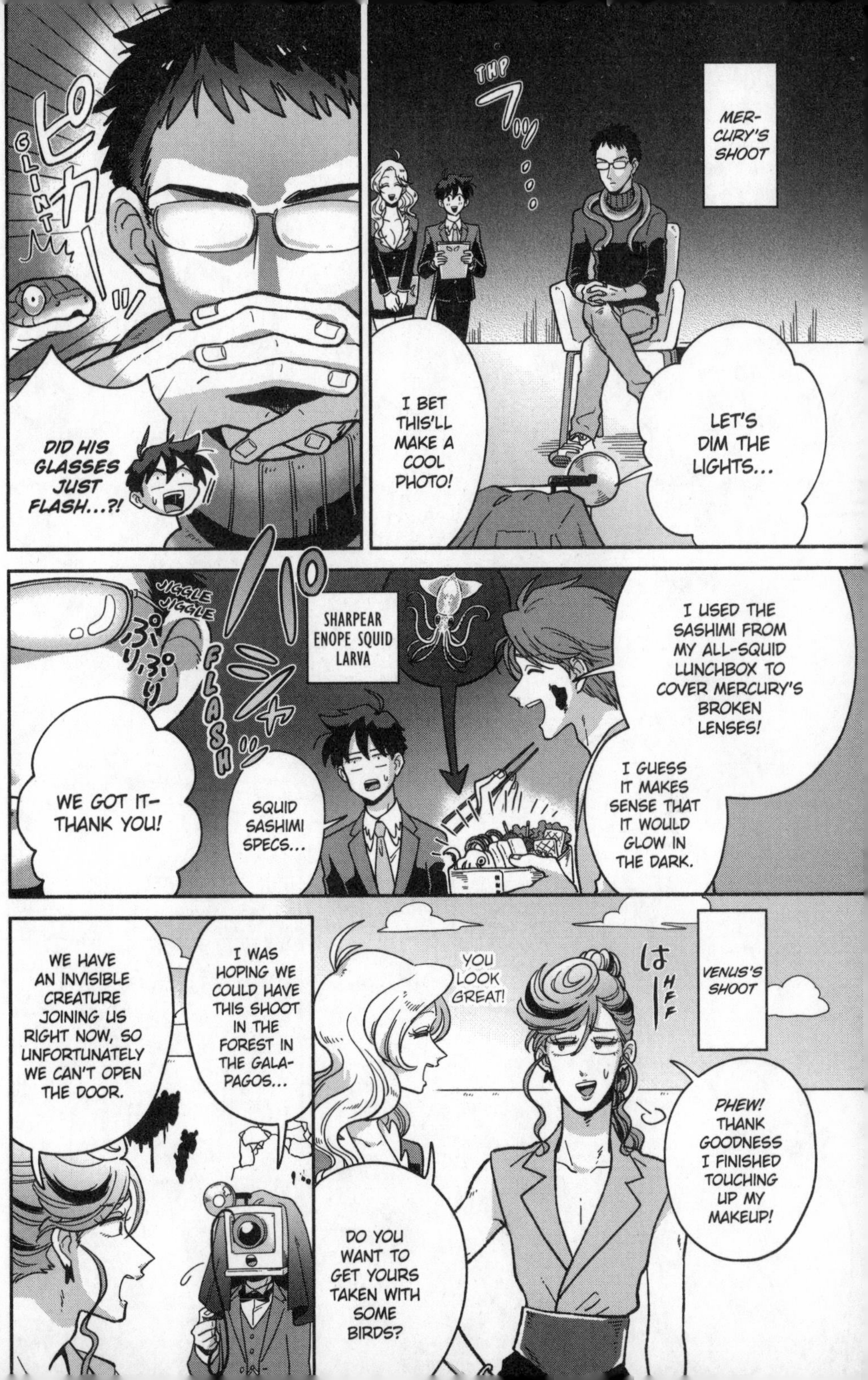
MERCURY'S SHOOT
THP
LET'S DIM THE LIGHTS...
I BET THIS'LL MAKE A COOL PHOTO!
GLINT
DID HIS GLASSES JUST FLASH...?!
I USED THE SASHIMI FROM MY ALL-SQUID LUNCHBOX TO COVER MERCURY'S BROKEN LENSES!
I GUESS IT MAKES SENSE THAT IT WOULD GLOW IN THE DARK.
SHARPEAR ENOPE SQUID LARVA
SQUID SASHIMI SPECS...
FLASH
JIGGLE JIGGLE
WE GOT IT— THANK YOU!
VENUS'S SHOOT
HFF
PHEW! THANK GOODNESS I FINISHED TOUCHING UP MY MAKEUP!
YOU LOOK GREAT!
I WAS HOPING WE COULD HAVE THIS SHOOT IN THE FOREST IN THE GALA-PAGOS...
WE HAVE AN INVISIBLE CREATURE JOINING US RIGHT NOW, SO UNFORTUNATELY WE CAN'T OPEN THE DOOR.
DO YOU WANT TO GET YOURS TAKEN WITH SOME BIRDS?

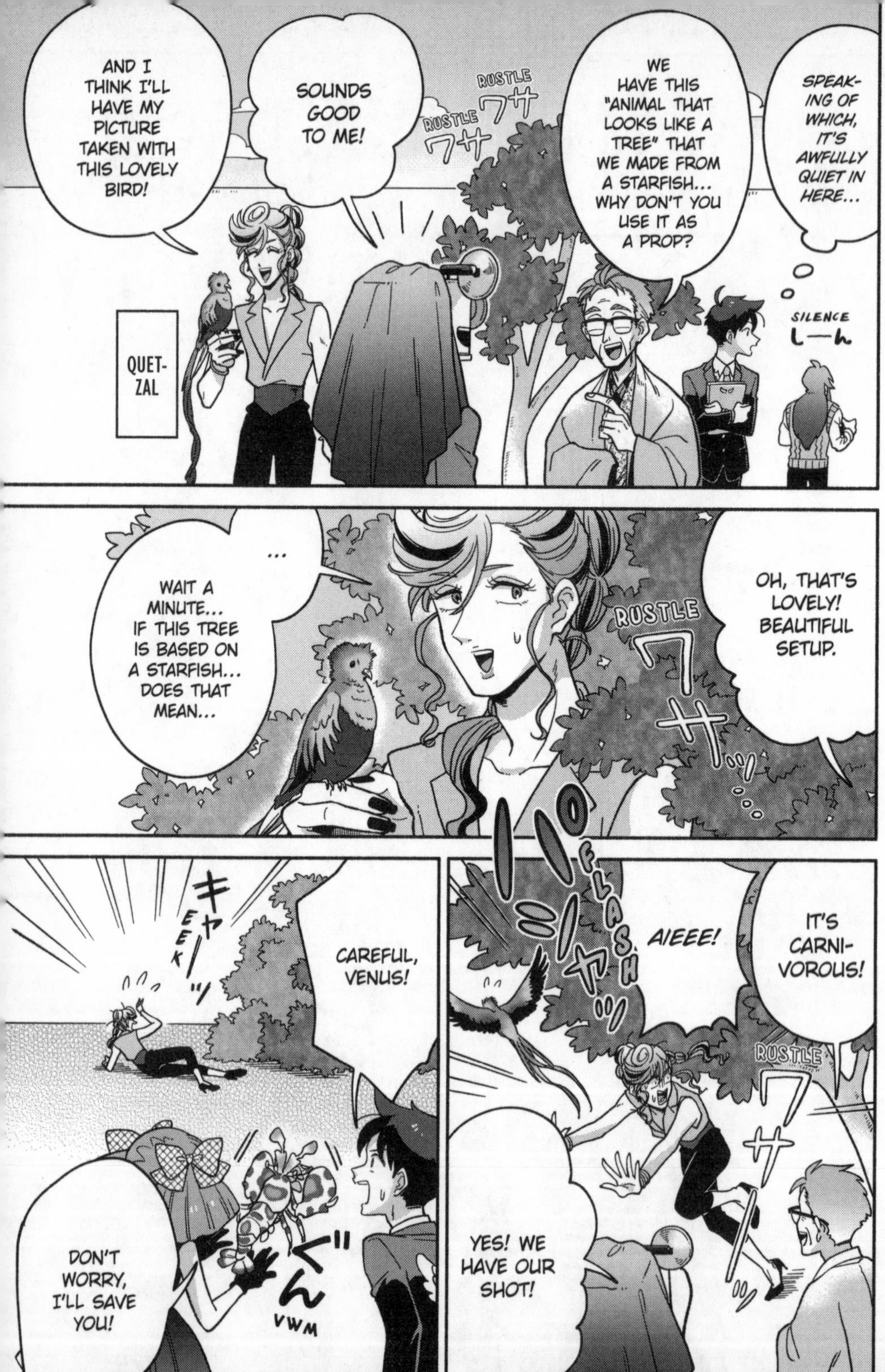
SPEAKING OF WHICH, IT'S AWFULLY QUIET IN HERE...
SILENCE
しーん
WE HAVE THIS "ANIMAL THAT LOOKS LIKE A TREE" THAT WE MADE FROM A STARFISH... WHY DON'T YOU USE IT AS A PROP?
RUSTLE
ワサ
RUSTLE
ワサ
SOUNDS GOOD TO ME!
AND I THINK I'LL HAVE MY PICTURE TAKEN WITH THIS LOVELY BIRD!
QUET-ZAL
OH, THAT'S LOVELY! BEAUTIFUL SETUP.
RUSTLE
ワサ
...
WAIT A MINUTE... IF THIS TREE IS BASED ON A STARFISH... DOES THAT MEAN...
IT'S CARNIVOROUS!
RUSTLE
ワサ
AIEEE!
FLASH
YES! WE HAVE OUR SHOT!
EEK
キャ
CAREFUL, VENUS!
VWM
DON'T WORRY, I'LL SAVE YOU!

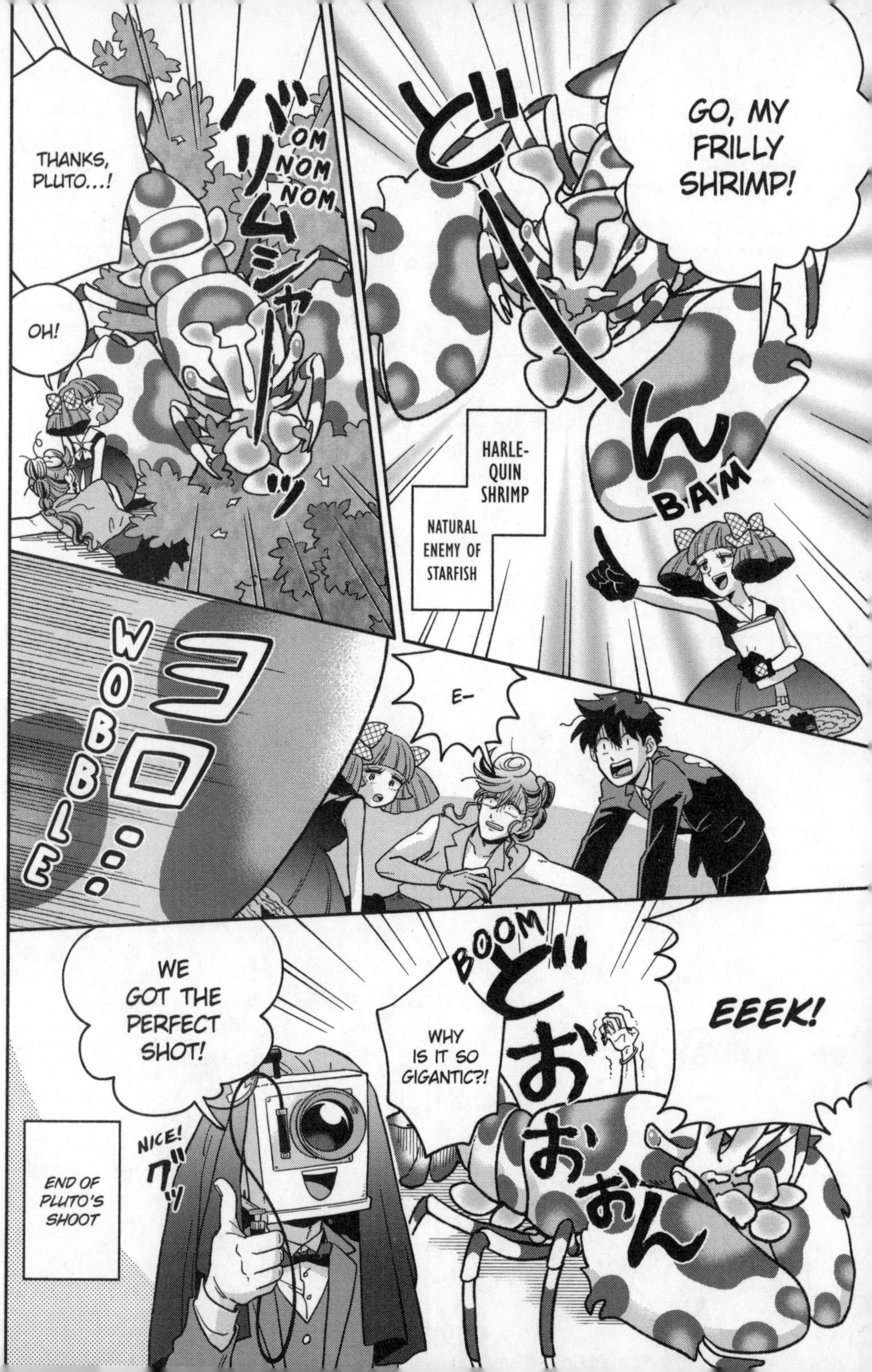

GO, MY FRILLY SHRIMP!
どーん
BAM
HARLEQUIN SHRIMP
NATURAL ENEMY OF STARFISH
バリムシャーッ
OM NOM NOM
THANKS, PLUTO...!
OH!
E-
ヨロ...
WOBBLE...
EEEK!
どおおおん
BOOM
WHY IS IT SO GIGANTIC?!
WE GOT THE PERFECT SHOT!
NICE!
グッ
END OF PLUTO'S SHOOT

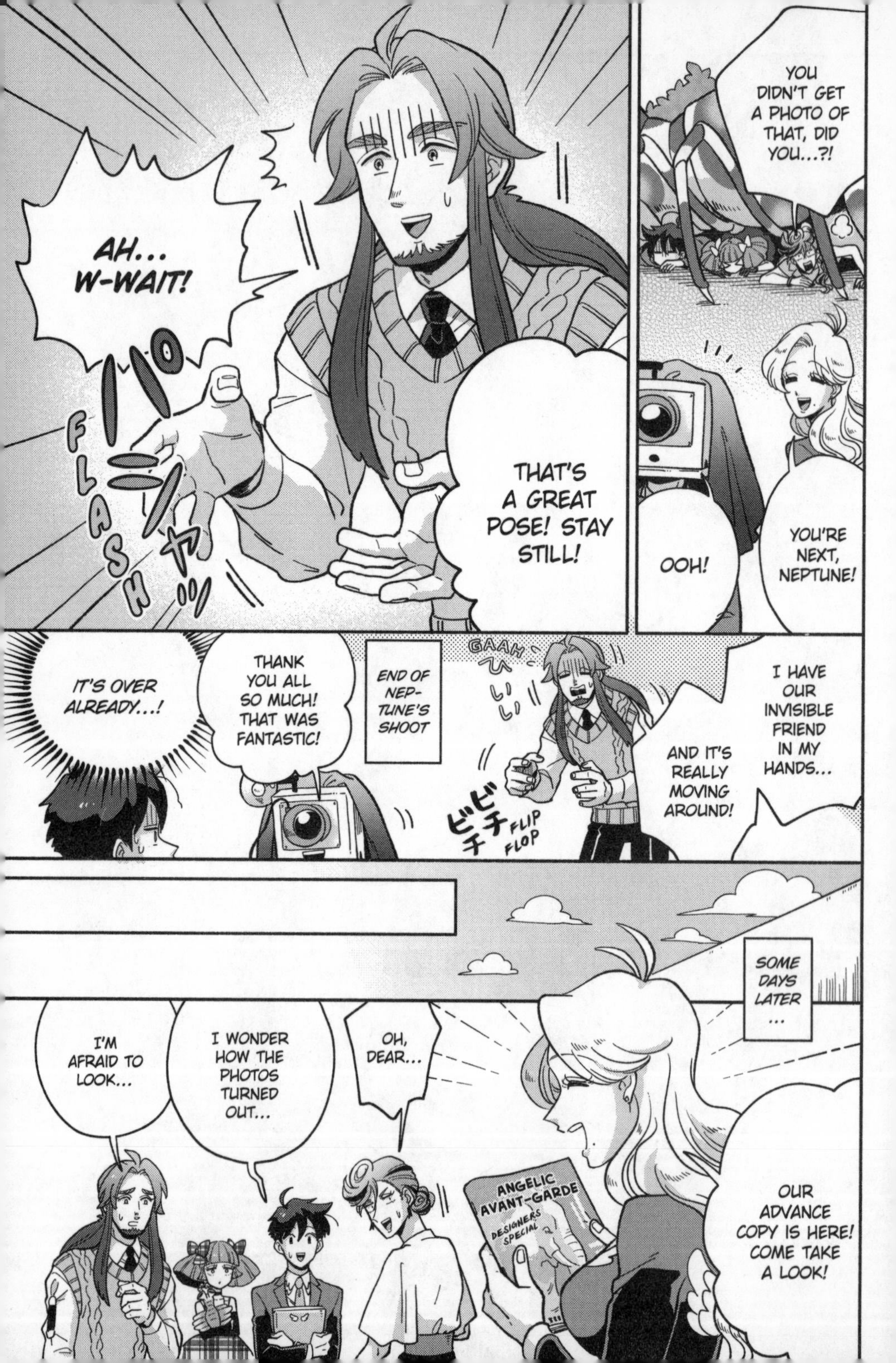
YOU DIDN'T GET A PHOTO OF THAT, DID YOU...?!
YOU'RE NEXT, NEPTUNE!
OOH!
THAT'S A GREAT POSE! STAY STILL!
AH... W-WAIT!
FLASH
I HAVE OUR INVISIBLE FRIEND IN MY HANDS...
AND IT'S REALLY MOVING AROUND!
GAAH
FLIP FLOP
END OF NEPTUNE'S SHOOT
THANK YOU ALL SO MUCH! THAT WAS FANTASTIC!
IT'S OVER ALREADY...!
SOME DAYS LATER...
OUR ADVANCE COPY IS HERE! COME TAKE A LOOK!
ANGELIC AVANT-GARDE
DESIGNERS SPECIAL
OH, DEAR...
I WONDER HOW THE PHOTOS TURNED OUT...
I'M AFRAID TO LOOK...

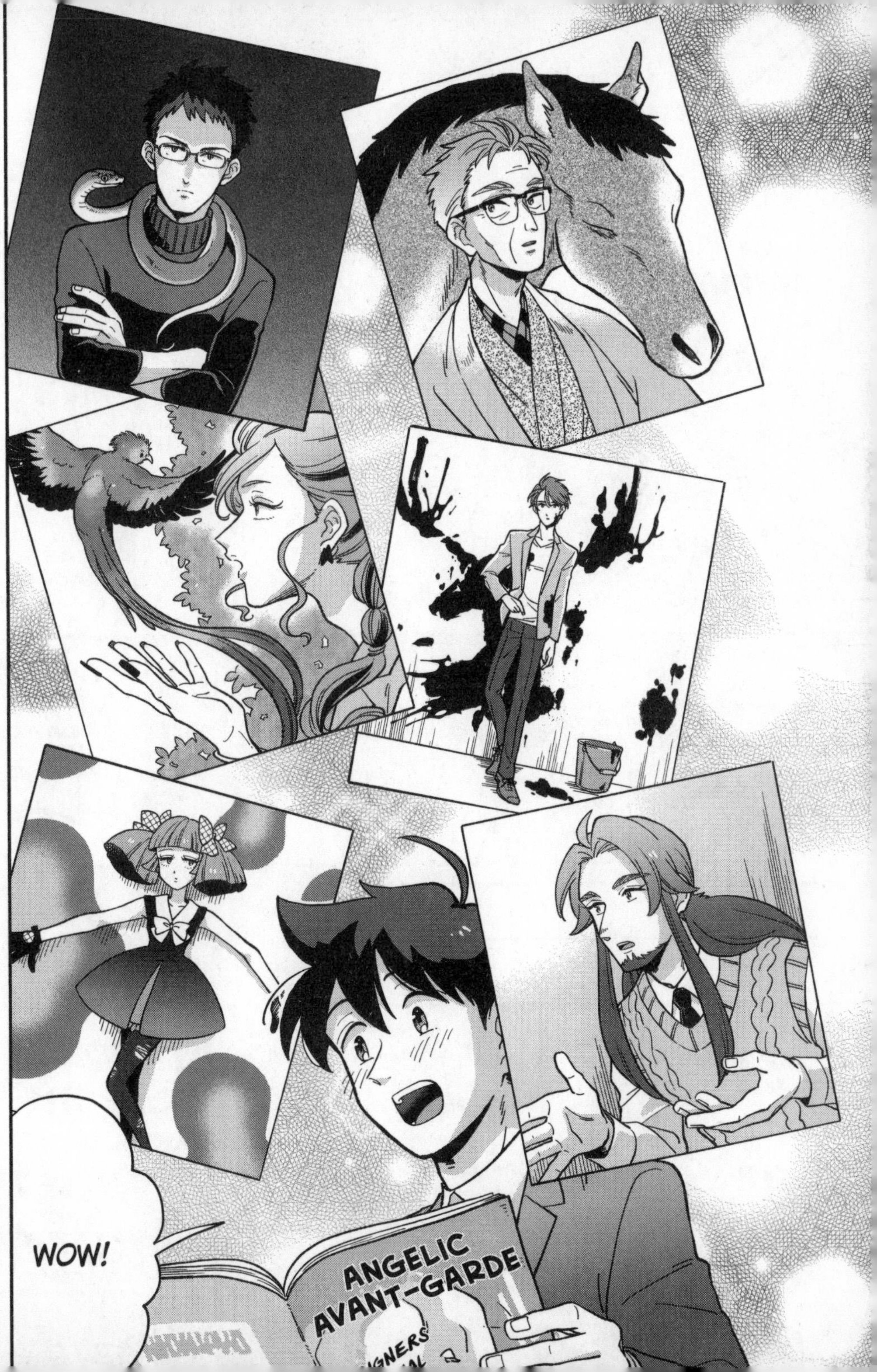
WOW!
ANGELIC AVANT-GARDE

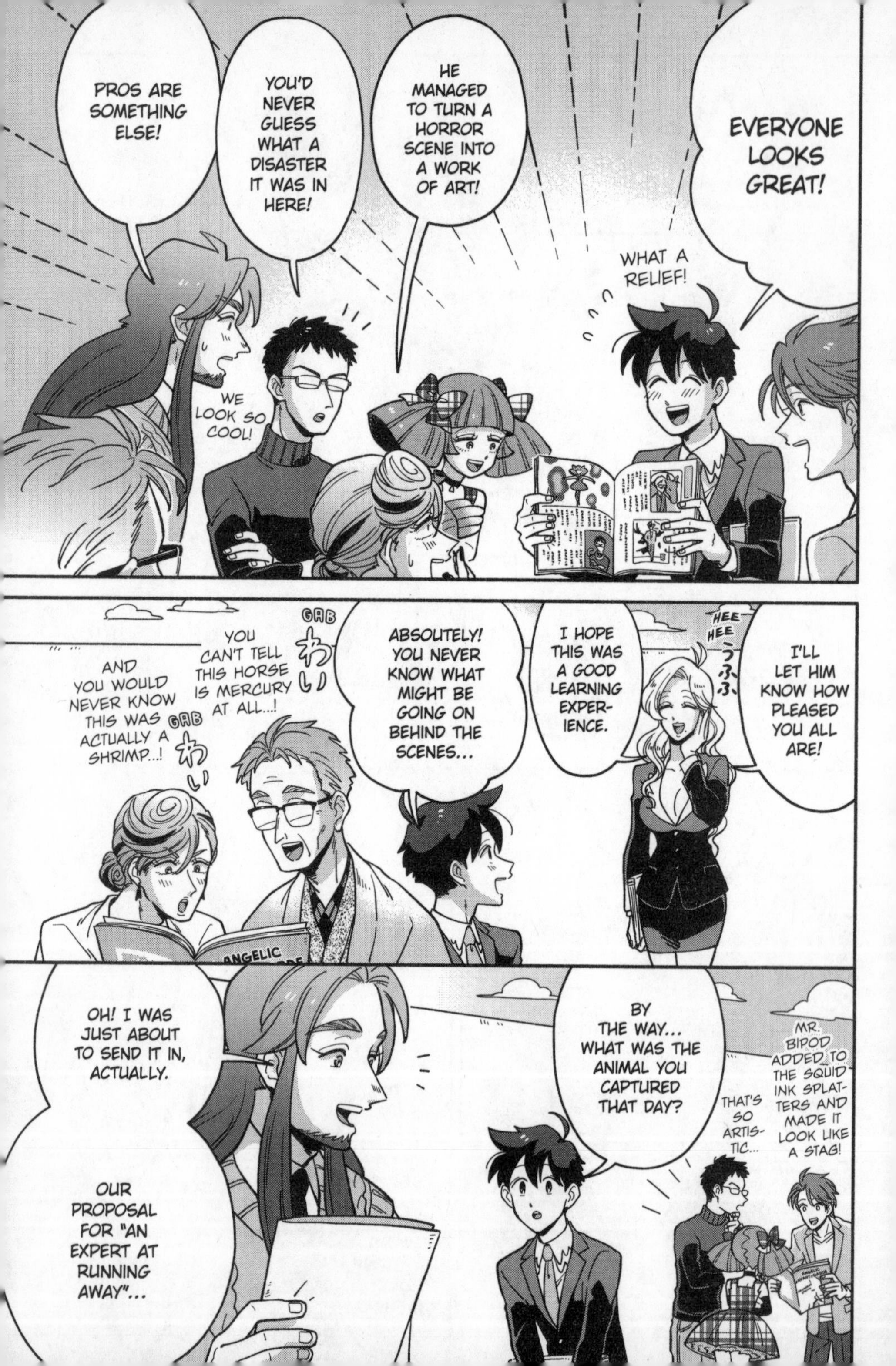
EVERYONE LOOKS GREAT!
WHAT A RELIEF!
HE MANAGED TO TURN A HORROR SCENE INTO A WORK OF ART!
YOU'D NEVER GUESS WHAT A DISASTER IT WAS IN HERE!
PROS ARE SOMETHING ELSE!
WE LOOK SO COOL!
I'LL LET HIM KNOW HOW PLEASED YOU ALL ARE!
HEE HEE うふふ
I HOPE THIS WAS A GOOD LEARNING EXPERIENCE.
ABSOUTELY! YOU NEVER KNOW WHAT MIGHT BE GOING ON BEHIND THE SCENES…
GAB わい
YOU CAN'T TELL THIS HORSE IS MERCURY AT ALL...!
GAB わい
AND YOU WOULD NEVER KNOW THIS WAS ACTUALLY A SHRIMP...!
MR. BIPOD ADDED TO THE SQUID INK SPLATTERS AND MADE IT LOOK LIKE A STAG!
THAT'S SO ARTISTIC...
BY THE WAY… WHAT WAS THE ANIMAL YOU CAPTURED THAT DAY?
OH! I WAS JUST ABOUT TO SEND IT IN, ACTUALLY.
OUR PROPOSAL FOR "AN EXPERT AT RUNNING AWAY"…

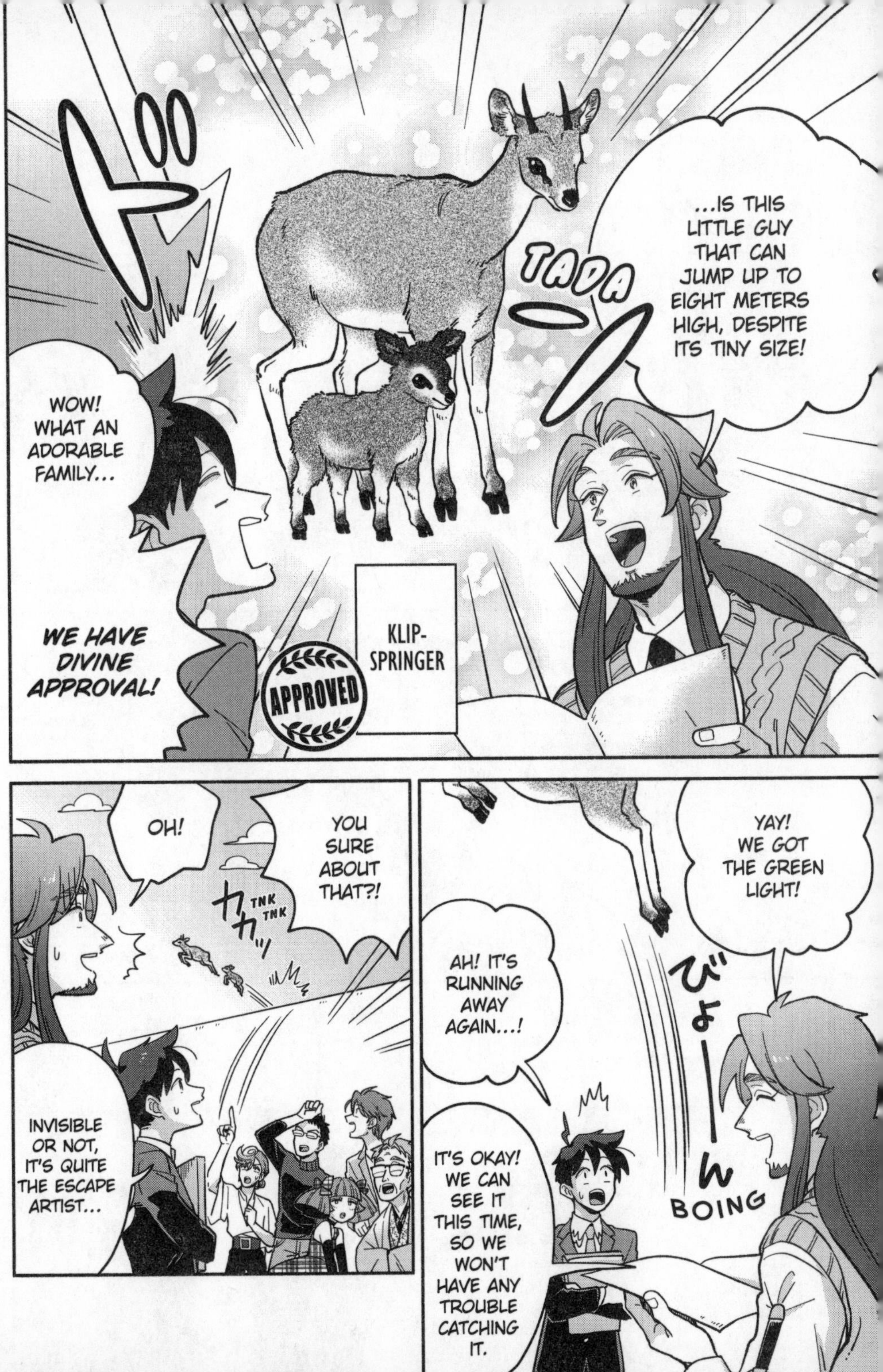
...IS THIS LITTLE GUY THAT CAN JUMP UP TO EIGHT METERS HIGH, DESPITE ITS TINY SIZE!
TADA
WOW! WHAT AN ADORABLE FAMILY...
KLIP-SPRINGER
WE HAVE DIVINE APPROVAL!
APPROVED
YAY! WE GOT THE GREEN LIGHT!
AH! IT'S RUNNING AWAY AGAIN...!
びょーーん
BOING
IT'S OKAY! WE CAN SEE IT THIS TIME, SO WE WON'T HAVE ANY TROUBLE CATCHING IT.
YOU SURE ABOUT THAT?!
OH!
TNK TNK
INVISIBLE OR NOT, IT'S QUITE THE ESCAPE ARTIST...

THE ENCYCLOPEDIA OF REAL ANIMALS 38

ANIMAL 88 KLIPSPRINGER

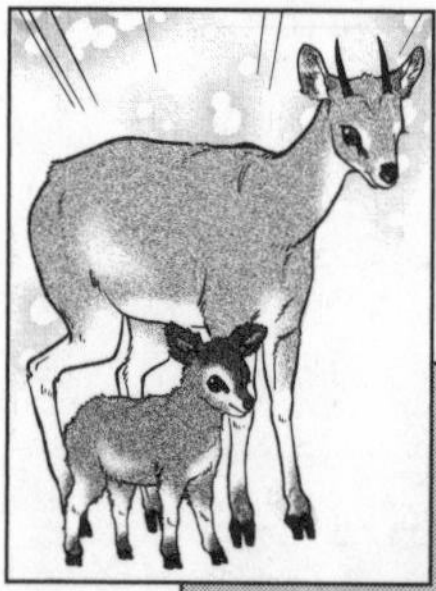

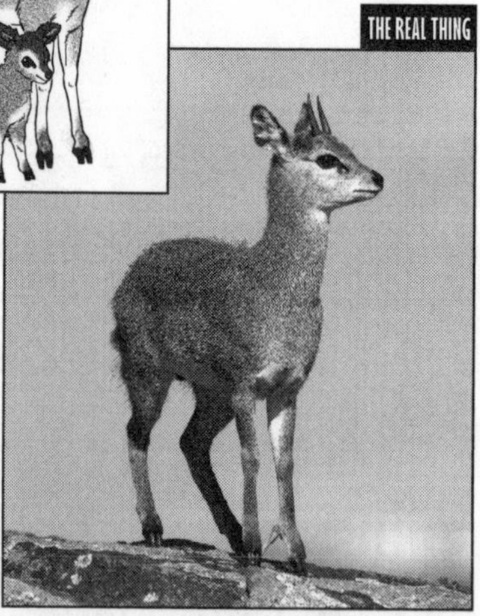
THE REAL THING

Another name for this species is klipbok. The females are larger than the males.
Photo: Minden Pictures/Aflo

The klipspringer is a small antelope that lives on steep, rocky terrain. Despite being the size of a medium-sized dog, it can jump over boulders several times its own height. Walking and leaping around on the tips of its cylindrical hooves, the klipspringer is as graceful and light on its feet as a ballerina dancing in toe shoes.

The klipspringer's slightly sloping back helps it keep all four feet on the ground in mountainous areas that lack many flat surfaces. Its dense fur and thick skin help protect it from falls and injuries. Because of its compact size, the klipspringer has a small stomach and is thus unable to store food internally for extended periods of time. For that reason, it prefers a diet of young shoots and fruit that's rich in nutrients and low in fiber.

[Name]	*Oreotragus oreotragus*
[Classification]	Class: Mammalia Order: Artiodactyla Family: Bovidae Genus: *Oreotragus*
[Habitat]	Africa
[Length]	75-90 cm (2.5-3 ft)

ANIMAL 89 HARLEQUIN SHRIMP

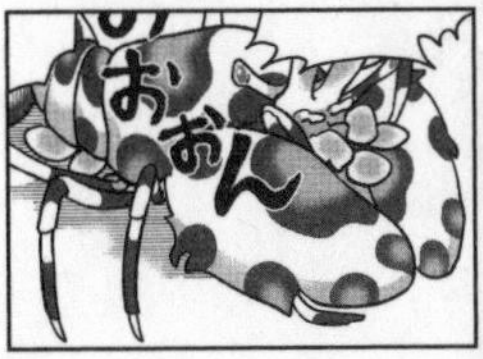
おおん

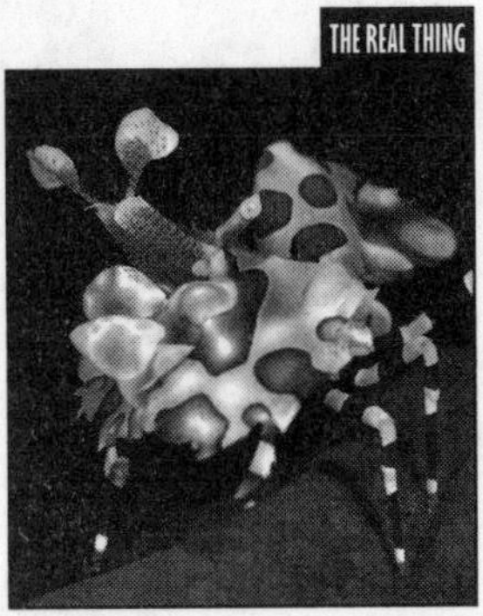
THE REAL THING

A harlequin shrimp on top of a starfish.

Photo: Minden Pictures/Aflo

The harlequin shrimp is one of the few animals to feed exclusively on starfish. Milky white with blue and/or pink polka-dots, this shrimp joins forces with a member of the opposite sex to hunt. When they find a starfish attached to the ocean floor, the smaller, speedier male quickly cuts off its arms. The two shrimp then work together to flip the starfish over and share a feast of internal organs.

[Name]	*Hymenocera picta*
[Classification]	Class: Malacostraca Order: Decapoda Family: Palaemonidae Genus: *Hymenocera*
[Habitat]	The coral reefs of the Pacific and Indian Oceans
[Length]	2-5 cm (0.8-2 in)

SPECIAL FEATURE FLEHMEN RESPONSE

The flehmen response is a behavior provoked by the pheromones of other members of the same species or by a particularly unusual smell. Ordinary smells are detected in the upper part of the nasal cavity, while pheromones are sensed via the vomeronasal organ located just above the roof of the mouth.

What's the best way to get the most odor molecules to stick to the roof of your mouth? Try a few different poses and you might understand the horse's reasoning behind lifting its head with its lips curled back.

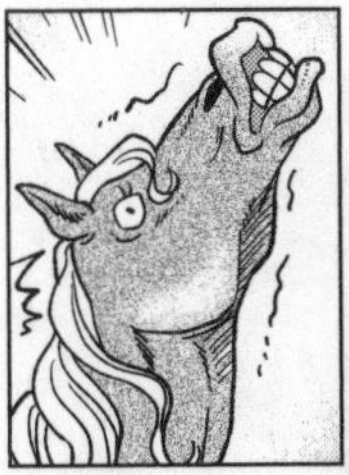

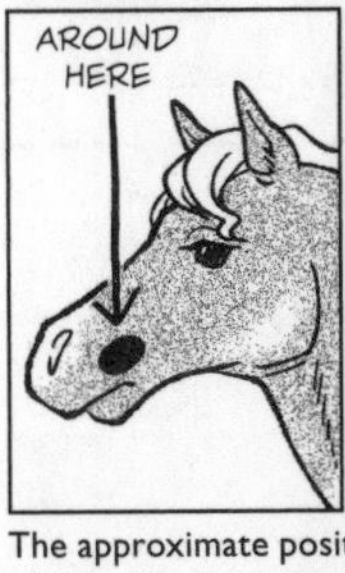
AROUND HERE

The approximate position of the vomeronasal organ.

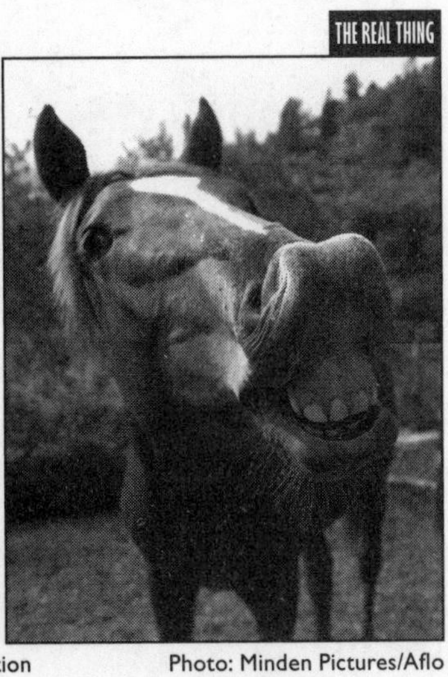
THE REAL THING

Photo: Minden Pictures/Aflo

HEAVEN'S DESIGN TEAM

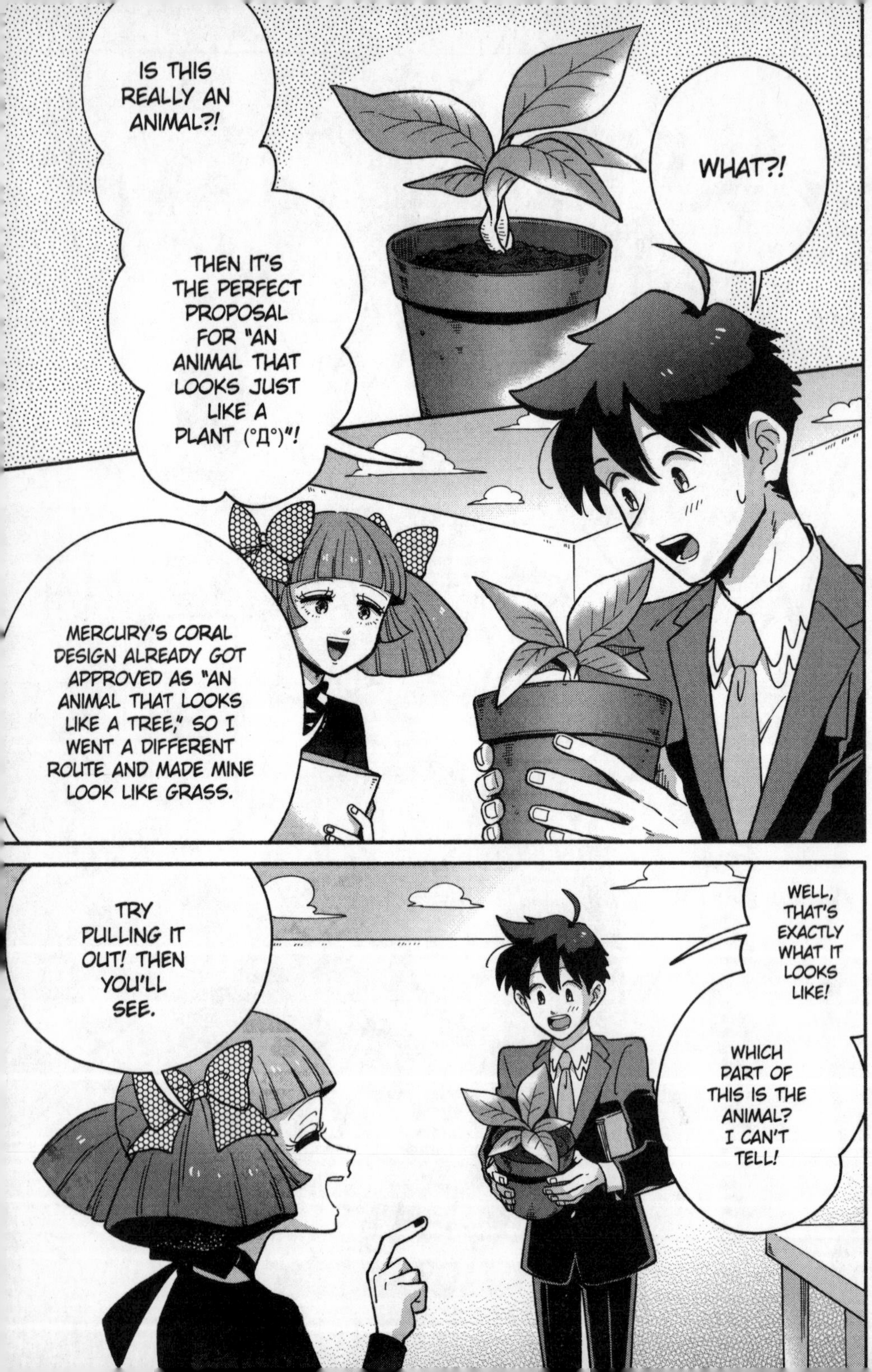
WHAT?!
IS THIS REALLY AN ANIMAL?!
THEN IT'S THE PERFECT PROPOSAL FOR "AN ANIMAL THAT LOOKS JUST LIKE A PLANT (°Д°)"!
MERCURY'S CORAL DESIGN ALREADY GOT APPROVED AS "AN ANIMAL THAT LOOKS LIKE A TREE," SO I WENT A DIFFERENT ROUTE AND MADE MINE LOOK LIKE GRASS.
WELL, THAT'S EXACTLY WHAT IT LOOKS LIKE!
WHICH PART OF THIS IS THE ANIMAL? I CAN'T TELL!
TRY PULLING IT OUT! THEN YOU'LL SEE.

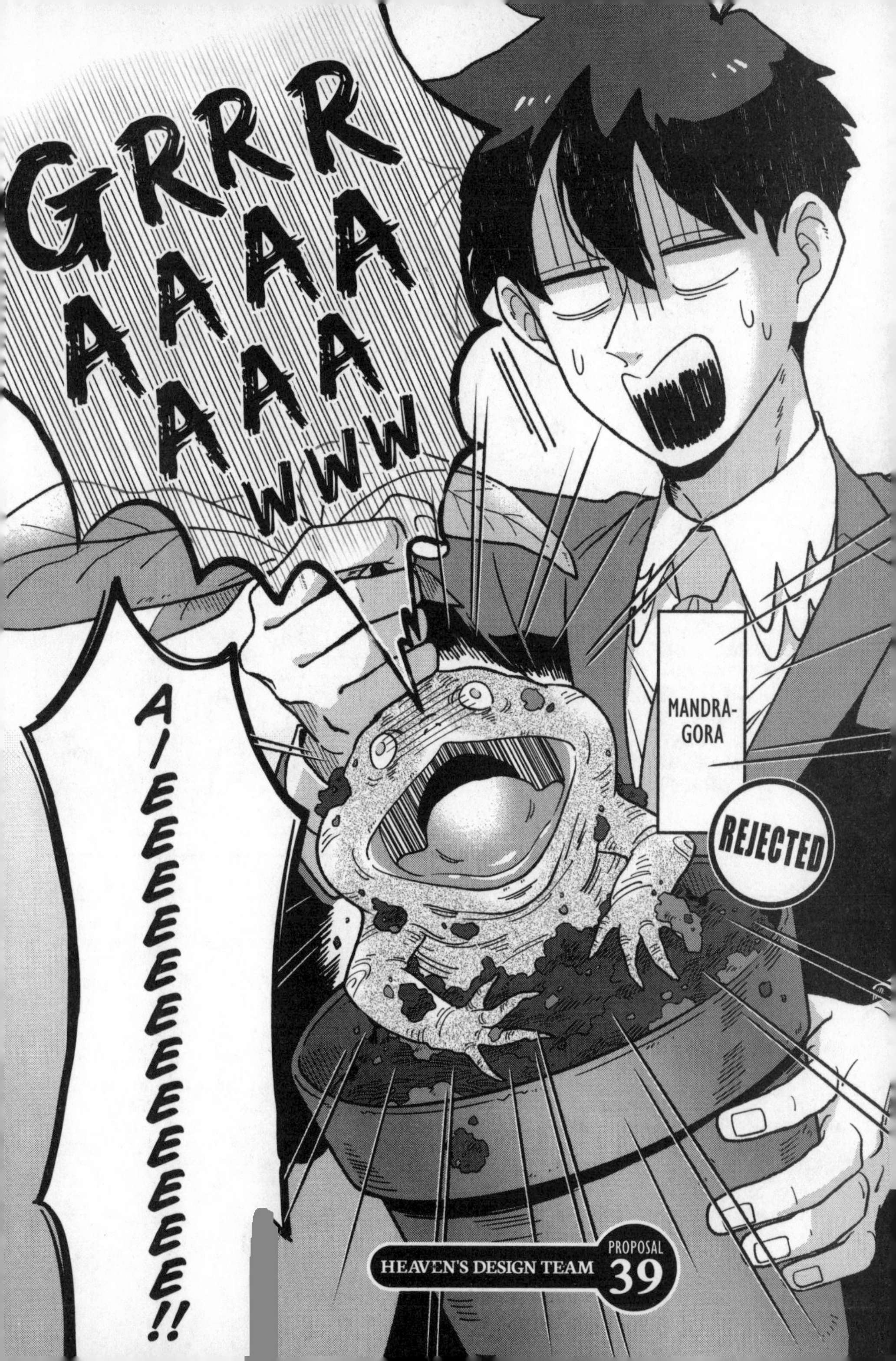
GRRRAAAAAAAWWW
MANDRA-GORA
REJECTED
AIEEEEEEEEEEEEEEEE!!
HEAVEN'S DESIGN TEAM PROPOSAL 39

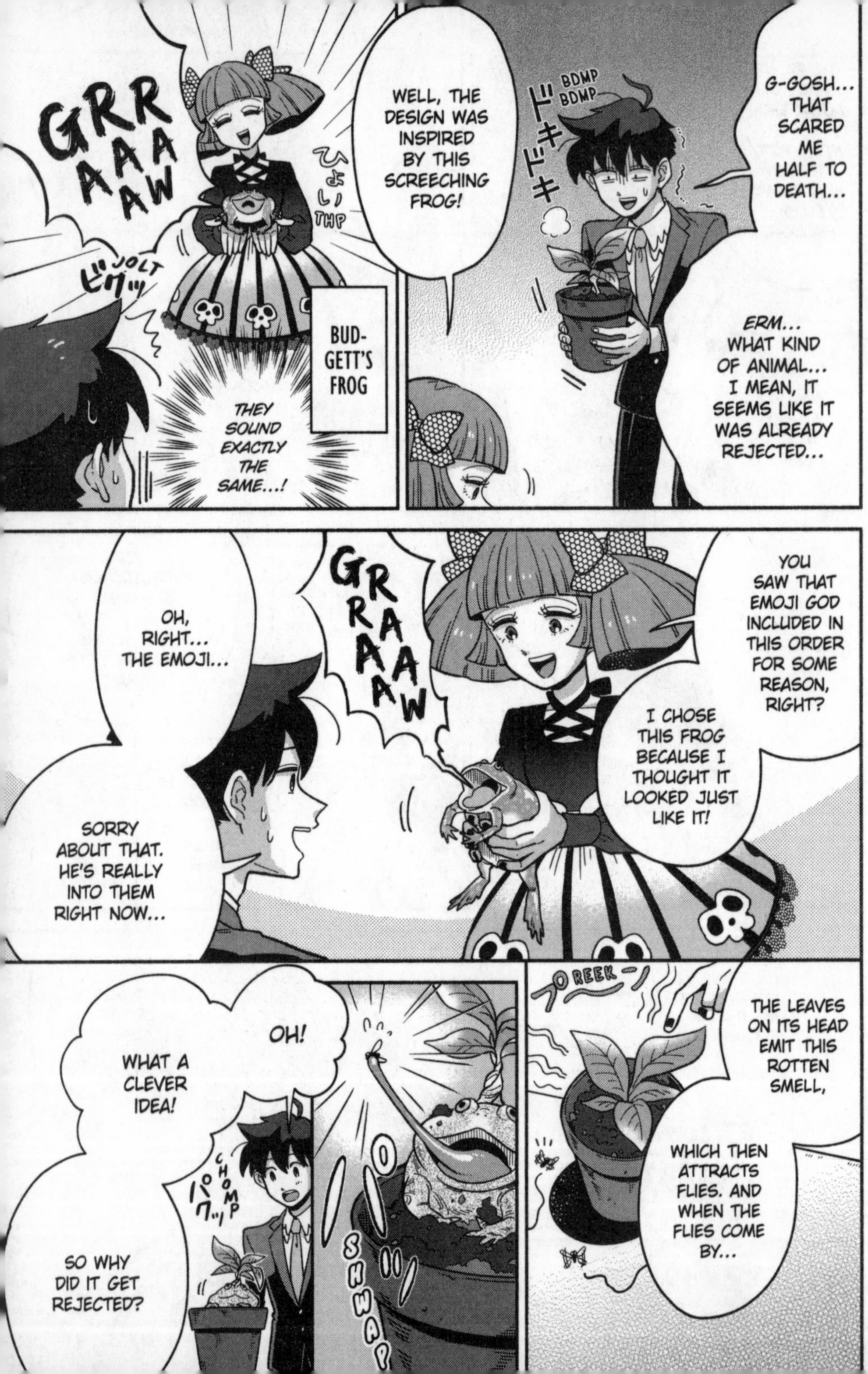
BDMP BDMP
ドキドキ
G-GOSH... THAT SCARED ME HALF TO DEATH...
ERM... WHAT KIND OF ANIMAL... I MEAN, IT SEEMS LIKE IT WAS ALREADY REJECTED...
WELL, THE DESIGN WAS INSPIRED BY THIS SCREECHING FROG!
ひょい THP
BUD-GETT'S FROG
GRRAAAAW
ビクッ JOLT
THEY SOUND EXACTLY THE SAME...!
YOU SAW THAT EMOJI GOD INCLUDED IN THIS ORDER FOR SOME REASON, RIGHT?
I CHOSE THIS FROG BECAUSE I THOUGHT IT LOOKED JUST LIKE IT!
GRRAAAAW
OH, RIGHT... THE EMOJI...
SORRY ABOUT THAT. HE'S REALLY INTO THEM RIGHT NOW...
REEK
THE LEAVES ON ITS HEAD EMIT THIS ROTTEN SMELL,
WHICH THEN ATTRACTS FLIES. AND WHEN THE FLIES COME BY...
SHWAP
パクッ CHOMP
OH!
WHAT A CLEVER IDEA!
SO WHY DID IT GET REJECTED?

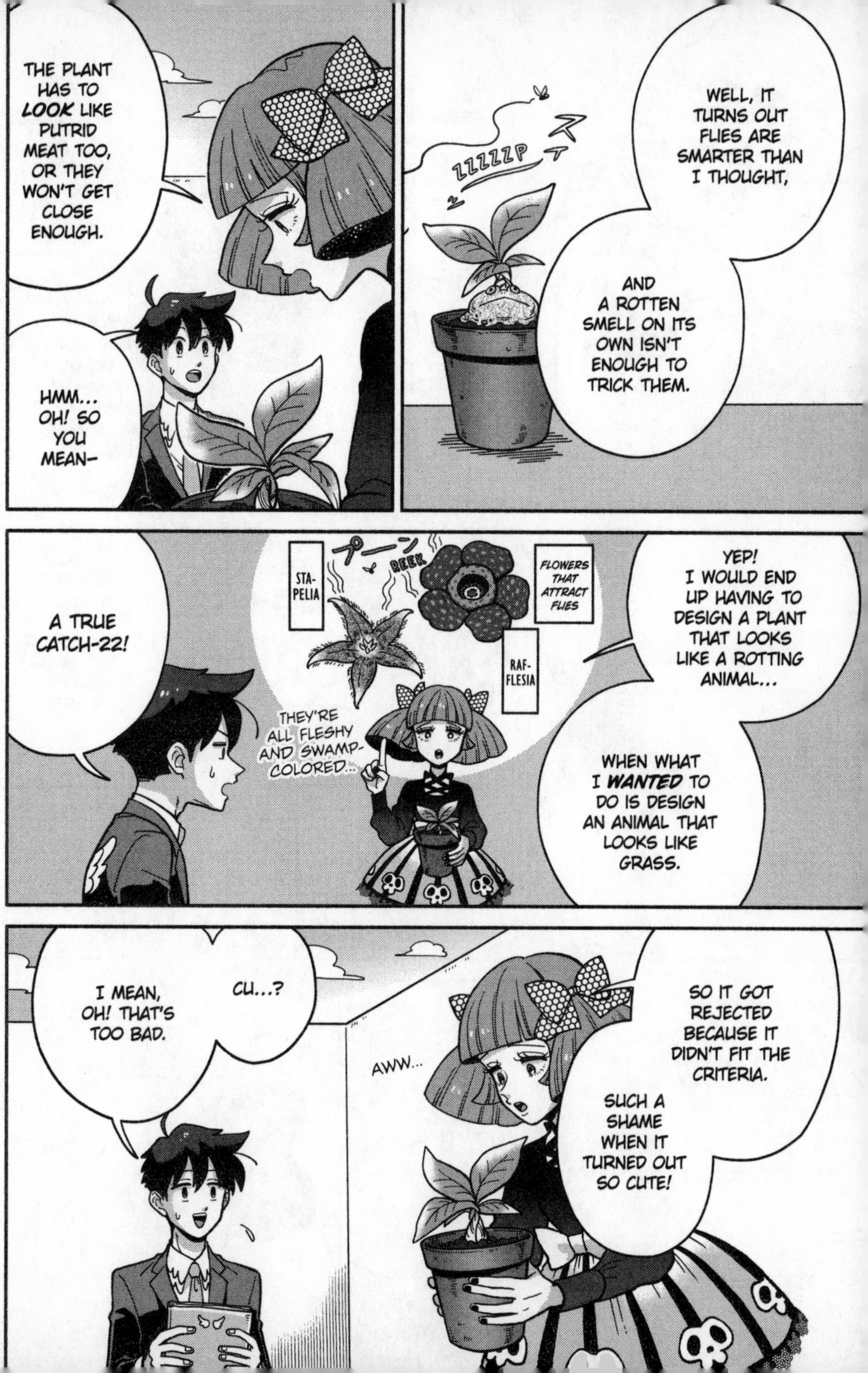
WELL, IT TURNS OUT FLIES ARE SMARTER THAN I THOUGHT,
ZZZZZP
AND A ROTTEN SMELL ON ITS OWN ISN'T ENOUGH TO TRICK THEM.
THE PLANT HAS TO LOOK LIKE PUTRID MEAT TOO, OR THEY WON'T GET CLOSE ENOUGH.
HMM... OH! SO YOU MEAN-
YEP! I WOULD END UP HAVING TO DESIGN A PLANT THAT LOOKS LIKE A ROTTING ANIMAL...
FLOWERS THAT ATTRACT FLIES
RAF-FLESIA
REEK
STA-PELIA
THEY'RE ALL FLESHY AND SWAMP-COLORED...
WHEN WHAT I WANTED TO DO IS DESIGN AN ANIMAL THAT LOOKS LIKE GRASS.
A TRUE CATCH-22!
SO IT GOT REJECTED BECAUSE IT DIDN'T FIT THE CRITERIA.
SUCH A SHAME WHEN IT TURNED OUT SO CUTE!
AWW...
CU...?
I MEAN, OH! THAT'S TOO BAD.

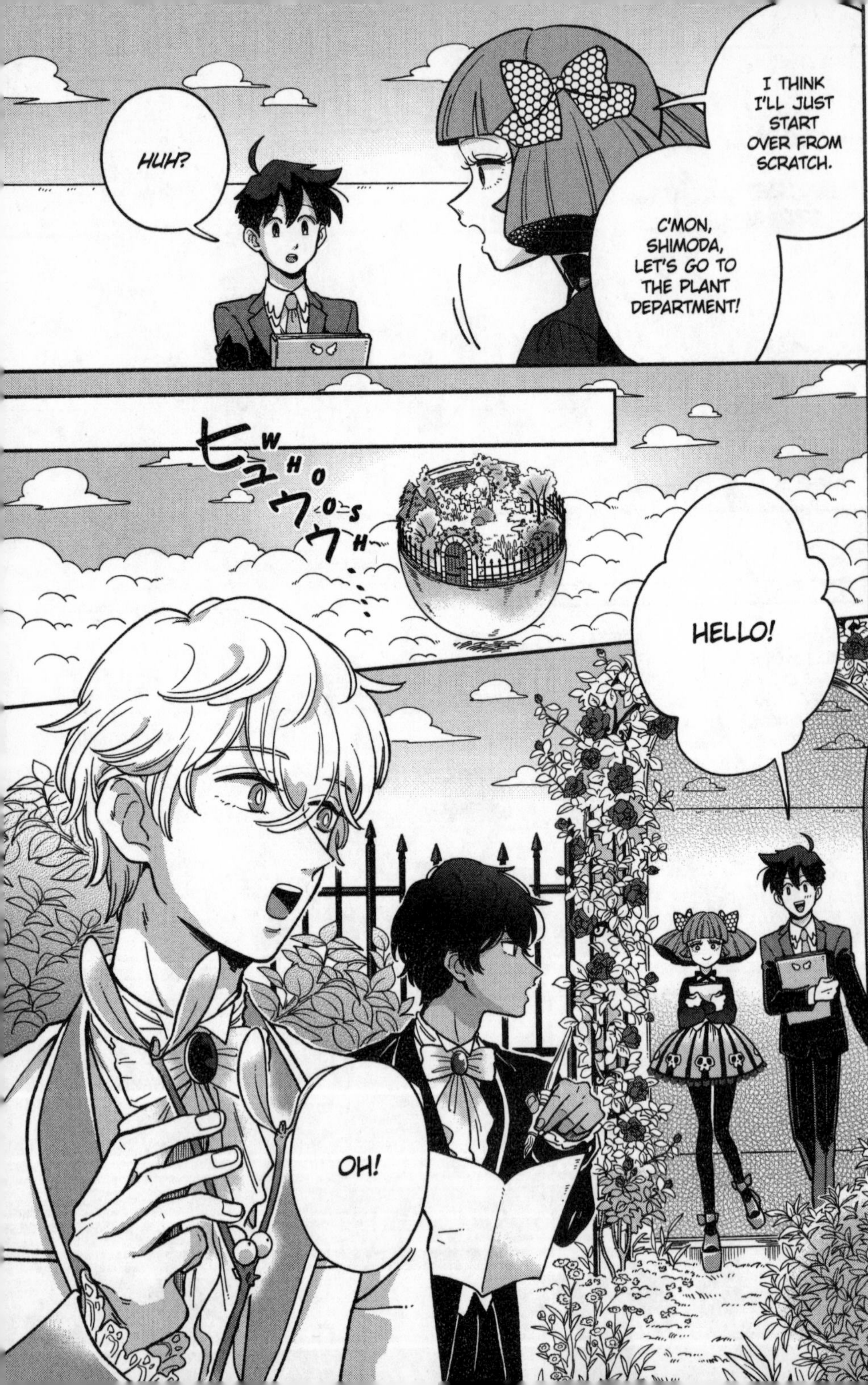
I THINK I'LL JUST START OVER FROM SCRATCH.
C'MON, SHIMODA, LET'S GO TO THE PLANT DEPARTMENT!
HUH?
ヒュウウ
WHOOSH
HELLO!
OH!

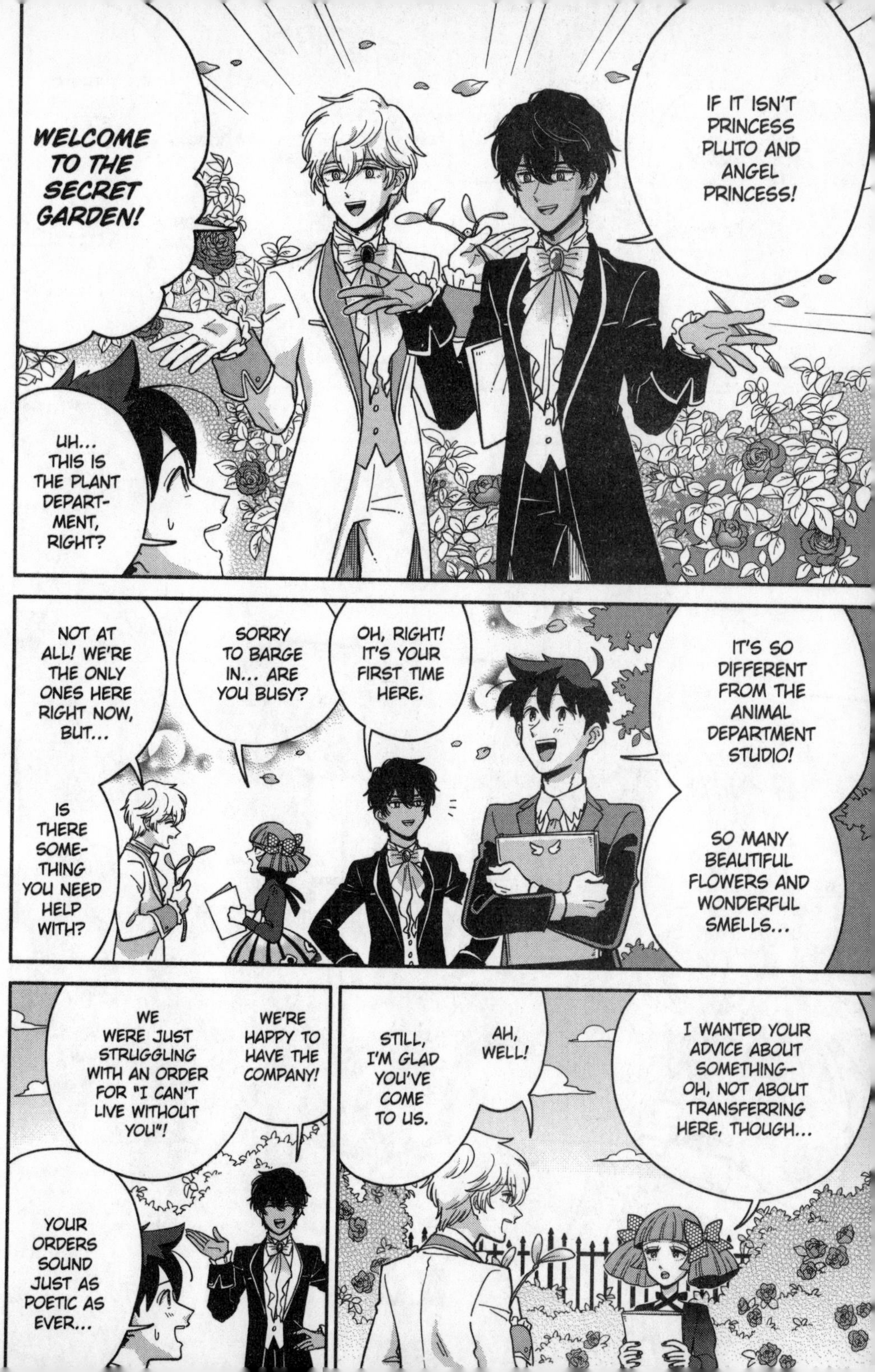
IF IT ISN'T PRINCESS PLUTO AND ANGEL PRINCESS!
WELCOME TO THE SECRET GARDEN!
UH... THIS IS THE PLANT DEPARTMENT, RIGHT?
IT'S SO DIFFERENT FROM THE ANIMAL DEPARTMENT STUDIO!
SO MANY BEAUTIFUL FLOWERS AND WONDERFUL SMELLS...
OH, RIGHT! IT'S YOUR FIRST TIME HERE.
SORRY TO BARGE IN... ARE YOU BUSY?
NOT AT ALL! WE'RE THE ONLY ONES HERE RIGHT NOW, BUT...
IS THERE SOMETHING YOU NEED HELP WITH?
I WANTED YOUR ADVICE ABOUT SOMETHING—OH, NOT ABOUT TRANSFERRING HERE, THOUGH...
AH, WELL!
STILL, I'M GLAD YOU'VE COME TO US.
WE'RE HAPPY TO HAVE THE COMPANY!
WE WERE JUST STRUGGLING WITH AN ORDER FOR "I CAN'T LIVE WITHOUT YOU"!
YOUR ORDERS SOUND JUST AS POETIC AS EVER...

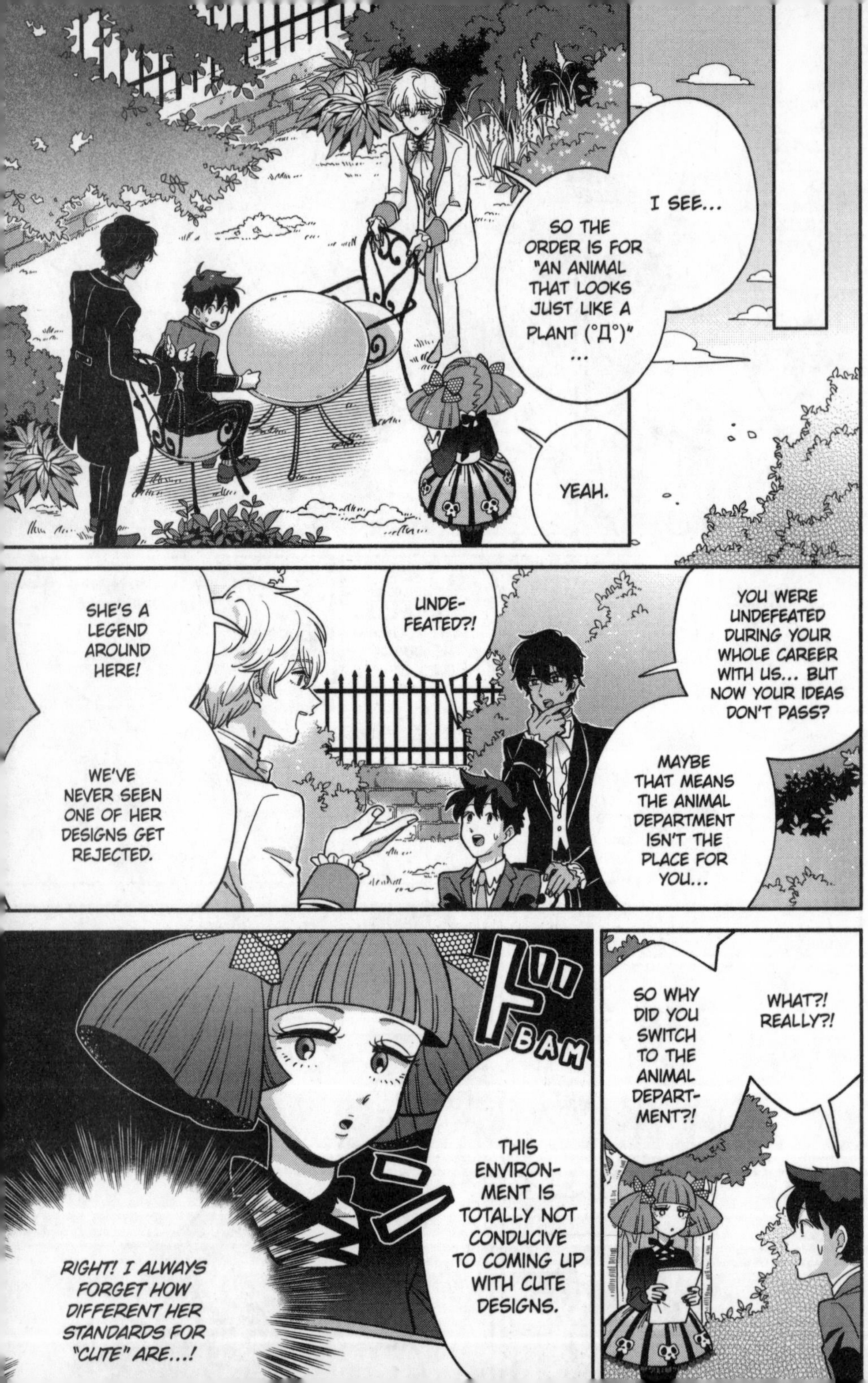
I SEE...
SO THE ORDER IS FOR "AN ANIMAL THAT LOOKS JUST LIKE A PLANT (°Д°)" ...
YEAH.
YOU WERE UNDEFEATED DURING YOUR WHOLE CAREER WITH US... BUT NOW YOUR IDEAS DON'T PASS?
MAYBE THAT MEANS THE ANIMAL DEPARTMENT ISN'T THE PLACE FOR YOU...
UNDE-FEATED?!
SHE'S A LEGEND AROUND HERE!
WE'VE NEVER SEEN ONE OF HER DESIGNS GET REJECTED.
WHAT?! REALLY?!
SO WHY DID YOU SWITCH TO THE ANIMAL DEPART-MENT?!
BAM
THIS ENVIRON-MENT IS TOTALLY NOT CONDUCIVE TO COMING UP WITH CUTE DESIGNS.
RIGHT! I ALWAYS FORGET HOW DIFFERENT HER STANDARDS FOR "CUTE" ARE...!

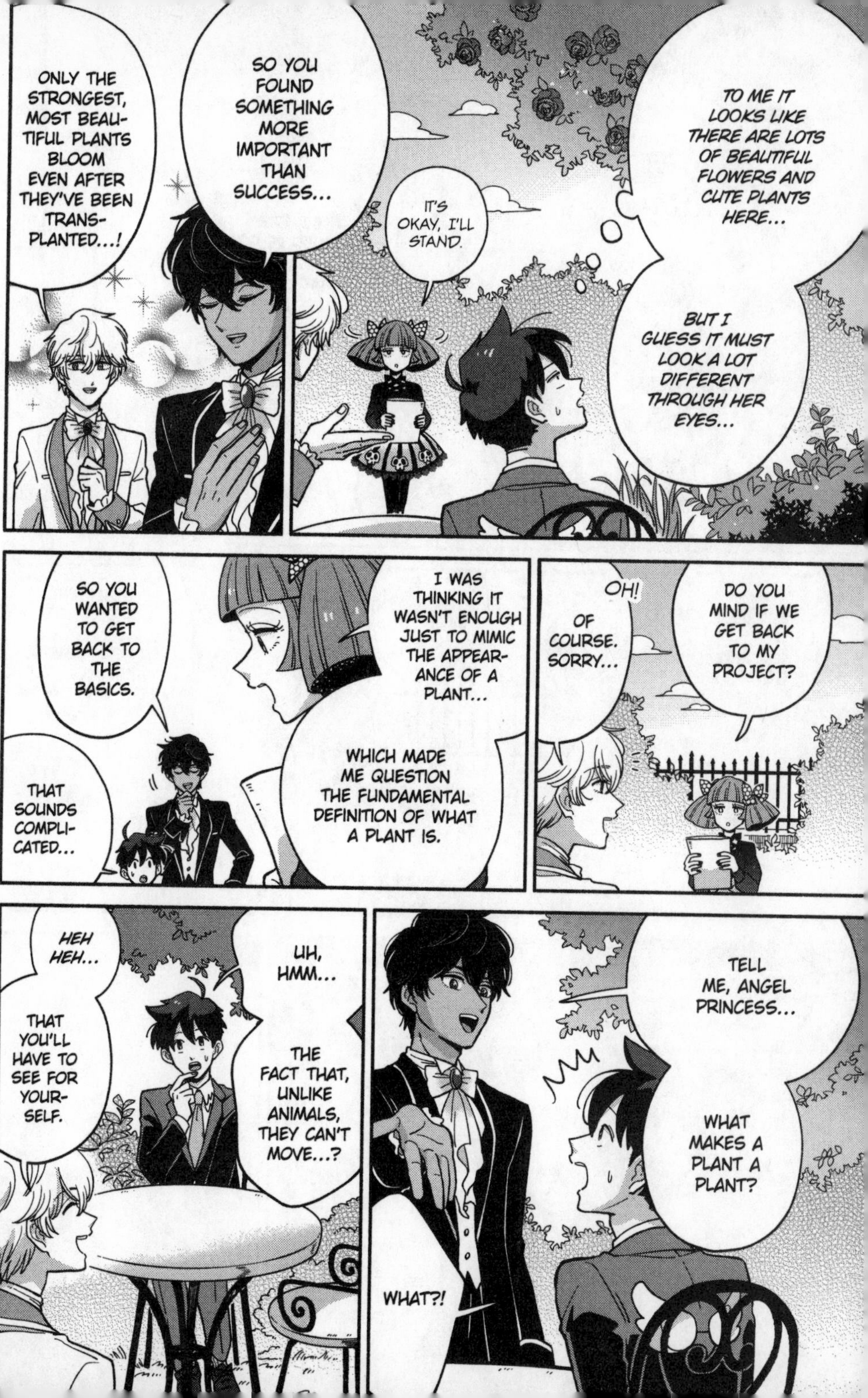
TO ME IT LOOKS LIKE THERE ARE LOTS OF BEAUTIFUL FLOWERS AND CUTE PLANTS HERE...
BUT I GUESS IT MUST LOOK A LOT DIFFERENT THROUGH HER EYES...
IT'S OKAY, I'LL STAND.
SO YOU FOUND SOMETHING MORE IMPORTANT THAN SUCCESS...
ONLY THE STRONGEST, MOST BEAUTIFUL PLANTS BLOOM EVEN AFTER THEY'VE BEEN TRANSPLANTED...!
DO YOU MIND IF WE GET BACK TO MY PROJECT?
OH!
OF COURSE. SORRY...
I WAS THINKING IT WASN'T ENOUGH JUST TO MIMIC THE APPEARANCE OF A PLANT...
WHICH MADE ME QUESTION THE FUNDAMENTAL DEFINITION OF WHAT A PLANT IS.
SO YOU WANTED TO GET BACK TO THE BASICS.
THAT SOUNDS COMPLICATED...
TELL ME, ANGEL PRINCESS...
WHAT MAKES A PLANT A PLANT?
MM
WHAT?!
UH, HMM...
THE FACT THAT, UNLIKE ANIMALS, THEY CAN'T MOVE...?
HEH HEH...
THAT YOU'LL HAVE TO SEE FOR YOURSELF.

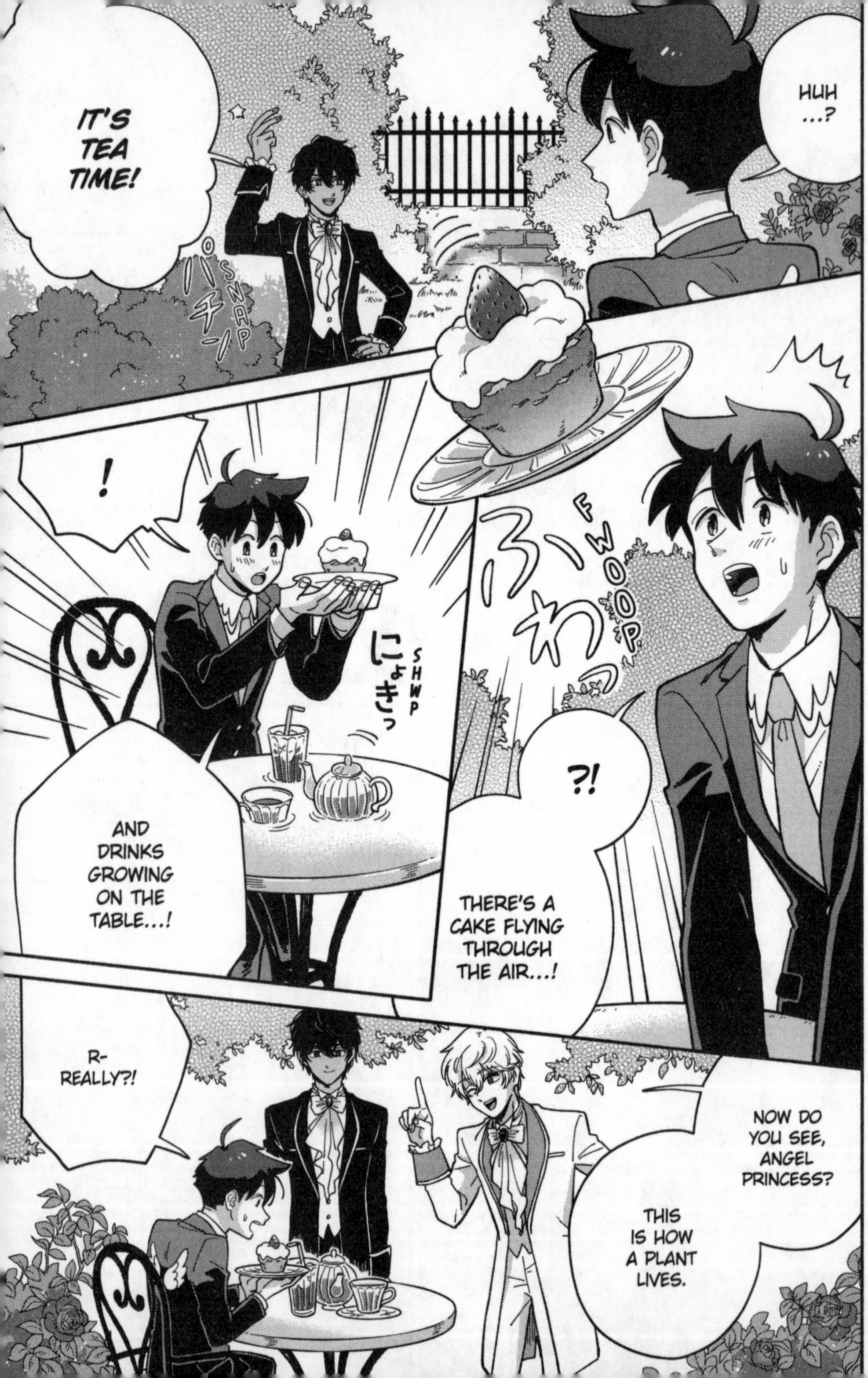
HUH ...?
IT'S TEA TIME!
パチーン
SNAP
ふわっ
FWOOP
?!
THERE'S A CAKE FLYING THROUGH THE AIR...!
!
にょきっ
SHWP
AND DRINKS GROWING ON THE TABLE...!
NOW DO YOU SEE, ANGEL PRINCESS?
THIS IS HOW A PLANT LIVES.
R-REALLY?!

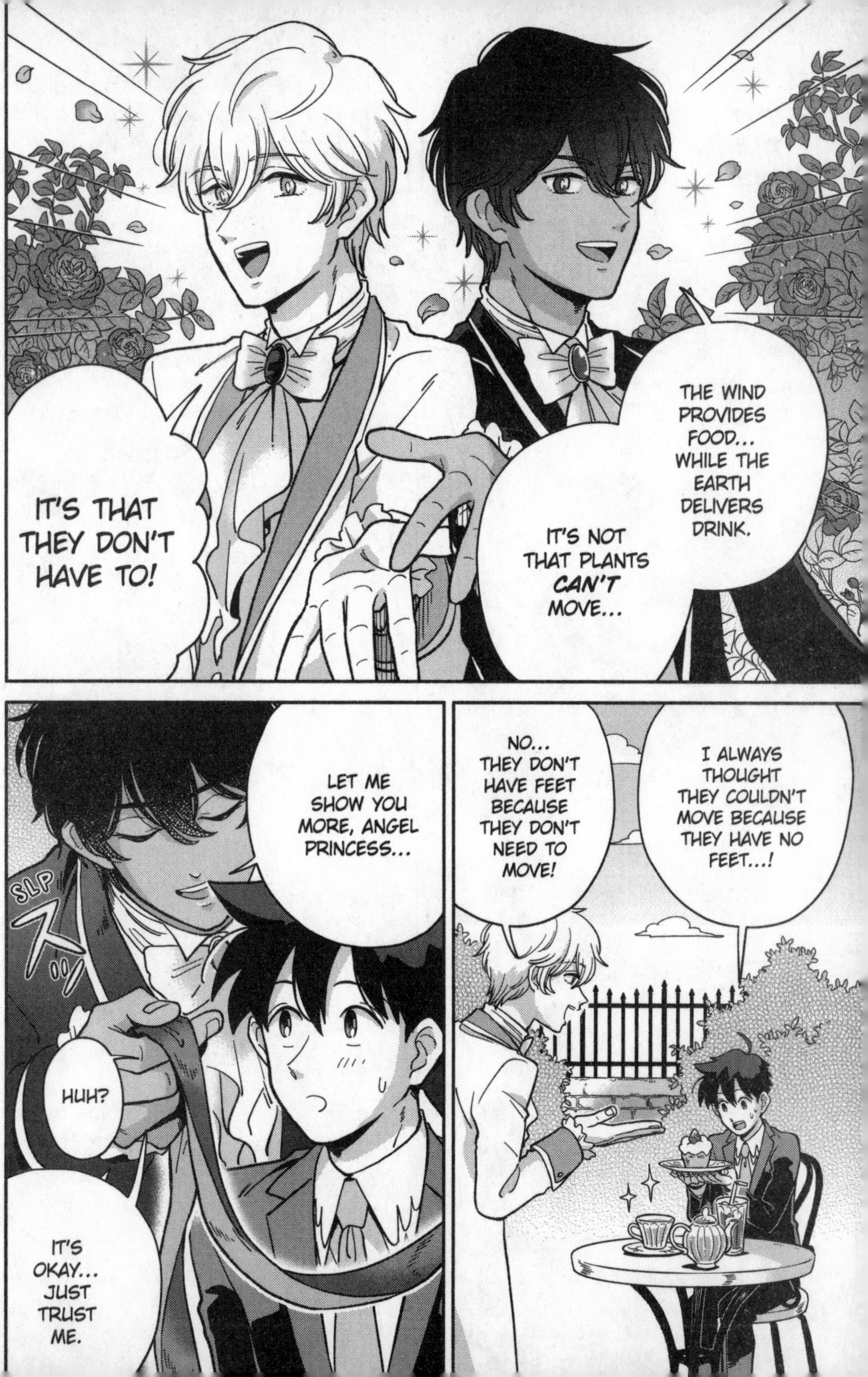
THE WIND PROVIDES FOOD... WHILE THE EARTH DELIVERS DRINK.
IT'S NOT THAT PLANTS *CAN'T* MOVE...
IT'S THAT THEY DON'T HAVE TO!
I ALWAYS THOUGHT THEY COULDN'T MOVE BECAUSE THEY HAVE NO FEET...!
NO... THEY DON'T HAVE FEET BECAUSE THEY DON'T NEED TO MOVE!
LET ME SHOW YOU MORE, ANGEL PRINCESS...
SLP
HUH?
IT'S OKAY... JUST TRUST ME.

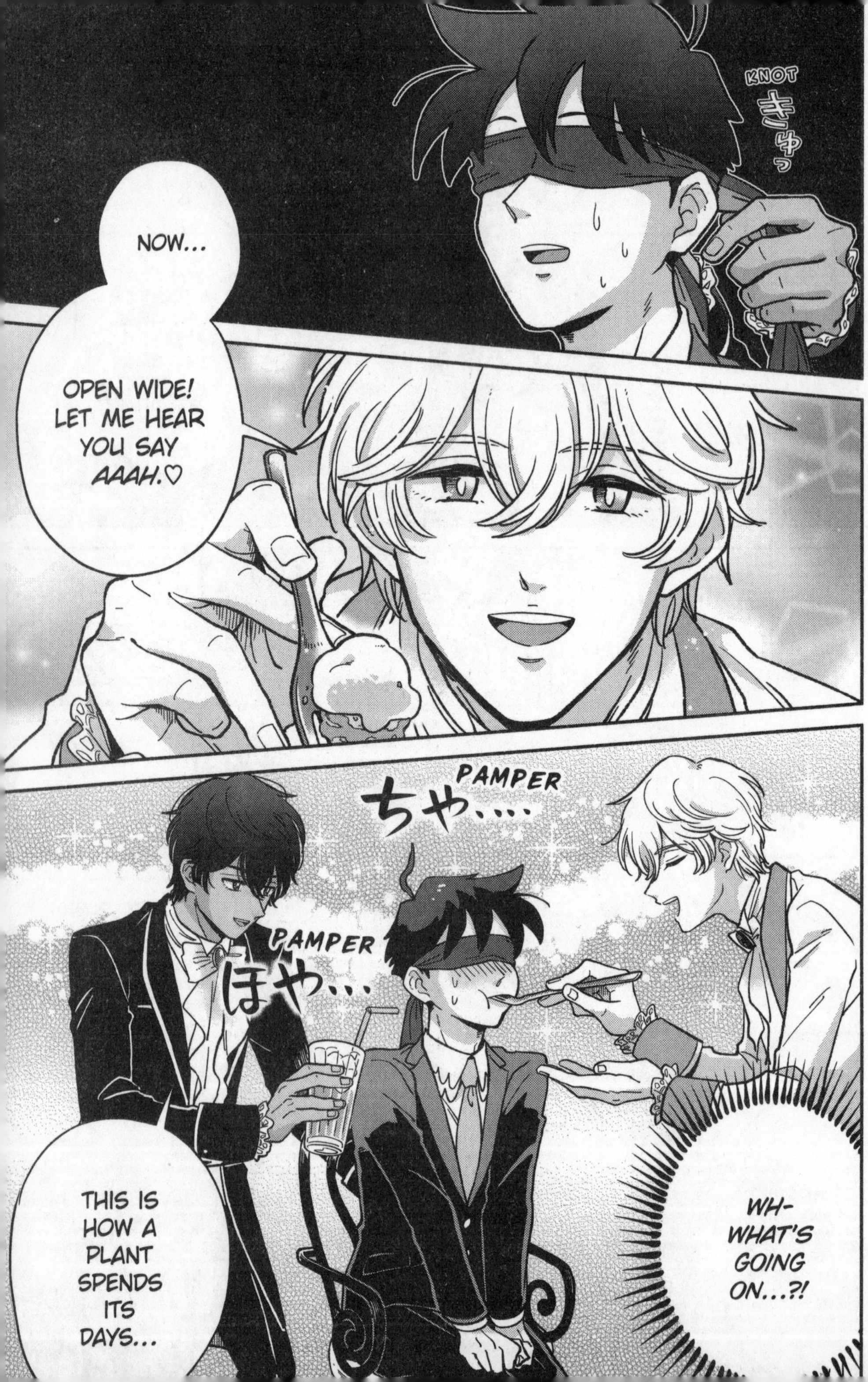
KNOT
きゅっ
NOW...
OPEN WIDE! LET ME HEAR YOU SAY *AAAH.*♡
PAMPER
ちや…...
PAMPER
ほや…
WH- WHAT'S GOING ON...?!
THIS IS HOW A PLANT SPENDS ITS DAYS...

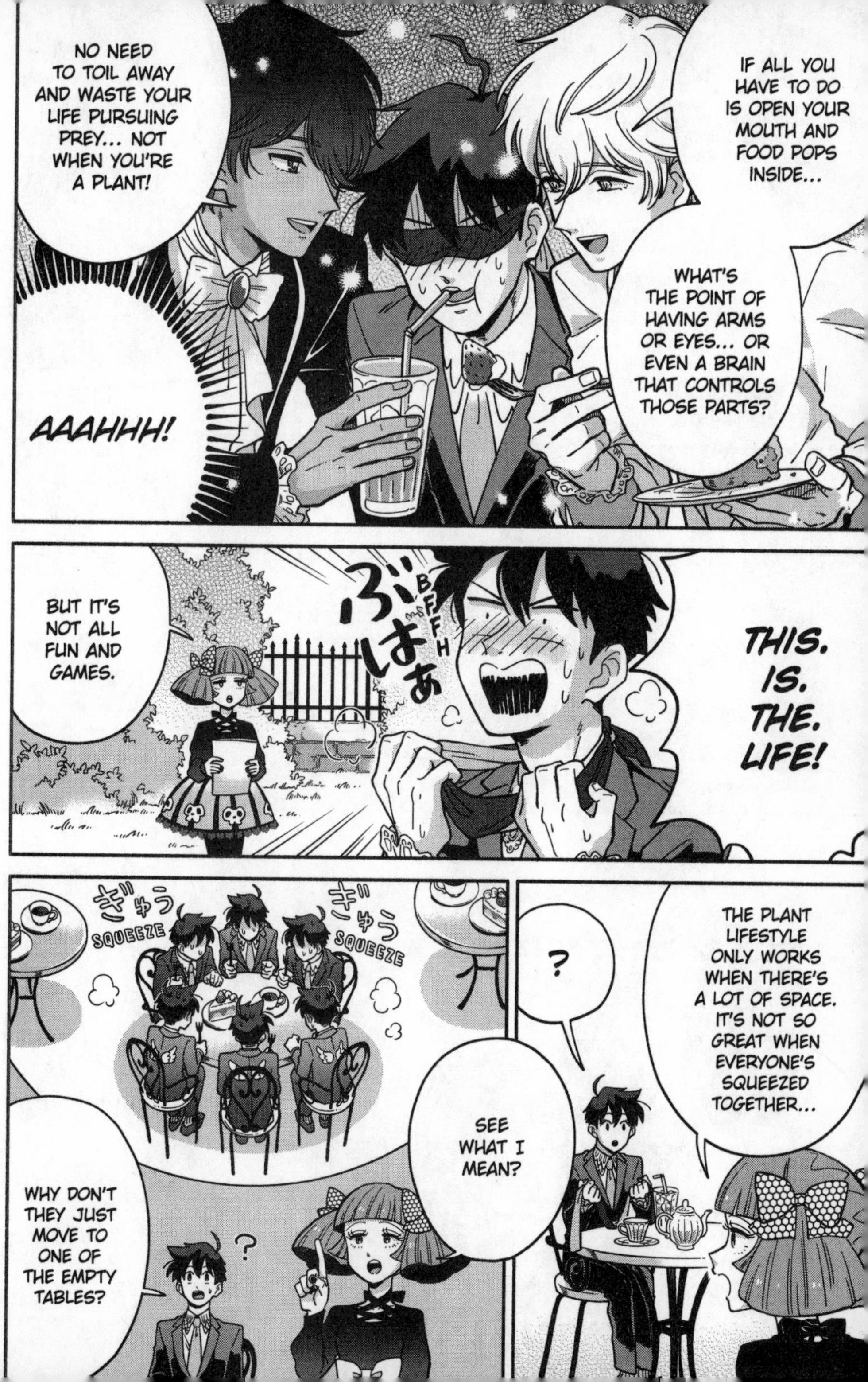

IF ALL YOU HAVE TO DO IS OPEN YOUR MOUTH AND FOOD POPS INSIDE...
WHAT'S THE POINT OF HAVING ARMS OR EYES... OR EVEN A BRAIN THAT CONTROLS THOSE PARTS?
NO NEED TO TOIL AWAY AND WASTE YOUR LIFE PURSUING PREY... NOT WHEN YOU'RE A PLANT!
AAAHHH!
THIS. IS. THE. LIFE!
ぶはぁ
BFFH
BUT IT'S NOT ALL FUN AND GAMES.
THE PLANT LIFESTYLE ONLY WORKS WHEN THERE'S A LOT OF SPACE. IT'S NOT SO GREAT WHEN EVERYONE'S SQUEEZED TOGETHER...
?
SEE WHAT I MEAN?
ぎゅう
SQUEEZE
ぎゅう
SQUEEZE
WHY DON'T THEY JUST MOVE TO ONE OF THE EMPTY TABLES?
?

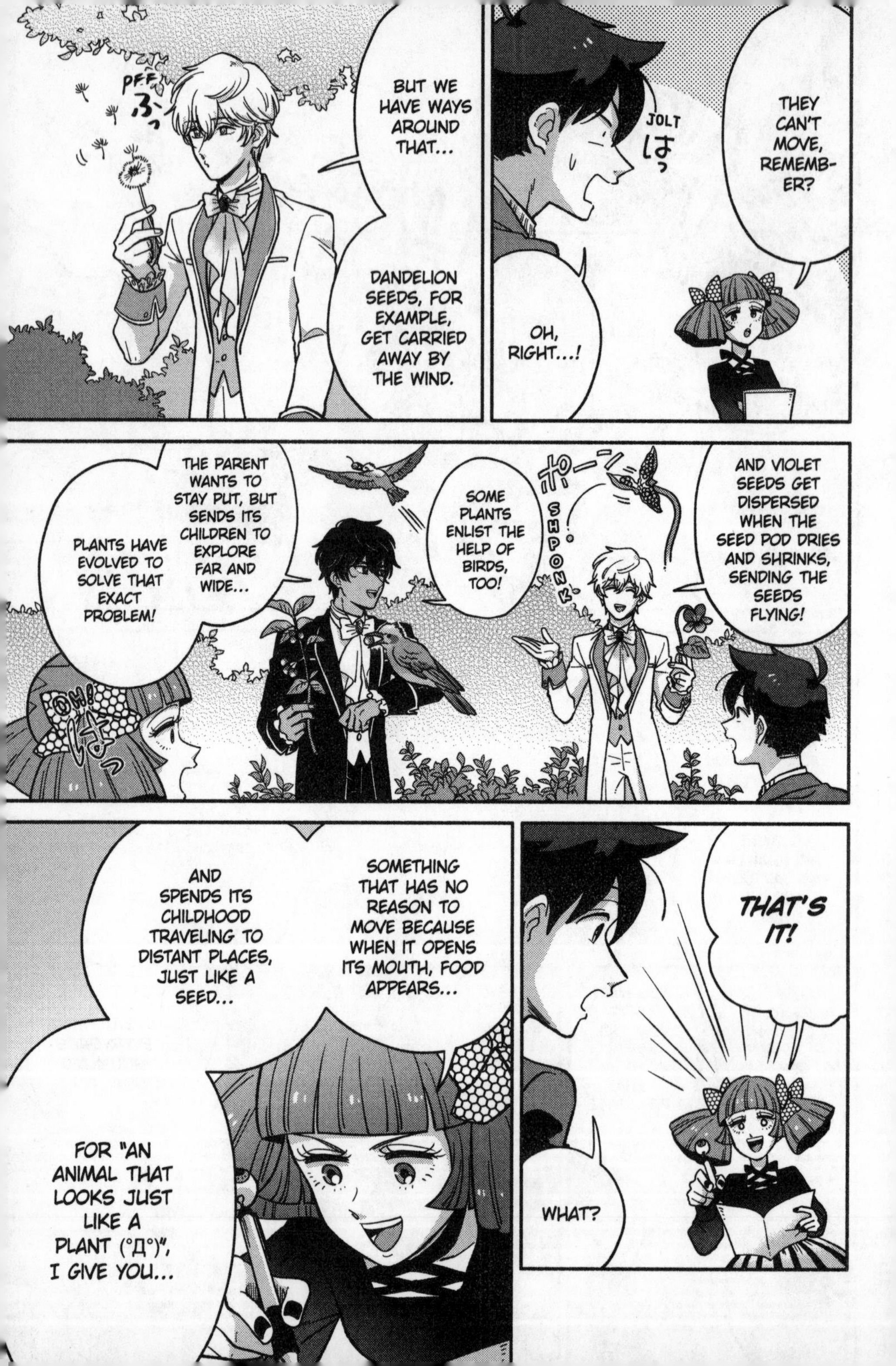
THEY CAN'T MOVE, REMEMB-ER?
JOLT
は
OH, RIGHT...!
PFF
ふっ
BUT WE HAVE WAYS AROUND THAT...
DANDELION SEEDS, FOR EXAMPLE, GET CARRIED AWAY BY THE WIND.
AND VIOLET SEEDS GET DISPERSED WHEN THE SEED POD DRIES AND SHRINKS, SENDING THE SEEDS FLYING!
ポーン
SHPONK
SOME PLANTS ENLIST THE HELP OF BIRDS, TOO!
THE PARENT WANTS TO STAY PUT, BUT SENDS ITS CHILDREN TO EXPLORE FAR AND WIDE...
PLANTS HAVE EVOLVED TO SOLVE THAT EXACT PROBLEM!
OH!
はっ
THAT'S IT!
WHAT?
SOMETHING THAT HAS NO REASON TO MOVE BECAUSE WHEN IT OPENS ITS MOUTH, FOOD APPEARS...
AND SPENDS ITS CHILDHOOD TRAVELING TO DISTANT PLACES, JUST LIKE A SEED...
FOR "AN ANIMAL THAT LOOKS JUST LIKE A PLANT (°Д°)", I GIVE YOU...

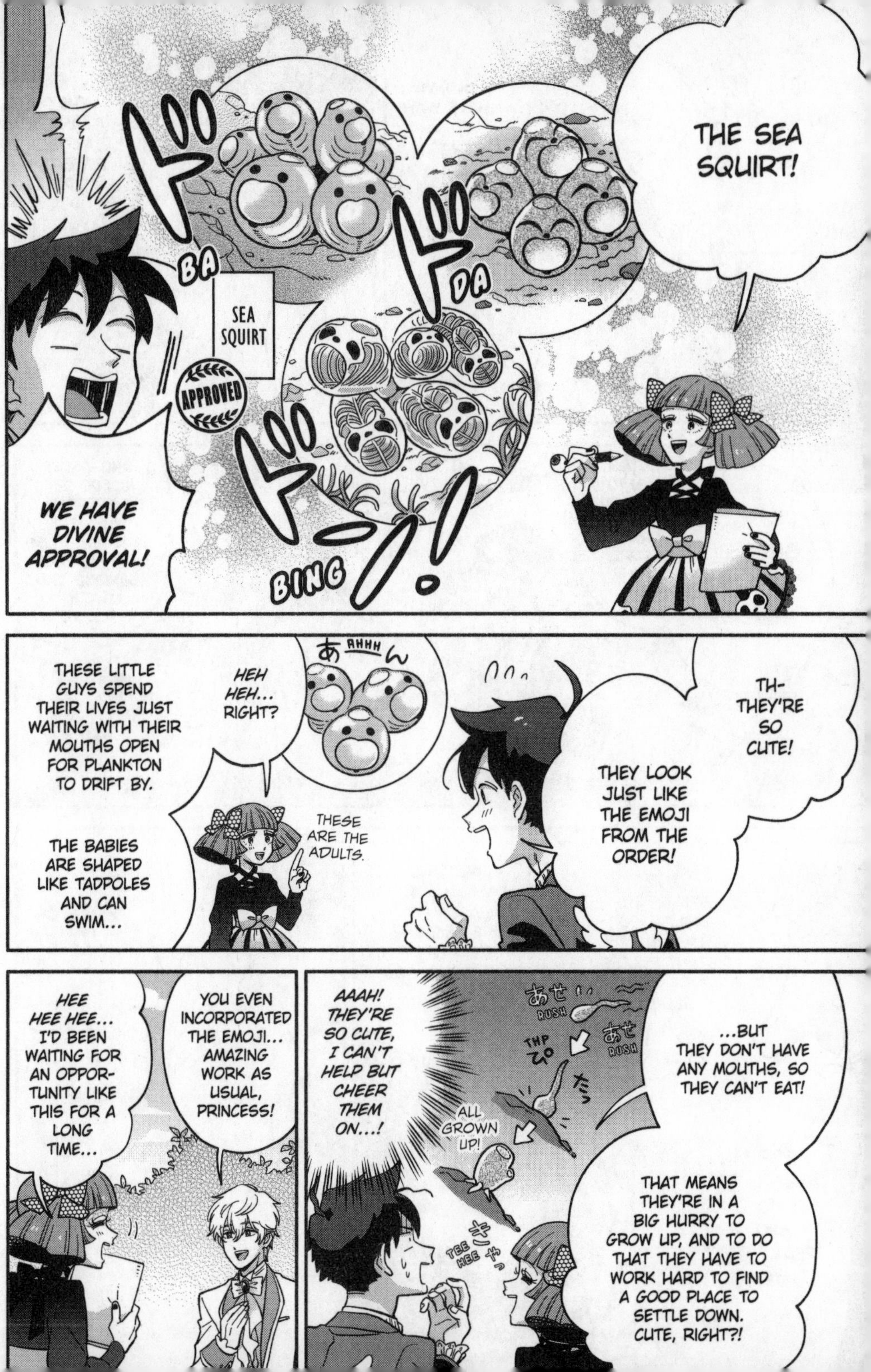
THE SEA SQUIRT!
DOO
DOO
DOO
BA
DA
BING
SEA SQUIRT
APPROVED
WE HAVE DIVINE APPROVAL!
TH-THEY'RE SO CUTE!
THEY LOOK JUST LIKE THE EMOJI FROM THE ORDER!
あAHHHん
HEH HEH... RIGHT?
THESE LITTLE GUYS SPEND THEIR LIVES JUST WAITING WITH THEIR MOUTHS OPEN FOR PLANKTON TO DRIFT BY.
THESE ARE THE ADULTS.
THE BABIES ARE SHAPED LIKE TADPOLES AND CAN SWIM...
...BUT THEY DON'T HAVE ANY MOUTHS, SO THEY CAN'T EAT!
あせ RUSH
あせ RUSH
THP
ALL GROWN UP!
THAT MEANS THEY'RE IN A BIG HURRY TO GROW UP, AND TO DO THAT THEY HAVE TO WORK HARD TO FIND A GOOD PLACE TO SETTLE DOWN. CUTE, RIGHT?!
TEE HEE
AAAH! THEY'RE SO CUTE, I CAN'T HELP BUT CHEER THEM ON...!
YOU EVEN INCORPORATED THE EMOJI... AMAZING WORK AS USUAL, PRINCESS!
HEE HEE HEE... I'D BEEN WAITING FOR AN OPPORTUNITY LIKE THIS FOR A LONG TIME...

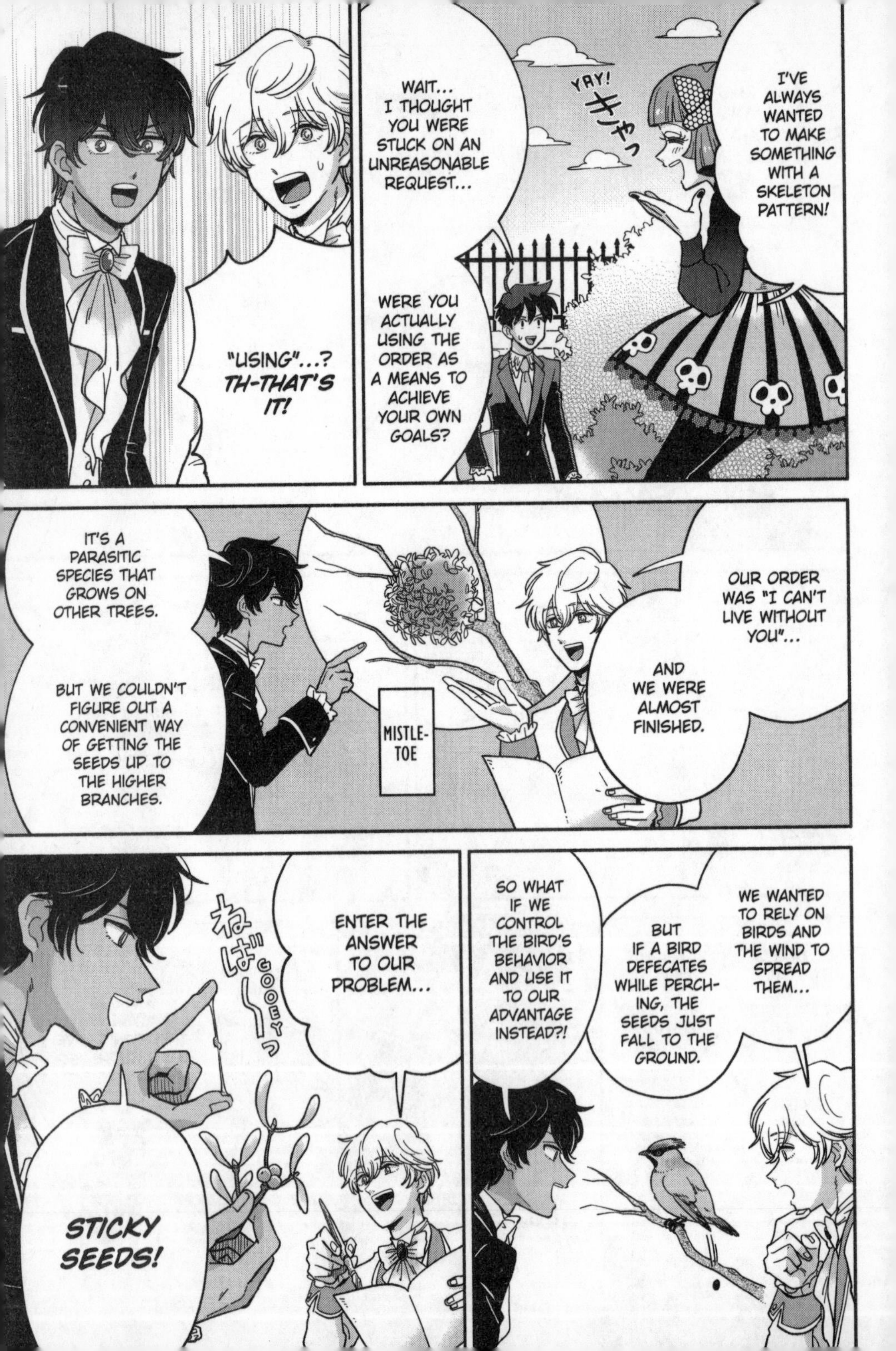
YAY!
キャッ
I'VE ALWAYS WANTED TO MAKE SOMETHING WITH A SKELETON PATTERN!
WAIT... I THOUGHT YOU WERE STUCK ON AN UNREASONABLE REQUEST...
WERE YOU ACTUALLY USING THE ORDER AS A MEANS TO ACHIEVE YOUR OWN GOALS?
"USING"...? TH-THAT'S IT!
OUR ORDER WAS "I CAN'T LIVE WITHOUT YOU"...
AND WE WERE ALMOST FINISHED.
MISTLE-TOE
IT'S A PARASITIC SPECIES THAT GROWS ON OTHER TREES.
BUT WE COULDN'T FIGURE OUT A CONVENIENT WAY OF GETTING THE SEEDS UP TO THE HIGHER BRANCHES.
WE WANTED TO RELY ON BIRDS AND THE WIND TO SPREAD THEM...
BUT IF A BIRD DEFECATES WHILE PERCHING, THE SEEDS JUST FALL TO THE GROUND.
SO WHAT IF WE CONTROL THE BIRD'S BEHAVIOR AND USE IT TO OUR ADVANTAGE INSTEAD?!
ENTER THE ANSWER TO OUR PROBLEM...
ねばー
GOOEY
っ
STICKY SEEDS!

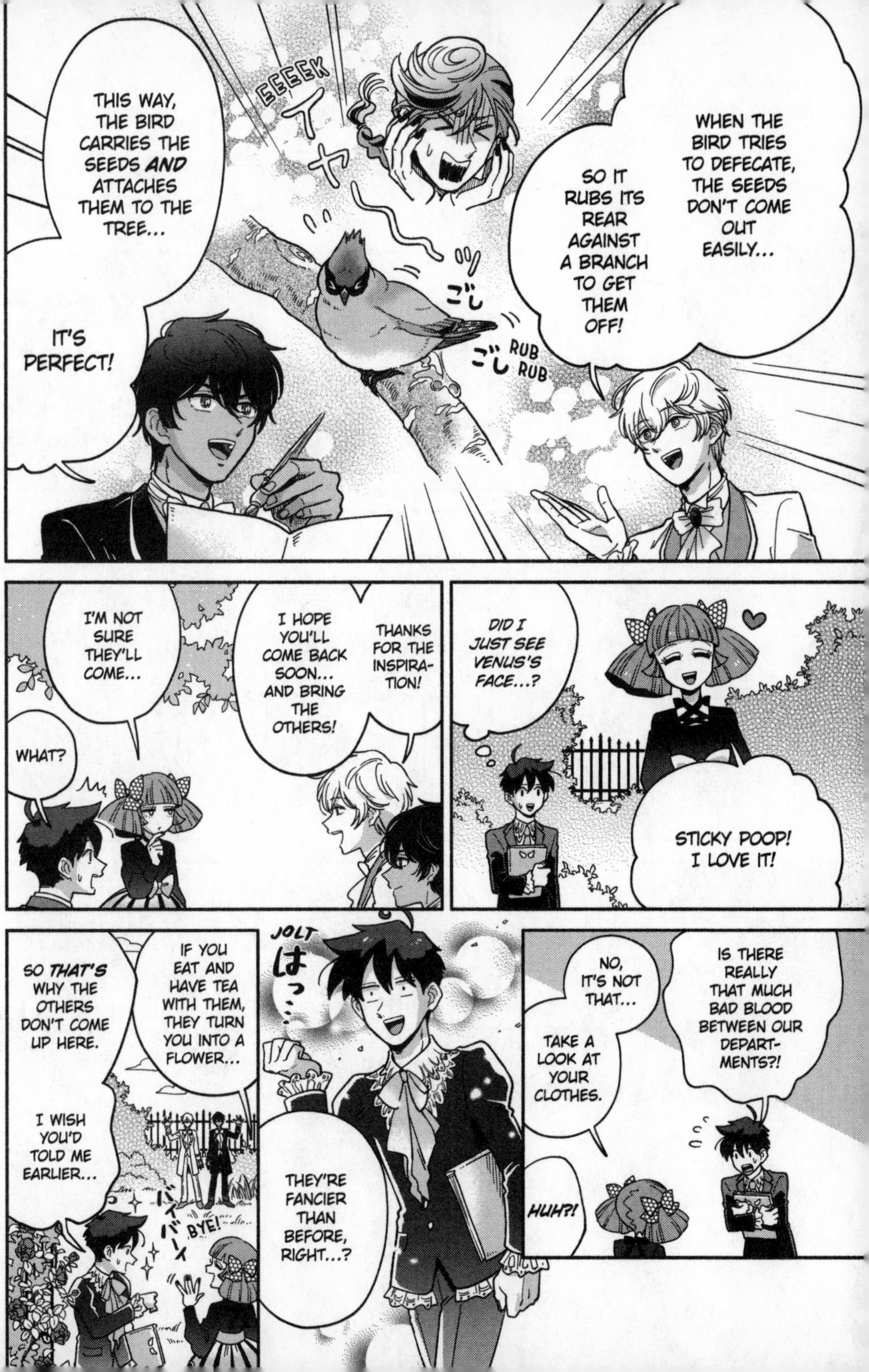
WHEN THE BIRD TRIES TO DEFECATE, THE SEEDS DON'T COME OUT EASILY...
SO IT RUBS ITS REAR AGAINST A BRANCH TO GET THEM OFF!
ごし ごし RUB RUB
イヤ EEEEK
THIS WAY, THE BIRD CARRIES THE SEEDS *AND* ATTACHES THEM TO THE TREE...
IT'S PERFECT!
DID I JUST SEE VENUS'S FACE...?
STICKY POOP! I LOVE IT!
THANKS FOR THE INSPIRA-TION!
I HOPE YOU'LL COME BACK SOON... AND BRING THE OTHERS!
I'M NOT SURE THEY'LL COME...
WHAT?
IS THERE REALLY THAT MUCH BAD BLOOD BETWEEN OUR DEPART-MENTS?!
NO, IT'S NOT THAT...
TAKE A LOOK AT YOUR CLOTHES.
HUH?!
はっ JOLT
THEY'RE FANCIER THAN BEFORE, RIGHT...?
IF YOU EAT AND HAVE TEA WITH THEM, THEY TURN YOU INTO A FLOWER...
SO *THAT'S* WHY THE OTHERS DON'T COME UP HERE.
I WISH YOU'D TOLD ME EARLIER...
バイバーイ BYE!

THE ENCYCLOPEDIA OF REAL ANIMALS 39

ANIMAL 90 | SEA SQUIRT

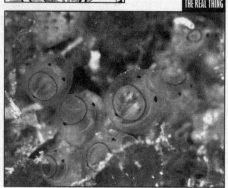

THE REAL THING

Currently unnamed sea squirts popular among divers in Okinawa, Japan.

Photo: Minden Pictures/Aflo

There are 2,300 known species of sea squirt living across the world's oceans. Some types, like those eaten as a delicacy in the Tohoku region of Japan, are solitary, while others, like the three shown in this chapter, form colonies. Though similar in appearance to anemones, sea squirts are actually more closely related to humans than to other invertebrates.

In their larval stage, sea squirts have long tails, muscles, nerves, and notochords, which give them a tadpole-like appearance. Once they attach to a rock or other surface, they metamorphize into their adult form. The adults' bodies are tube-shaped, with siphons on either end where water enters and exits. From then on, sea squirts feed by waiting for food to pass through their open mouths and thus live a plant-like existence. Their diet consists mainly of plankton.

Sea squirts are unusual in the animal kingdom because of their ability to produce cellulose.

[Name]	Sea squirt
[Classification]	Class: Ascidiacea
[Habitat]	Oceans of the world
[Height]	0.5-10 cm (0.2-4 in)

| # RAFFLESIA

THE REAL THING

Rafflesias grow enormous flowers to spread their scent as far away as possible.

Photo: Minden Pictures/Aflo

Rafflesias use petals resembling rotting meat and a strong, putrid odor to attract flies—not to eat, but to enlist as pollinators. Lured by the smell, the flies crawl through the narrow passageways deep within the flowers and get coated in pollen.

Rafflesias are parasites of vine plants in the grape family. While the plant may take two years to flower, it withers in about 3 days.

[Name]	*Rafflesia*
[Classification]	Order: Malpighiales
	Family: Rafflesiaceae
	Genus: *Rafflesia*
[Habitat]	Tropical rainforests of Southeast Asia
[Length]	15-100 cm (6-39 in)

| # MISTLETOE

Viscum album is a hemiparasitic species that grows on the branches and trunks of deciduous trees. Birds feed on its berries and carry the seeds up into the branches of potential hosts. When the seeds are excreted, they are covered in a sticky substance that helps them adhere to a host tree. Once it germinates, the mistletoe extends its roots into the branches of its host to extract water and nutrients. After approximately three years, it grows leaves of its own and starts photosynthesis.

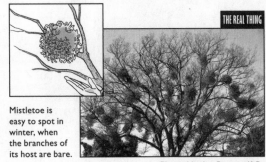

THE REAL THING

Mistletoe is easy to spot in winter, when the branches of its host are bare.

Photo: Minden Pictures/Aflo

[Name]	*Viscum album*
[Classification]	Order: Santalales
	Family: Santalaceae
	Genus: *Viscum*
[Habitat]	Europe; western and southern Asia
[Length]	50-80 cm (1.6-2.6 ft)

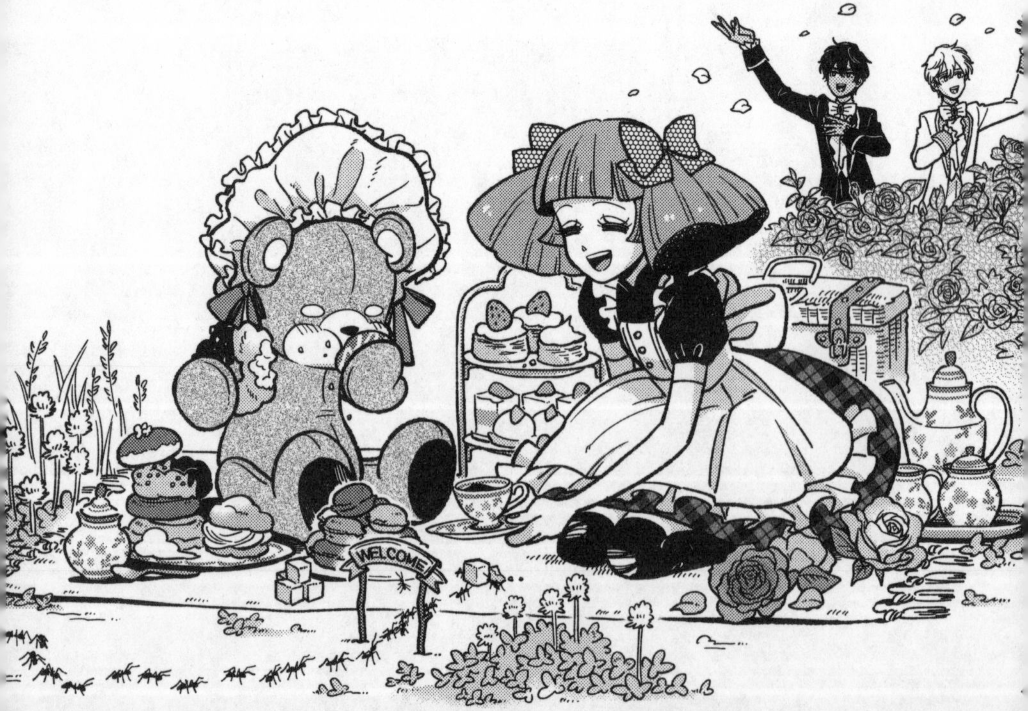
WELCOME

HEAVEN'S DESIGN TEAM

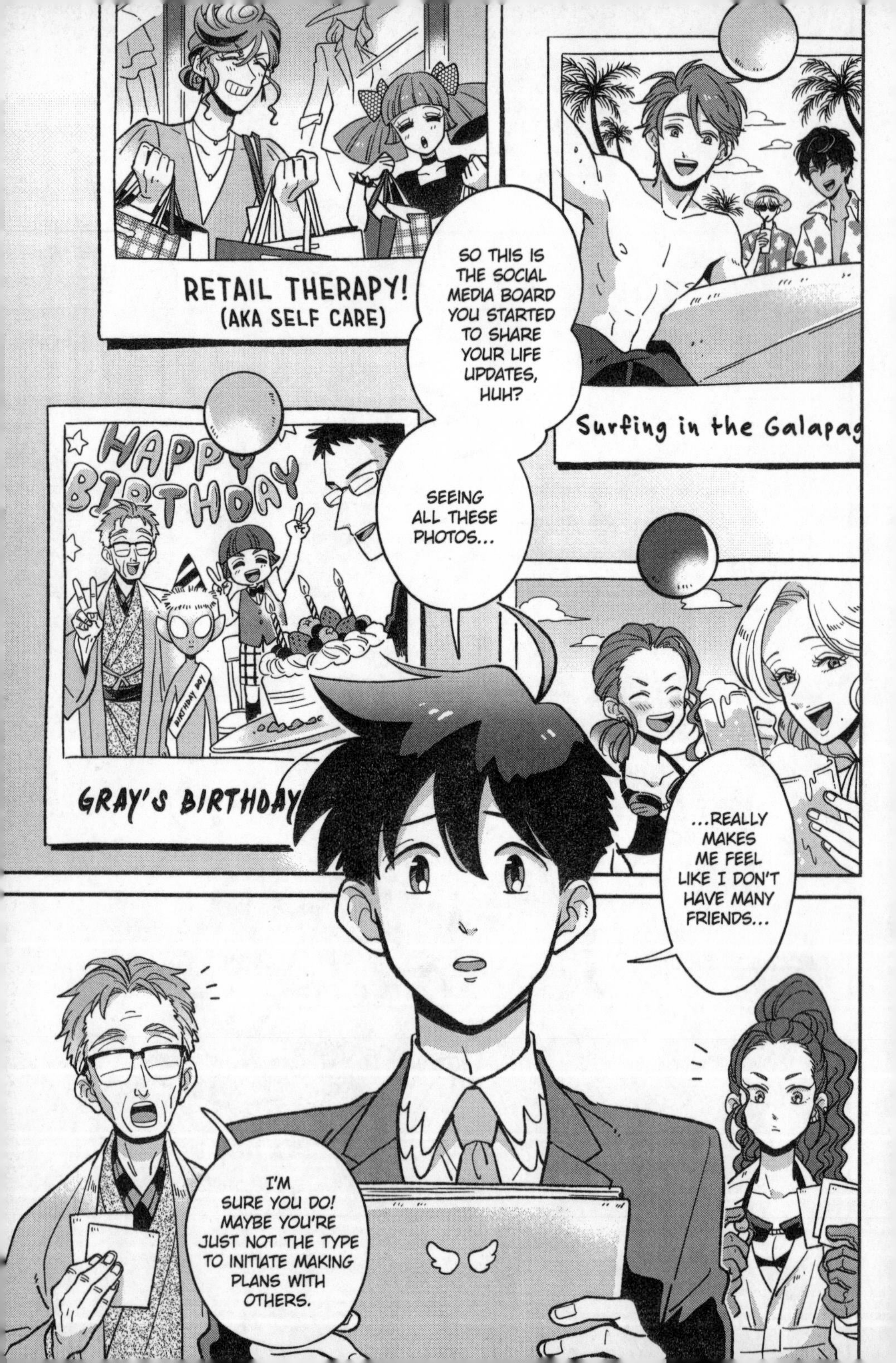
Surfing in the Galapag
RETAIL THERAPY!
(AKA SELF CARE)
SO THIS IS THE SOCIAL MEDIA BOARD YOU STARTED TO SHARE YOUR LIFE UPDATES, HUH?
HAPPY BIRTHDAY
BIRTHDAY BOY
GRAY'S BIRTHDAY
SEEING ALL THESE PHOTOS...
...REALLY MAKES ME FEEL LIKE I DON'T HAVE MANY FRIENDS...
I'M SURE YOU DO! MAYBE YOU'RE JUST NOT THE TYPE TO INITIATE MAKING PLANS WITH OTHERS.

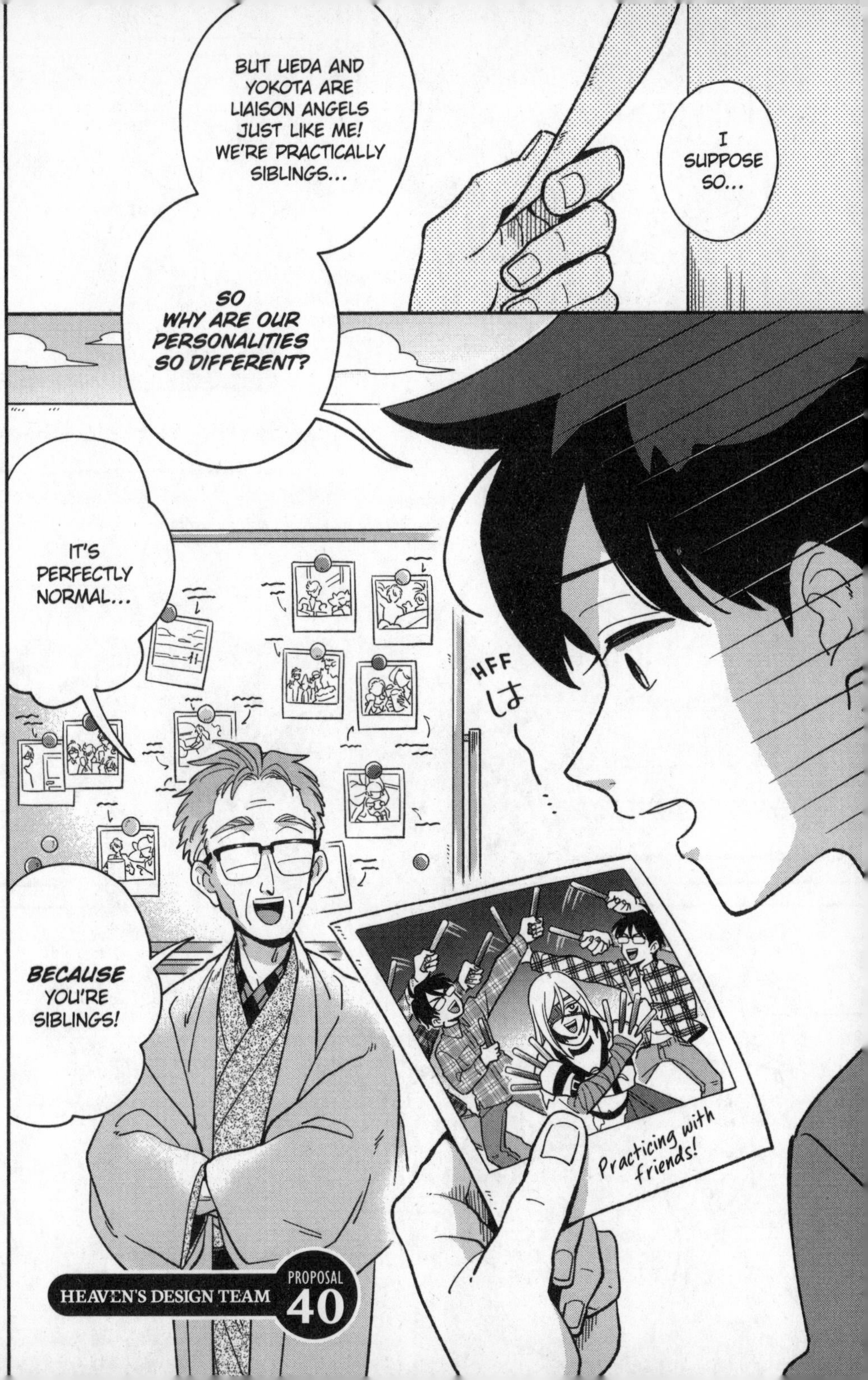

BUT UEDA AND YOKOTA ARE LIAISON ANGELS JUST LIKE ME! WE'RE PRACTICALLY SIBLINGS...
I SUPPOSE SO...
SO WHY ARE OUR PERSONALITIES SO DIFFERENT?
HFF は
IT'S PERFECTLY NORMAL...
BECAUSE YOU'RE SIBLINGS!
Practicing with friends!
HEAVEN'S DESIGN TEAM
PROPOSAL 40

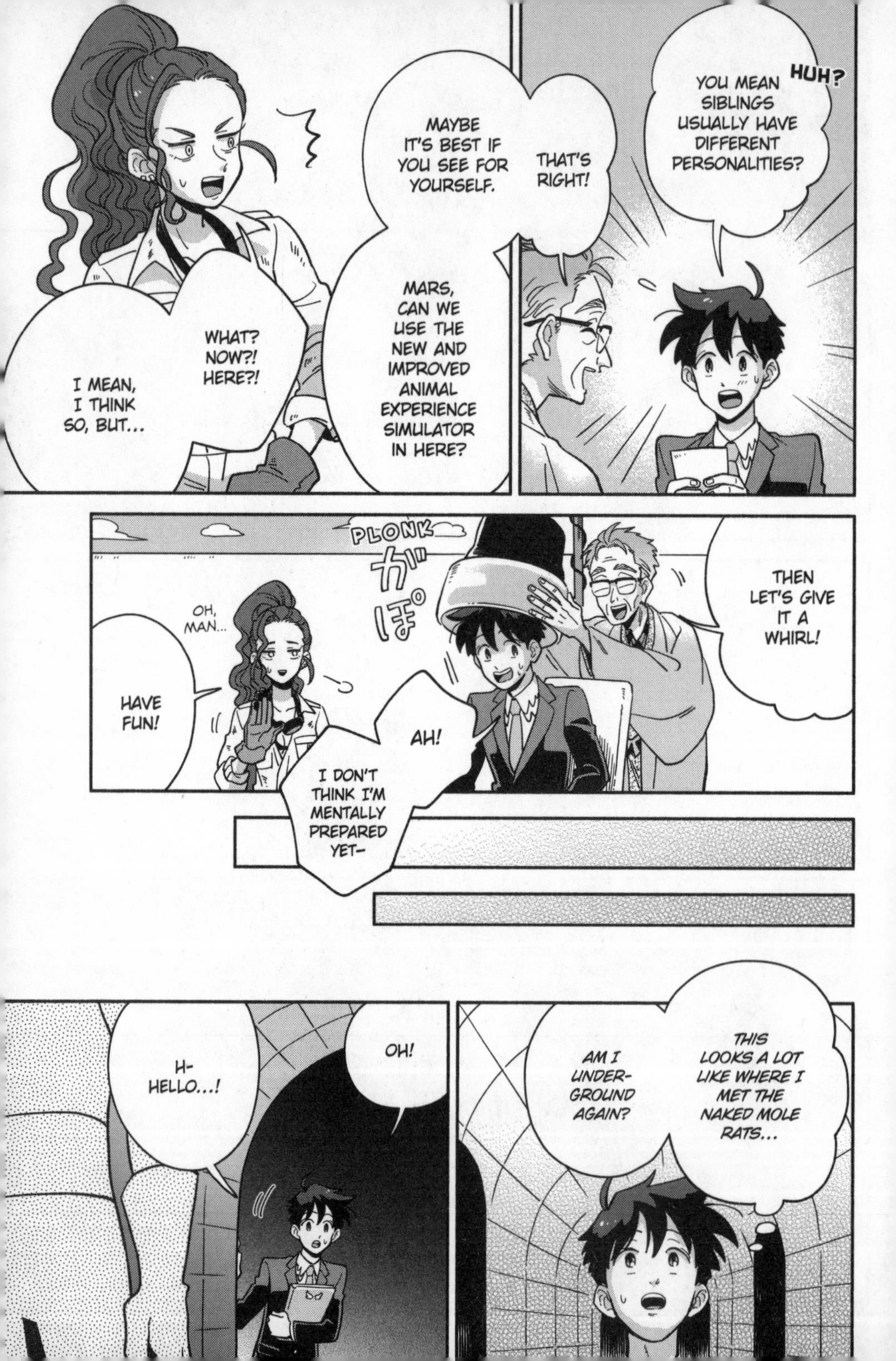
HUH?
YOU MEAN SIBLINGS USUALLY HAVE DIFFERENT PERSONALITIES?
THAT'S RIGHT!
MAYBE IT'S BEST IF YOU SEE FOR YOURSELF.
MARS, CAN WE USE THE NEW AND IMPROVED ANIMAL EXPERIENCE SIMULATOR IN HERE?
WHAT? NOW?! HERE?!
I MEAN, I THINK SO, BUT...
THEN LET'S GIVE IT A WHIRL!
PLONK
がぽ
AH!
I DON'T THINK I'M MENTALLY PREPARED YET-
OH, MAN...
HAVE FUN!
THIS LOOKS A LOT LIKE WHERE I MET THE NAKED MOLE RATS...
AM I UNDER-GROUND AGAIN?
OH!
H- HELLO...!

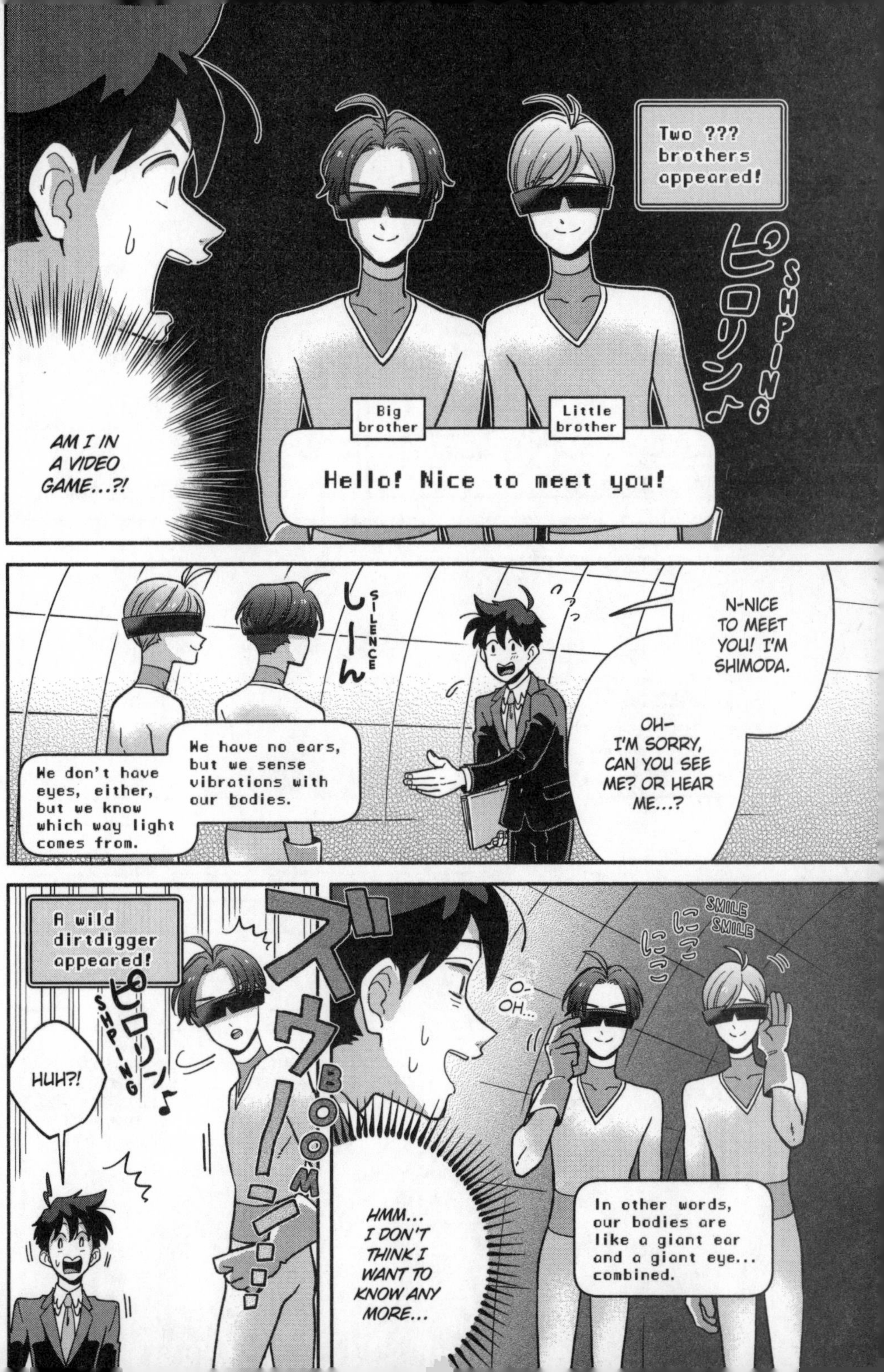
Two ??? brothers appeared!
ピロリン♪
SHPING
Big brother
Little brother
Hello! Nice to meet you!
AM I IN A VIDEO GAME...?!
N-NICE TO MEET YOU! I'M SHIMODA.
OH— I'M SORRY, CAN YOU SEE ME? OR HEAR ME...?
しーん
SILENCE
We have no ears, but we sense vibrations with our bodies.
We don't have eyes, either, but we know which way light comes from.
にこにこ
SMILE SMILE
O-OH...
In other words, our bodies are like a giant ear and a giant eye... combined.
HMM... I DON'T THINK I WANT TO KNOW ANY MORE...
ズウーン
BOOM
A wild dirtdigger appeared!
ピロリーン♪
SHPING
HUH?!

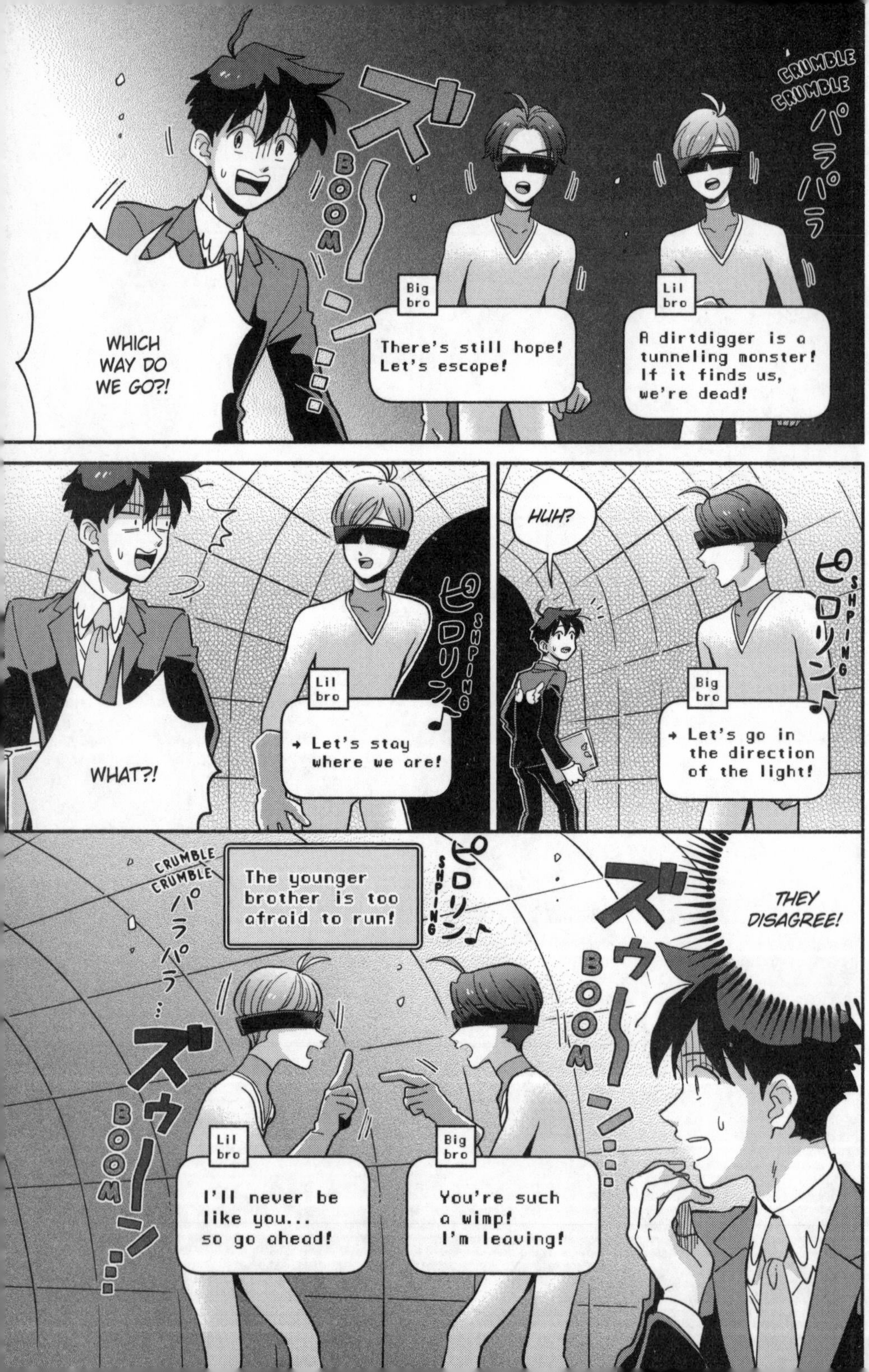
CRUMBLE CRUMBLE
パラパラ
Lil bro
A dirtdigger is a tunneling monster! If it finds us, we're dead!
Big bro
There's still hope! Let's escape!
ズ〜ン…
BOOM
WHICH WAY DO WE GO?!
HUH?
ピロリン♪
SHPING
Big bro
→ Let's go in the direction of the light!
ピロリン♪
SHPING
Lil bro
→ Let's stay where we are!
WHAT?!
THEY DISAGREE!
ズ〜ン…
BOOM
ピロリン♪
SHPING
The younger brother is too afraid to run!
CRUMBLE CRUMBLE
パラパラ…
Big bro
You're such a wimp! I'm leaving!
Lil bro
I'll never be like you... so go ahead!
ズ〜ン…
BOOM

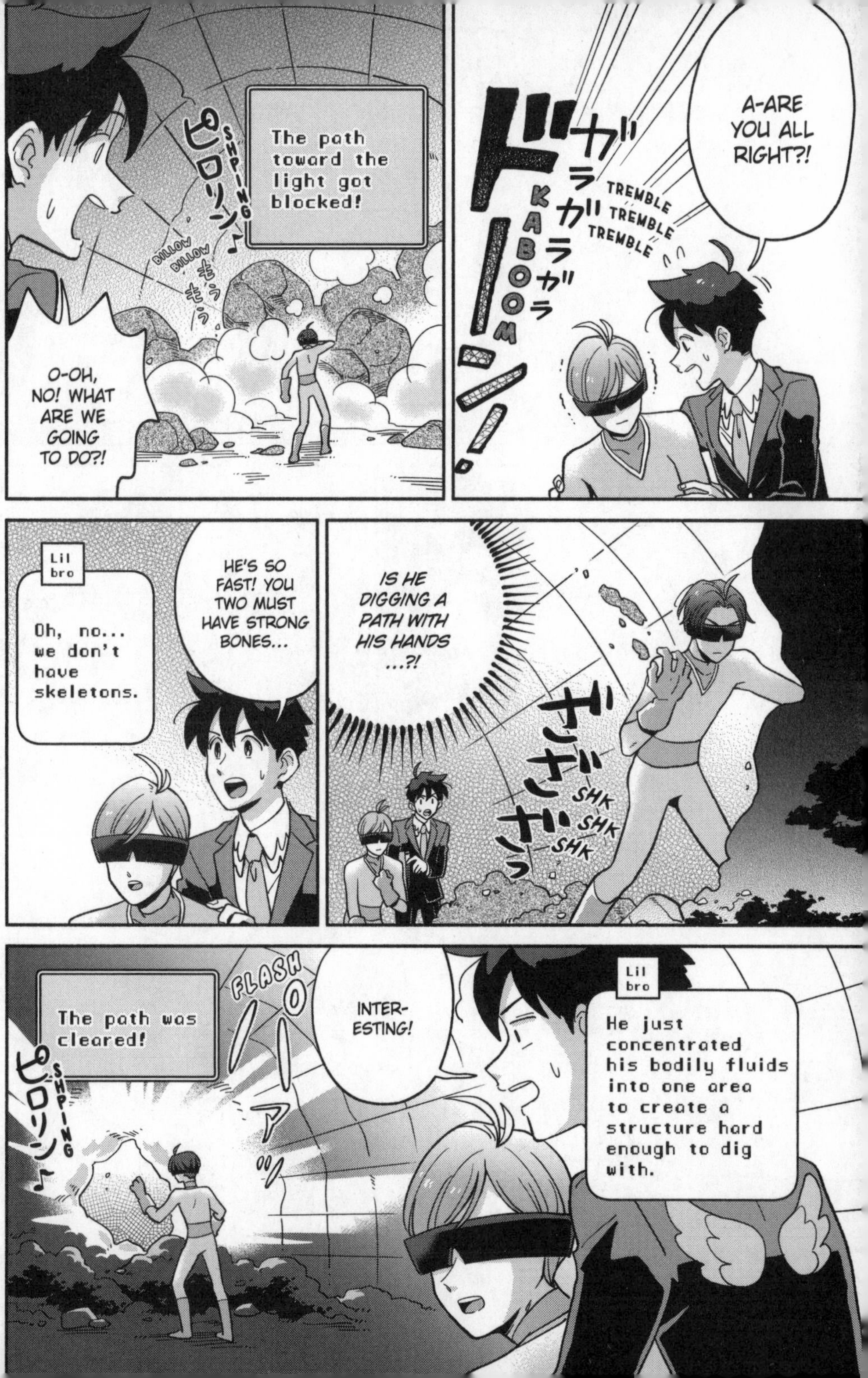
KABOOM
TREMBLE TREMBLE TREMBLE
A-ARE YOU ALL RIGHT?!
The path toward the light got blocked!
ピロリン♪
SHPING
BILLOW BILLOW
O-OH, NO! WHAT ARE WE GOING TO DO?!
IS HE DIGGING A PATH WITH HIS HANDS ...?!
SHK SHK SHK
HE'S SO FAST! YOU TWO MUST HAVE STRONG BONES...
Lil bro
Oh, no... we don't have skeletons.
Lil bro
He just concentrated his bodily fluids into one area to create a structure hard enough to dig with.
INTER-ESTING!
FLASH
The path was cleared!
ピロリン♪
SHPING

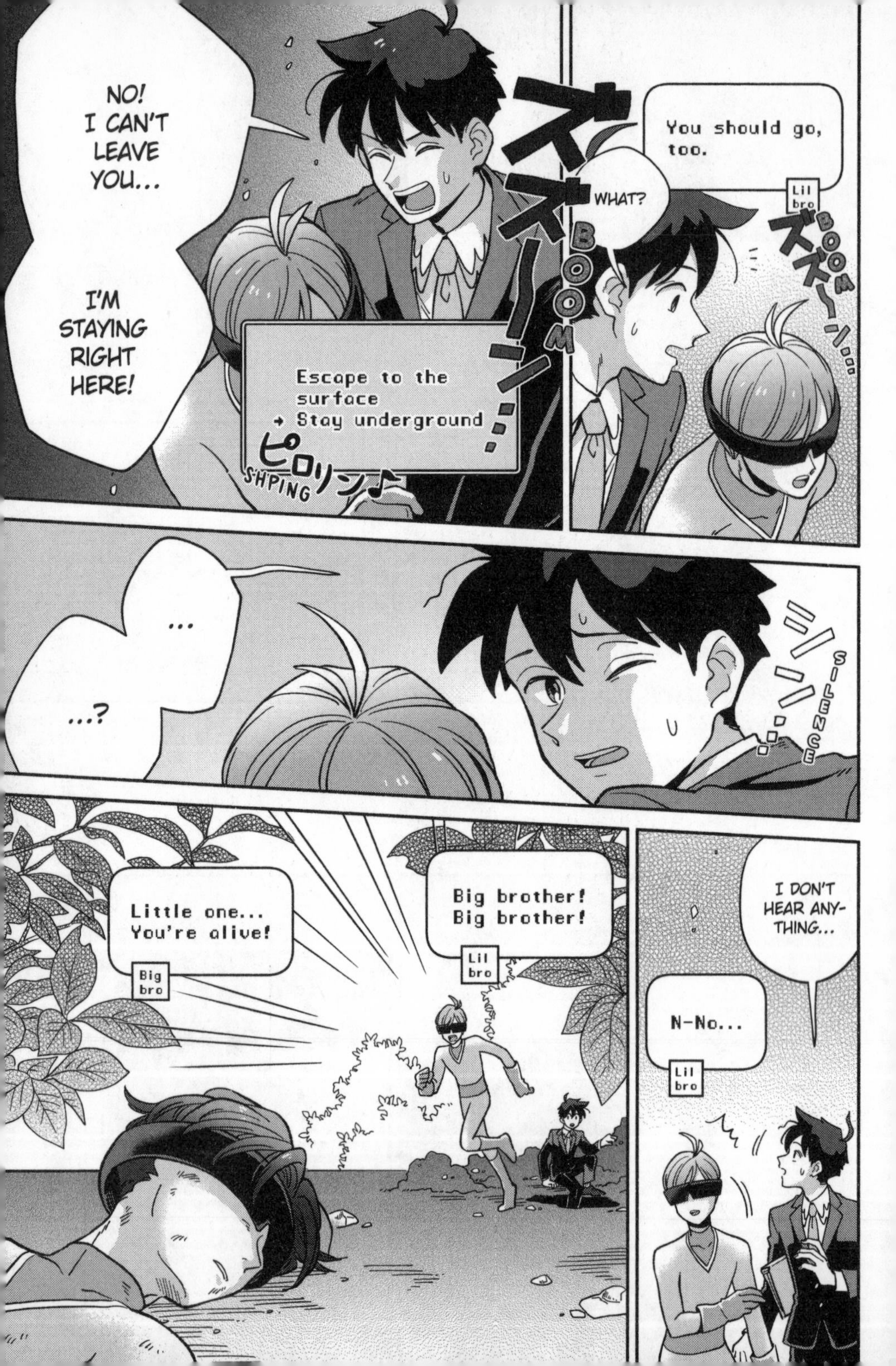
You should go, too.
Lil bro
ズズーン…
BOOM
WHAT?
ズズーン…
BOOM
NO! I CAN'T LEAVE YOU...
I'M STAYING RIGHT HERE!
Escape to the surface
→ Stay underground
ピロリン♪
SHPING
...
...?
シーン…
SILENCE
I DON'T HEAR ANYTHING...
N-No...
Lil bro
Big brother! Big brother!
Lil bro
Little one... You're alive!
Big bro

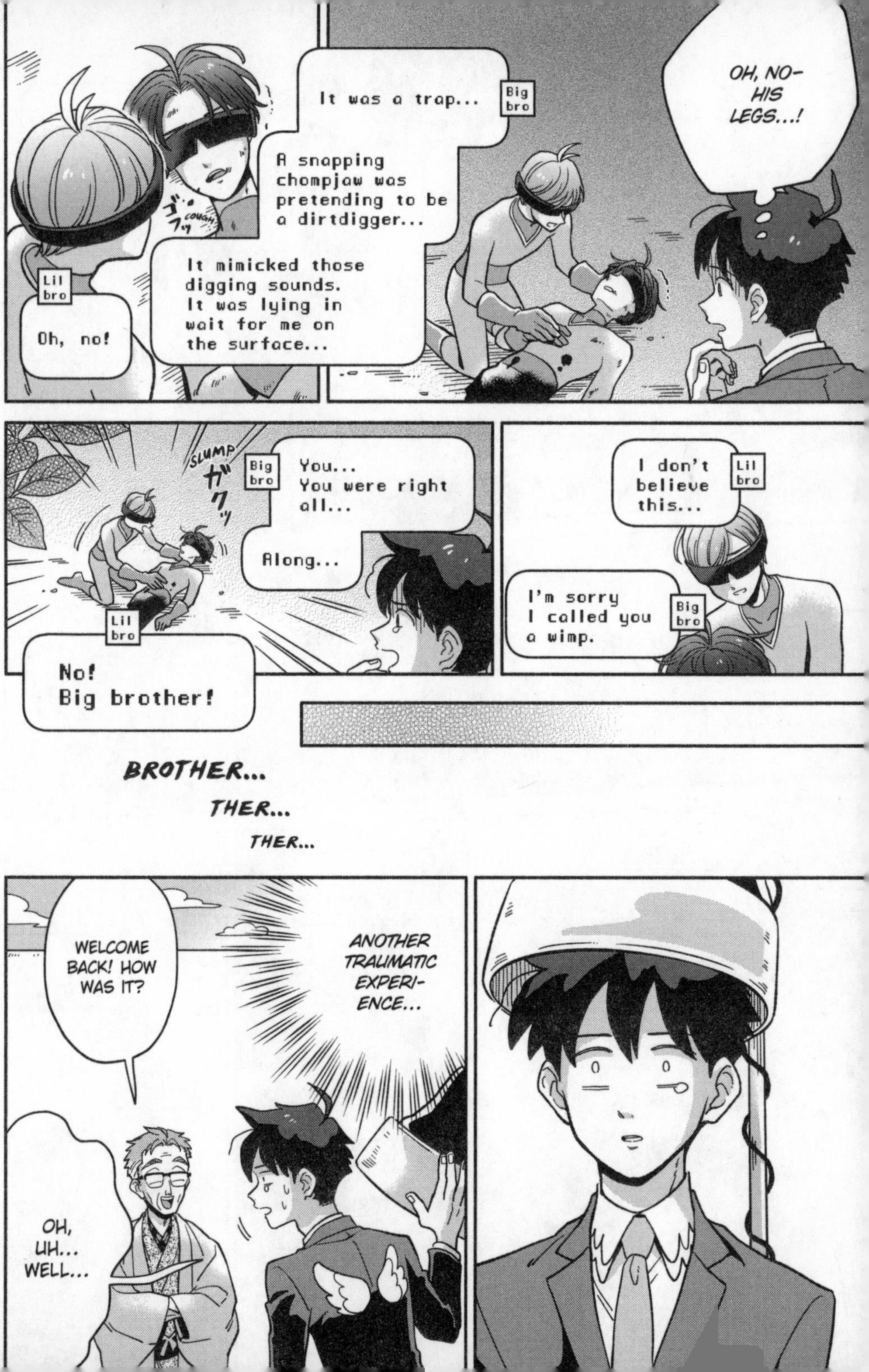

OH, NO- HIS LEGS...!
Big bro
It was a trap...
A snapping chompjaw was pretending to be a dirtdigger...
COUGH
It mimicked those digging sounds. It was lying in wait for me on the surface...
Lil bro
Oh, no!
Lil bro
I don't believe this...
Big bro
I'm sorry I called you a wimp.
SLUMP
Big bro
You... You were right all...
Along...
Lil bro
No! Big brother!
BROTHER...
THER...
THER...
WELCOME BACK! HOW WAS IT?
ANOTHER TRAUMATIC EXPERI-ENCE...
OH, UH... WELL...

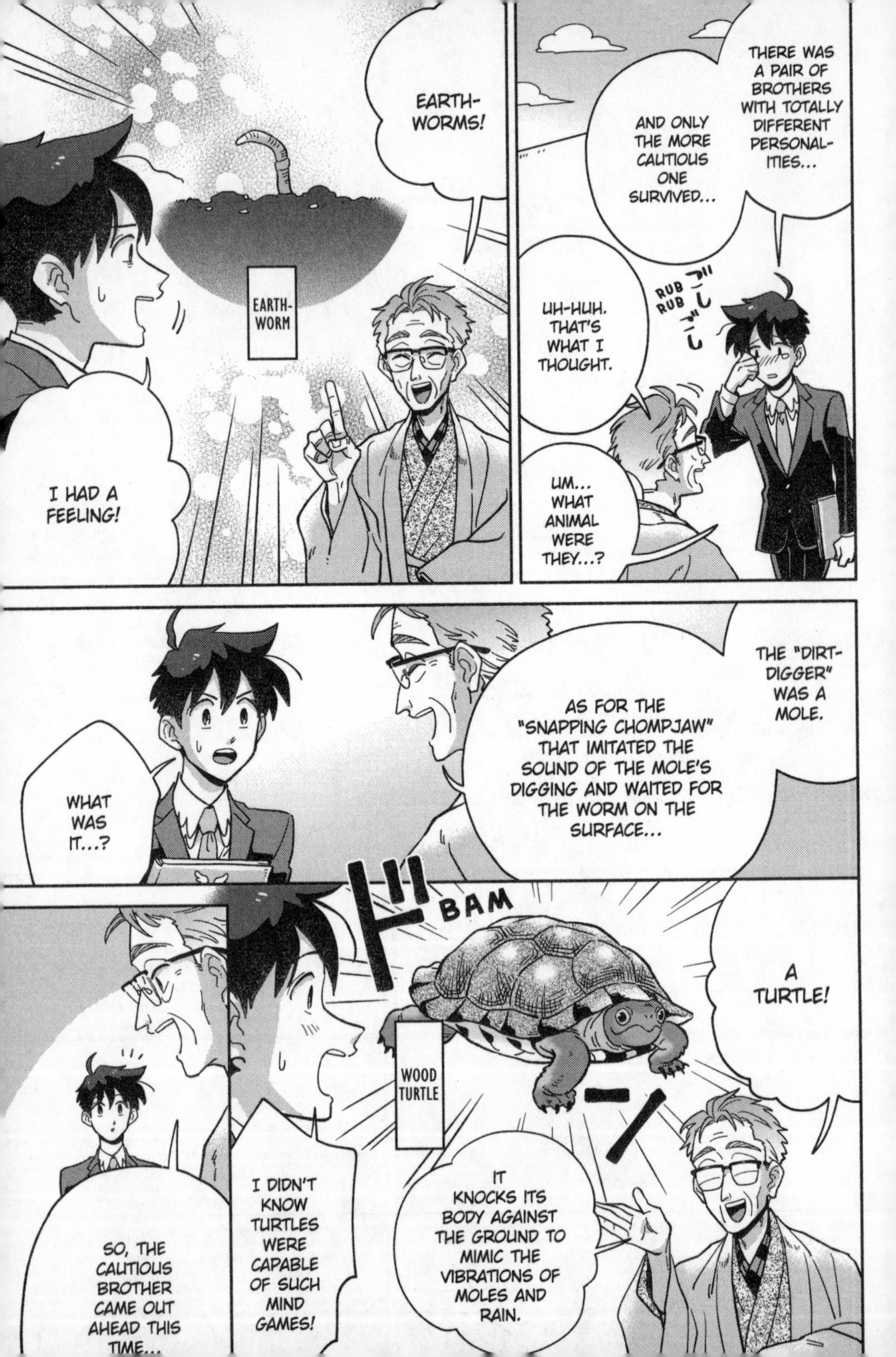

THERE WAS A PAIR OF BROTHERS WITH TOTALLY DIFFERENT PERSONALITIES...
AND ONLY THE MORE CAUTIOUS ONE SURVIVED...
RUB RUB
ごしごし
UH-HUH. THAT'S WHAT I THOUGHT.
UM... WHAT ANIMAL WERE THEY...?
EARTHWORMS!
EARTHWORM
I HAD A FEELING!
THE "DIRT-DIGGER" WAS A MOLE.
AS FOR THE "SNAPPING CHOMPJAW" THAT IMITATED THE SOUND OF THE MOLE'S DIGGING AND WAITED FOR THE WORM ON THE SURFACE...
WHAT WAS IT...?
ドッ
BAM
A TURTLE!
WOOD TURTLE
IT KNOCKS ITS BODY AGAINST THE GROUND TO MIMIC THE VIBRATIONS OF MOLES AND RAIN.
I DIDN'T KNOW TURTLES WERE CAPABLE OF SUCH MIND GAMES!
SO, THE CAUTIOUS BROTHER CAME OUT AHEAD THIS TIME...

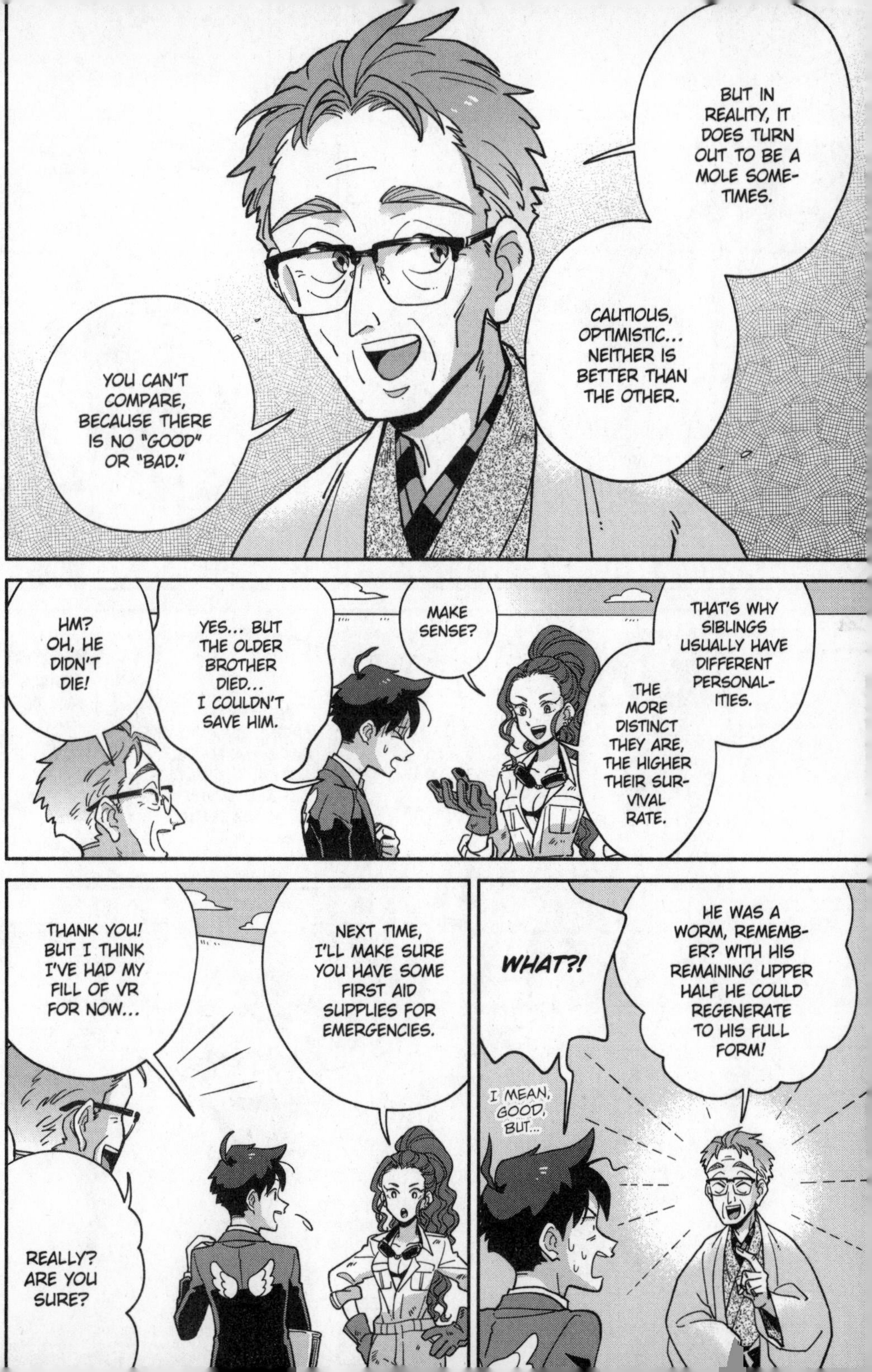
BUT IN REALITY, IT DOES TURN OUT TO BE A MOLE SOME-TIMES.
CAUTIOUS, OPTIMISTIC... NEITHER IS BETTER THAN THE OTHER.
YOU CAN'T COMPARE, BECAUSE THERE IS NO "GOOD" OR "BAD."
THAT'S WHY SIBLINGS USUALLY HAVE DIFFERENT PERSONAL-ITIES.
THE MORE DISTINCT THEY ARE, THE HIGHER THEIR SUR-VIVAL RATE.
MAKE SENSE?
YES... BUT THE OLDER BROTHER DIED... I COULDN'T SAVE HIM.
HM? OH, HE DIDN'T DIE!
HE WAS A WORM, REMEMB-ER? WITH HIS REMAINING UPPER HALF HE COULD REGENERATE TO HIS FULL FORM!
WHAT?!
I MEAN, GOOD, BUT...
NEXT TIME, I'LL MAKE SURE YOU HAVE SOME FIRST AID SUPPLIES FOR EMERGENCIES.
THANK YOU! BUT I THINK I'VE HAD MY FILL OF VR FOR NOW...
REALLY? ARE YOU SURE?

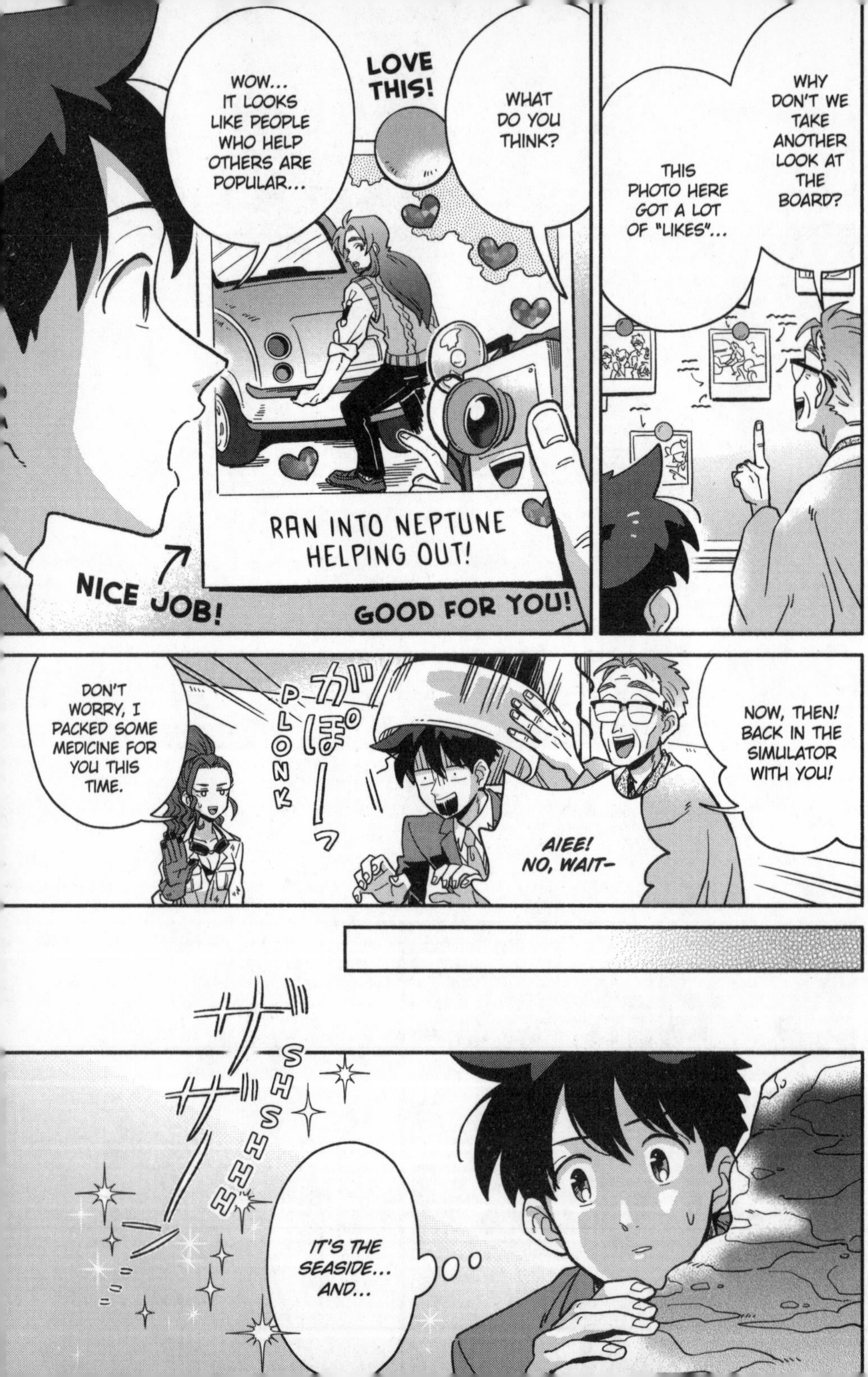
WHY DON'T WE TAKE ANOTHER LOOK AT THE BOARD?
THIS PHOTO HERE GOT A LOT OF "LIKES"...
WHAT DO YOU THINK?
LOVE THIS!
WOW... IT LOOKS LIKE PEOPLE WHO HELP OTHERS ARE POPULAR...
RAN INTO NEPTUNE HELPING OUT!
GOOD FOR YOU!
NICE JOB!
NOW, THEN! BACK IN THE SIMULATOR WITH YOU!
AIEE! NO, WAIT-
がぽーっ
PLONK
DON'T WORRY, I PACKED SOME MEDICINE FOR YOU THIS TIME.
SHHHHHHH
IT'S THE SEASIDE... AND...

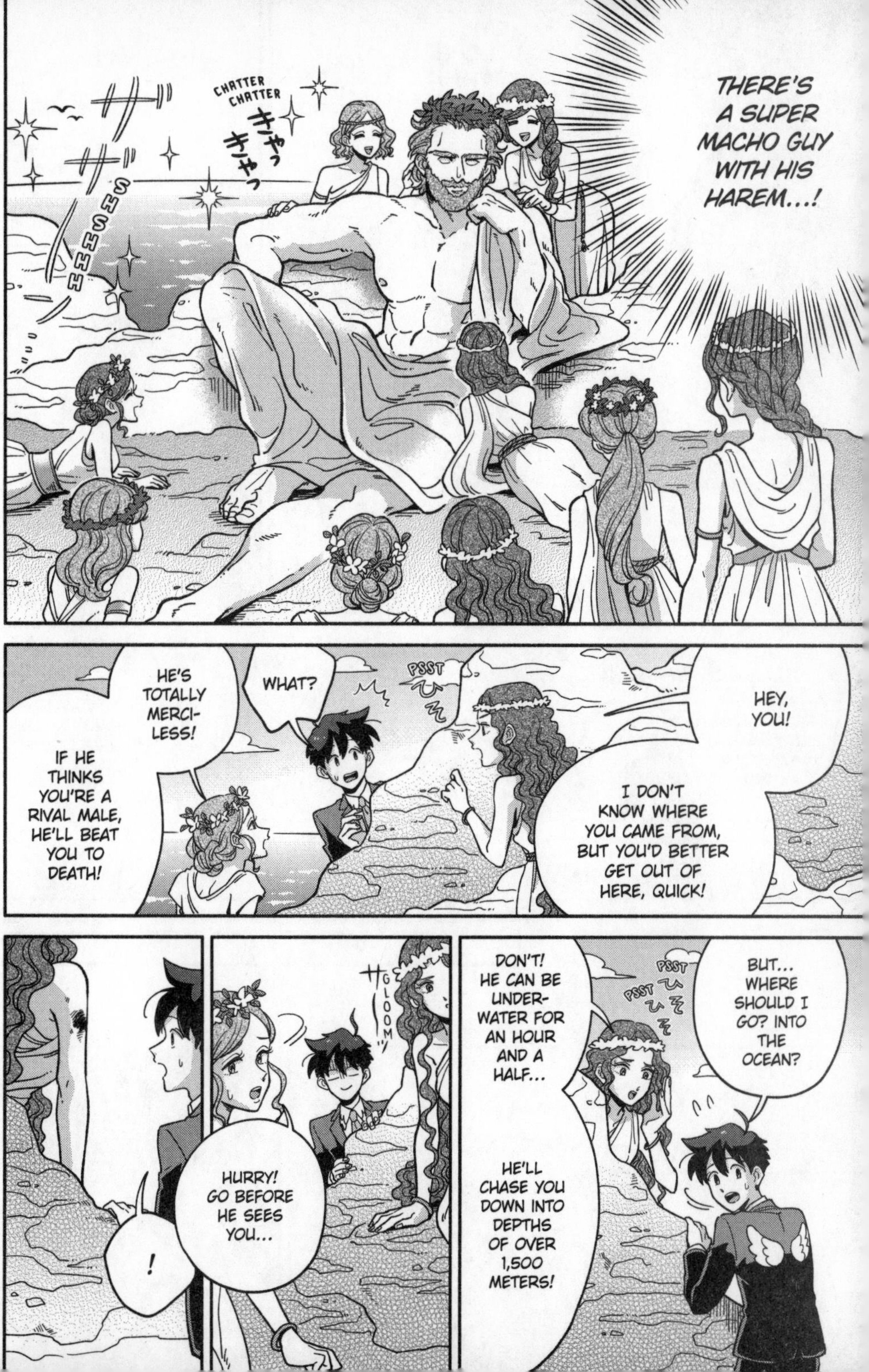
THERE'S A SUPER MACHO GUY WITH HIS HAREM...!
CHATTER CHATTER
きゃっ きゃっ
ザザ
SHHHHHH
HEY, YOU!
I DON'T KNOW WHERE YOU CAME FROM, BUT YOU'D BETTER GET OUT OF HERE, QUICK!
PSST
ひそ
WHAT?
HE'S TOTALLY MERCI-LESS!
IF HE THINKS YOU'RE A RIVAL MALE, HE'LL BEAT YOU TO DEATH!
BUT... WHERE SHOULD I GO? INTO THE OCEAN?
PSST ひそ
PSST ひそ
DON'T! HE CAN BE UNDER-WATER FOR AN HOUR AND A HALF...
HE'LL CHASE YOU DOWN INTO DEPTHS OF OVER 1,500 METERS!
GLOOM
HURRY! GO BEFORE HE SEES YOU...
!

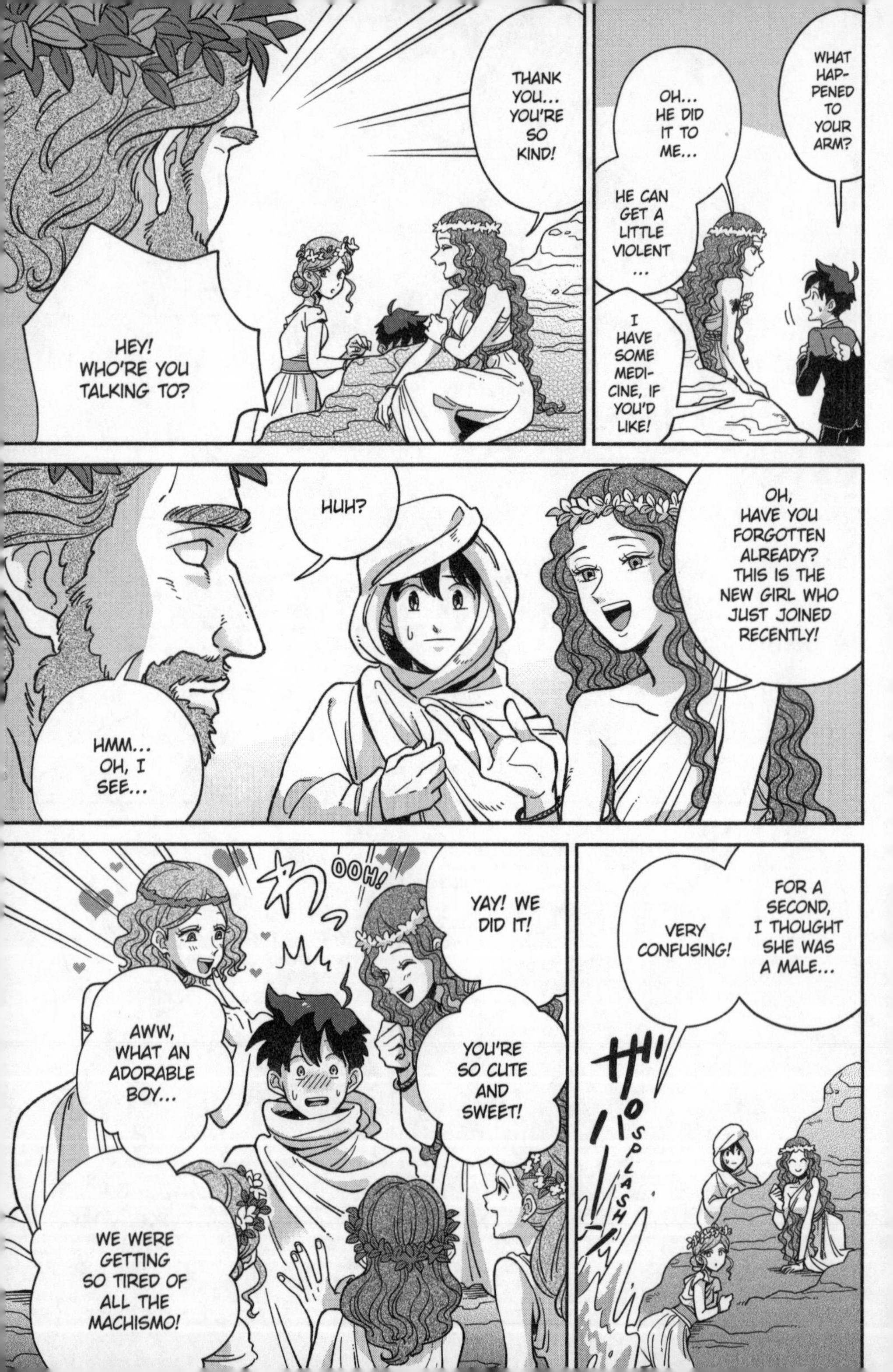
WHAT HAPPENED TO YOUR ARM?
OH... HE DID IT TO ME...
HE CAN GET A LITTLE VIOLENT ...
I HAVE SOME MEDICINE, IF YOU'D LIKE!
THANK YOU... YOU'RE SO KIND!
HEY! WHO'RE YOU TALKING TO?
OH, HAVE YOU FORGOTTEN ALREADY? THIS IS THE NEW GIRL WHO JUST JOINED RECENTLY!
HUH?
HMM... OH, I SEE...
FOR A SECOND, I THOUGHT SHE WAS A MALE...
VERY CONFUSING!
SPLASH
YAY! WE DID IT!
OOH!
YOU'RE SO CUTE AND SWEET!
AWW, WHAT AN ADORABLE BOY...
WE WERE GETTING SO TIRED OF ALL THE MACHISMO!

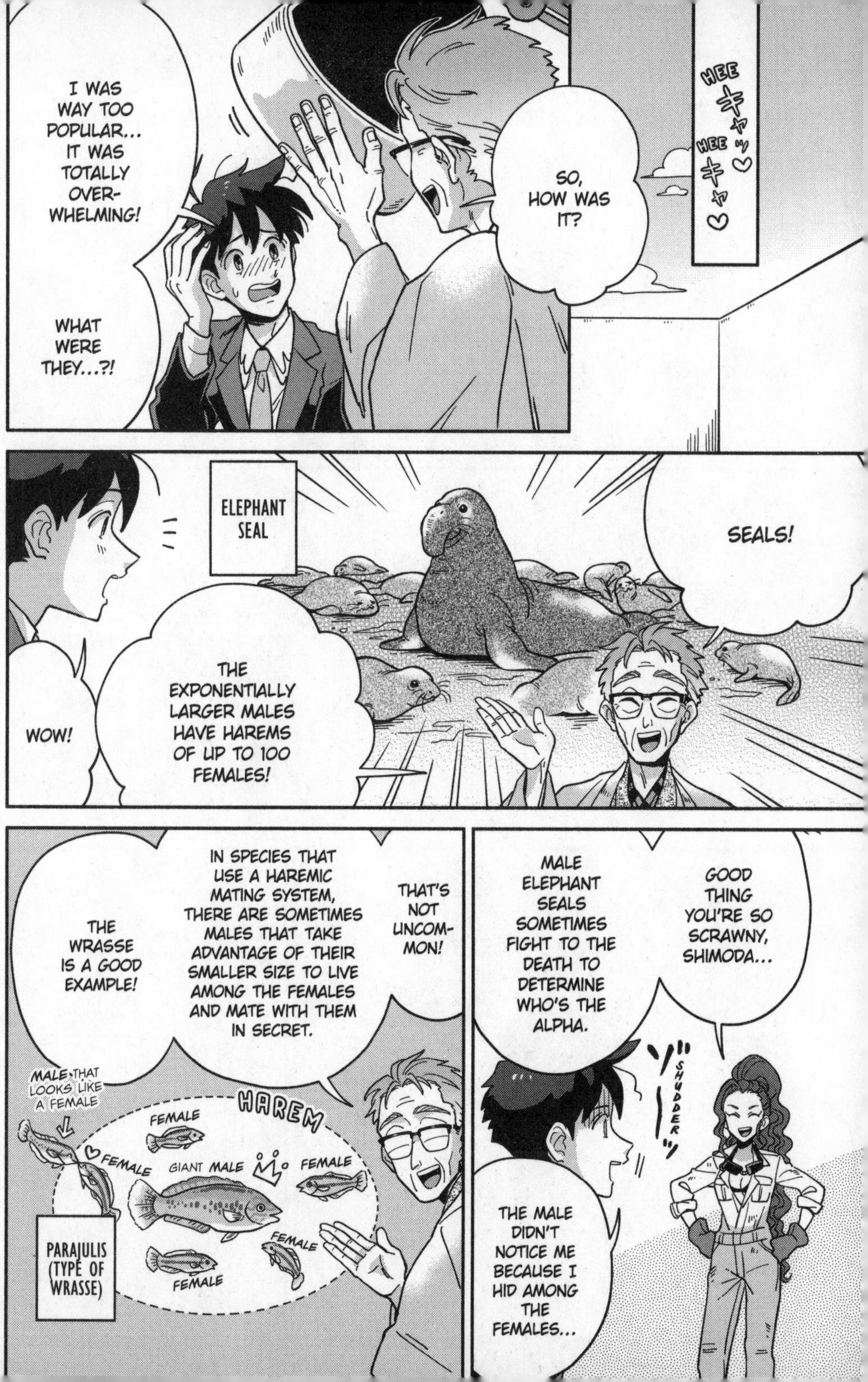

HEE キャ
HEE キャ
SO, HOW WAS IT?
I WAS WAY TOO POPULAR... IT WAS TOTALLY OVER-WHELMING!
WHAT WERE THEY...?!
SEALS!
ELEPHANT SEAL
THE EXPONENTIALLY LARGER MALES HAVE HAREMS OF UP TO 100 FEMALES!
WOW!
GOOD THING YOU'RE SO SCRAWNY, SHIMODA...
MALE ELEPHANT SEALS SOMETIMES FIGHT TO THE DEATH TO DETERMINE WHO'S THE ALPHA.
SHUDDER
THE MALE DIDN'T NOTICE ME BECAUSE I HID AMONG THE FEMALES...
THAT'S NOT UNCOMMON!
IN SPECIES THAT USE A HAREMIC MATING SYSTEM, THERE ARE SOMETIMES MALES THAT TAKE ADVANTAGE OF THEIR SMALLER SIZE TO LIVE AMONG THE FEMALES AND MATE WITH THEM IN SECRET.
THE WRASSE IS A GOOD EXAMPLE!
HAREM
MALE THAT LOOKS LIKE A FEMALE
FEMALE
FEMALE
GIANT MALE
FEMALE
FEMALE
FEMALE
PARAJULIS (TYPE OF WRASSE)

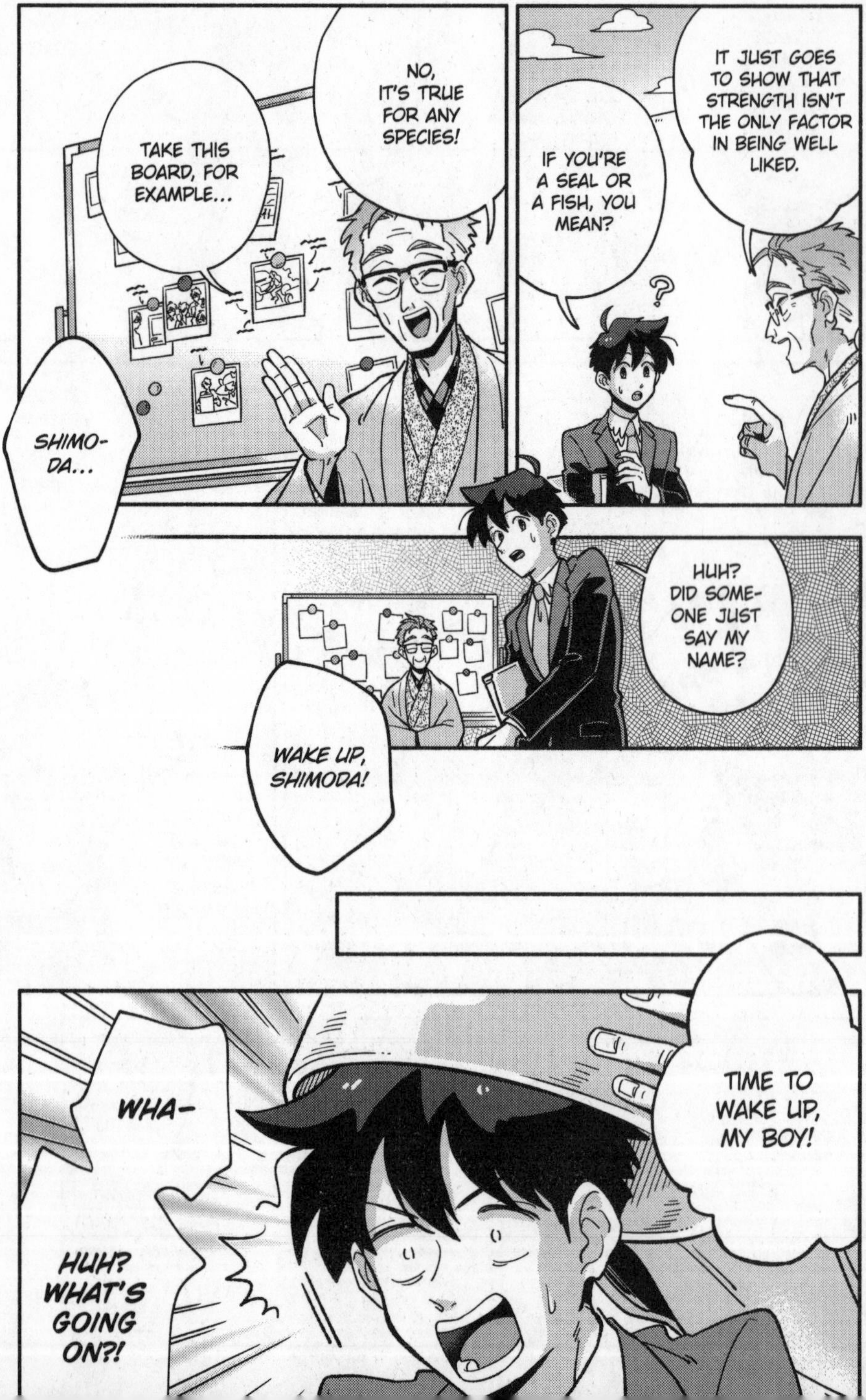
IT JUST GOES TO SHOW THAT STRENGTH ISN'T THE ONLY FACTOR IN BEING WELL LIKED.
IF YOU'RE A SEAL OR A FISH, YOU MEAN?
NO, IT'S TRUE FOR ANY SPECIES!
TAKE THIS BOARD, FOR EXAMPLE...
SHIMODA...
HUH? DID SOME-ONE JUST SAY MY NAME?
WAKE UP, SHIMODA!
TIME TO WAKE UP, MY BOY!
WHA-
HUH? WHAT'S GOING ON?!

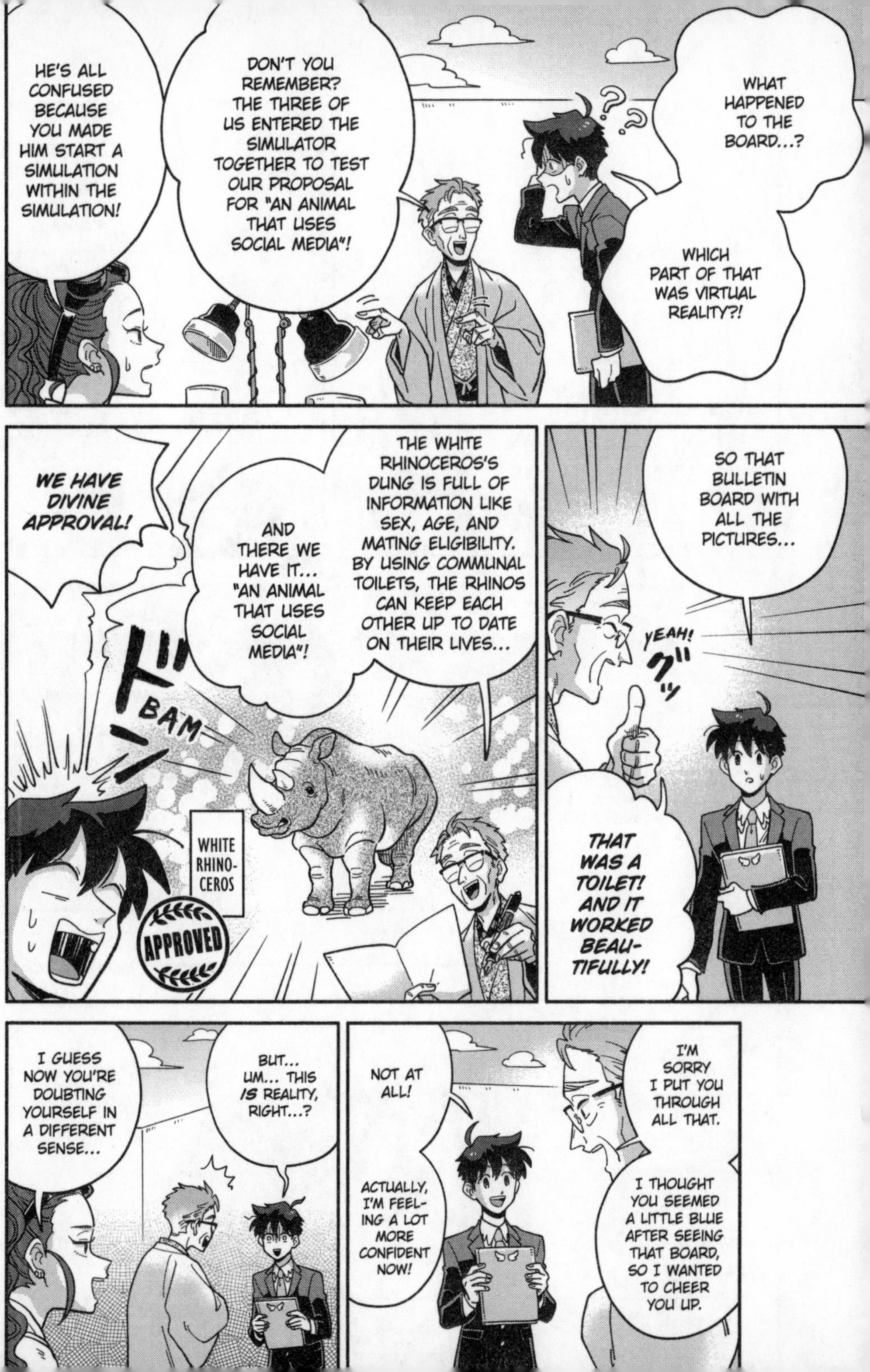
WHAT HAPPENED TO THE BOARD...?
WHICH PART OF THAT WAS VIRTUAL REALITY?!
DON'T YOU REMEMBER? THE THREE OF US ENTERED THE SIMULATOR TOGETHER TO TEST OUR PROPOSAL FOR "AN ANIMAL THAT USES SOCIAL MEDIA"!
HE'S ALL CONFUSED BECAUSE YOU MADE HIM START A SIMULATION WITHIN THE SIMULATION!
SO THAT BULLETIN BOARD WITH ALL THE PICTURES...
YEAH!
THAT WAS A TOILET! AND IT WORKED BEAU-TIFULLY!
THE WHITE RHINOCEROS'S DUNG IS FULL OF INFORMATION LIKE SEX, AGE, AND MATING ELIGIBILITY. BY USING COMMUNAL TOILETS, THE RHINOS CAN KEEP EACH OTHER UP TO DATE ON THEIR LIVES...
AND THERE WE HAVE IT... "AN ANIMAL THAT USES SOCIAL MEDIA"!
WE HAVE DIVINE APPROVAL!
BAM
WHITE RHINO-CEROS
APPROVED
I'M SORRY I PUT YOU THROUGH ALL THAT.
NOT AT ALL!
I THOUGHT YOU SEEMED A LITTLE BLUE AFTER SEEING THAT BOARD, SO I WANTED TO CHEER YOU UP.
ACTUALLY, I'M FEEL-ING A LOT MORE CONFIDENT NOW!
BUT... UM... THIS *IS* REALITY, RIGHT...?
I GUESS NOW YOU'RE DOUBTING YOURSELF IN A DIFFERENT SENSE...

THE ENCYCLOPEDIA OF REAL ANIMALS 40

ANIMAL 93 | WORM

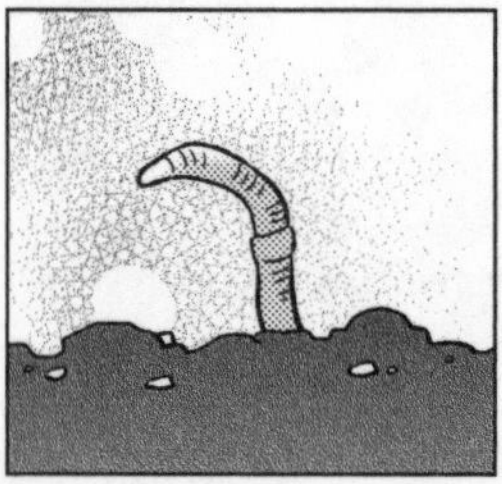

DIAGRAM

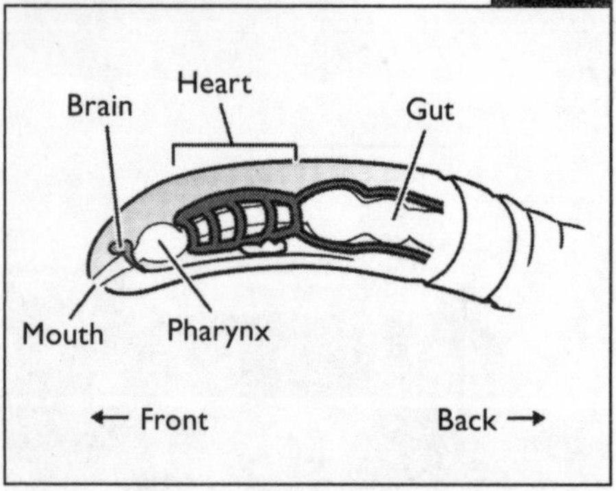
Heart
Brain
Gut
Mouth
Pharynx
← Front
Back →

A cross-section of a worm. The brain, heart, and blood vessels are visible.

Illustration: Hebizou

[Name] Earthworm
[Classification] Class: Oligochaeta
[Habitat] Worldwide, as long as the soil is neither frozen nor too dry
[Length] <1 mm - 300 cm (<0.04 in - 10 ft)

Though resembling parasitic nematodes in appearance, earthworms are actually in the same phylum as the more advanced ragworm and are thought to have evolved into their current legless form as a means of better adapting to life underground.

Earthworms, though smooth at first glance, are actually covered in short, stiff hairs. These act as spikes that help propel the worms through soil. Despite their lack of eyes and ears, they are able to sense the direction of light via photosensitive cells and are very sensitive to vibrations. Earthworms also have a primitive brain, digestive system, heart, and blood vessels. They do not have lungs, and respire through their mucus-covered skin.

Earthworms are able to regenerate when injured. When this happens, the upper half generally regrows a bottom half to form a complete worm. *Enchytraeus japonensis* has the ability to regenerate from a segment without reproductive organs into a fully-grown individual complete with reproductive capabilities.

ANIMAL 94 ELEPHANT SEAL

THE REAL THING

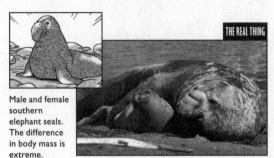

Male and female southern elephant seals. The difference in body mass is extreme.

Photo: Minden Pictures/Aflo

[Name] *Mirounga*
[Classification] Class: Mammalia
Order: Carnivora
Family: Phocidae
Genus: *Mirounga*
[Habitat] Eastern to central Pacific Ocean (northern); Drift ice in the northern subantarctic (southern)
[Length] Males: 420-470 cm (13.8-15.4 ft)
Females: 250-280 cm (8-9 ft)

With males weighing up to 2,000 kilograms (4,400 pounds) and females reaching up to 500 kilograms (1,100 pounds), the sexual dimorphism of elephant seals is extreme. A dominant male of this highly polygynous species may have a harem consisting of 50 to 300 females.

After furious and sometimes fatal fighting, only the most dominant males win the right to control a harem. Smaller, subdominant males determined to pass on their genetic material sometimes hide among the females and mate with them in secret.

ANIMAL 95 WHITE RHINOCEROS

White rhinoceros defecate in a communal area known as a midden, where they collect information such as the sex, age, and reproductive status of other individuals. In other words, a midden serves as both a public toilet and a social media network used to exchange personal information.

There are two subspecies of white rhinoceros: the southern white rhinoceros and the northern white rhinoceros. As of 2020, only two females remain of the northern subspecies.

THE REAL THING

A family of white rhinoceros. Their mouths are wider than those of the black rhioceros.

Photo: Minden Pictures/Aflo

[Name] *Ceratotherium simum*
[Classification] Class: Mammalia
Order: Perissodactyla
Family: Rhinocerotidae
Genus: *Ceratotherium*
[Habitat] South Africa
[Length] 335-420 cm (11-13.8 ft)

HEAVEN'S
DESIGN TEAM

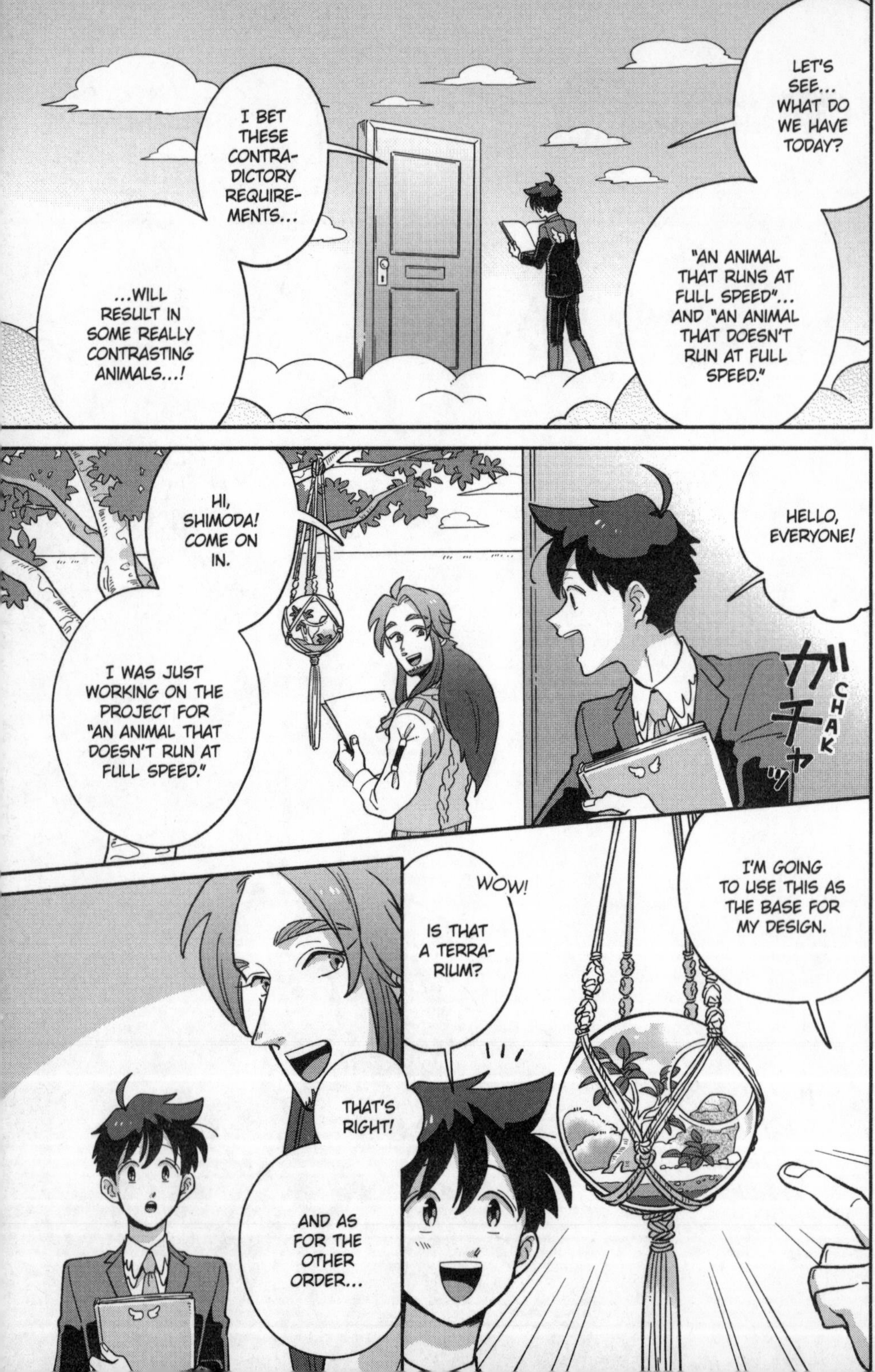
LET'S SEE... WHAT DO WE HAVE TODAY?
"AN ANIMAL THAT RUNS AT FULL SPEED"... AND "AN ANIMAL THAT DOESN'T RUN AT FULL SPEED."
I BET THESE CONTRA-DICTORY REQUIRE-MENTS...
...WILL RESULT IN SOME REALLY CONTRASTING ANIMALS...!
HELLO, EVERYONE!
ガチャッ
CHAK
HI, SHIMODA! COME ON IN.
I WAS JUST WORKING ON THE PROJECT FOR "AN ANIMAL THAT DOESN'T RUN AT FULL SPEED."
I'M GOING TO USE THIS AS THE BASE FOR MY DESIGN.
WOW!
IS THAT A TERRA-RIUM?
THAT'S RIGHT!
AND AS FOR THE OTHER ORDER...

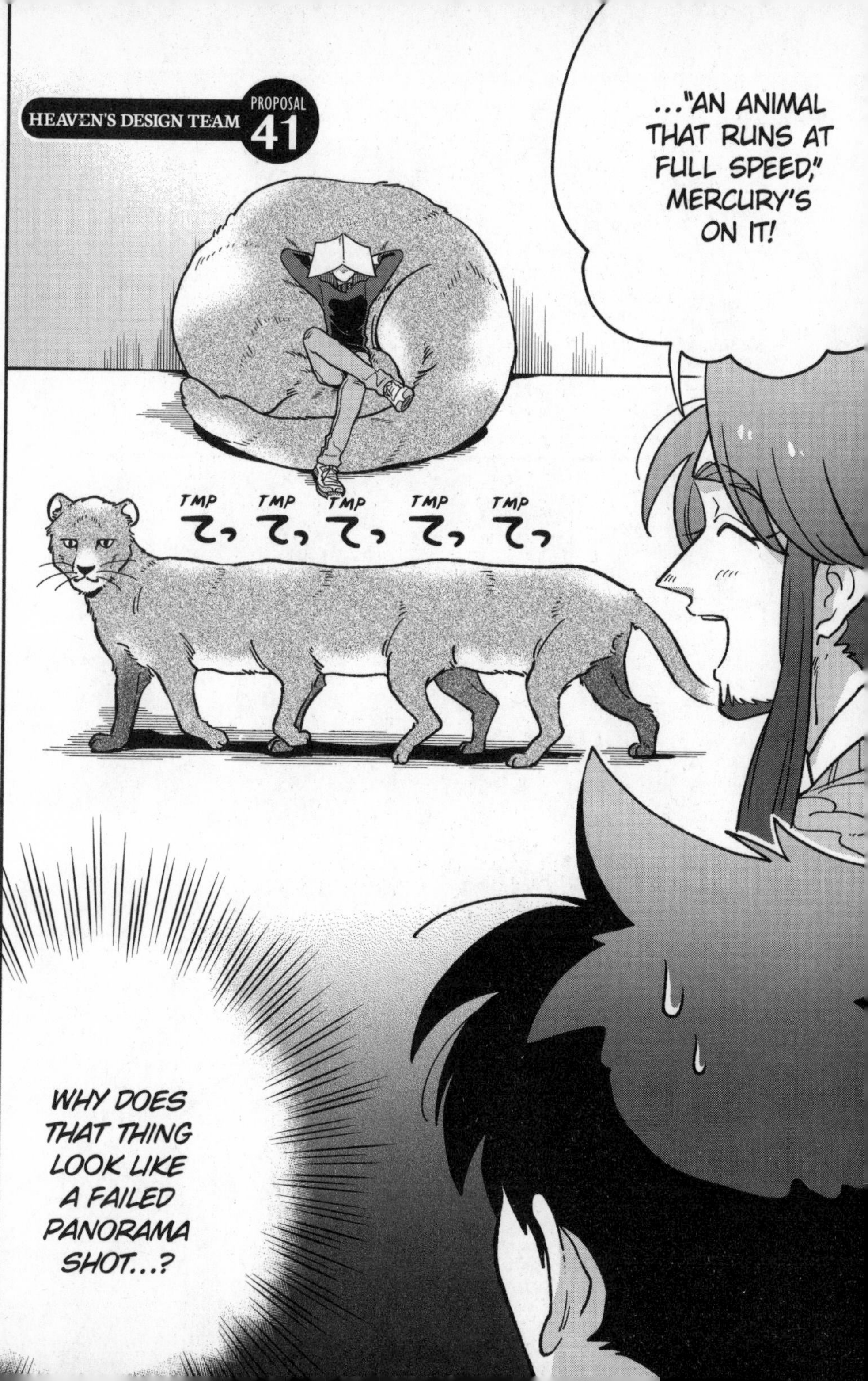
HEAVEN'S DESIGN TEAM
PROPOSAL
41
..."AN ANIMAL THAT RUNS AT FULL SPEED," MERCURY'S ON IT!
TMP TMP TMP TMP TMP
てっ てっ てっ てっ てっ
WHY DOES THAT THING LOOK LIKE A FAILED PANORAMA SHOT...?

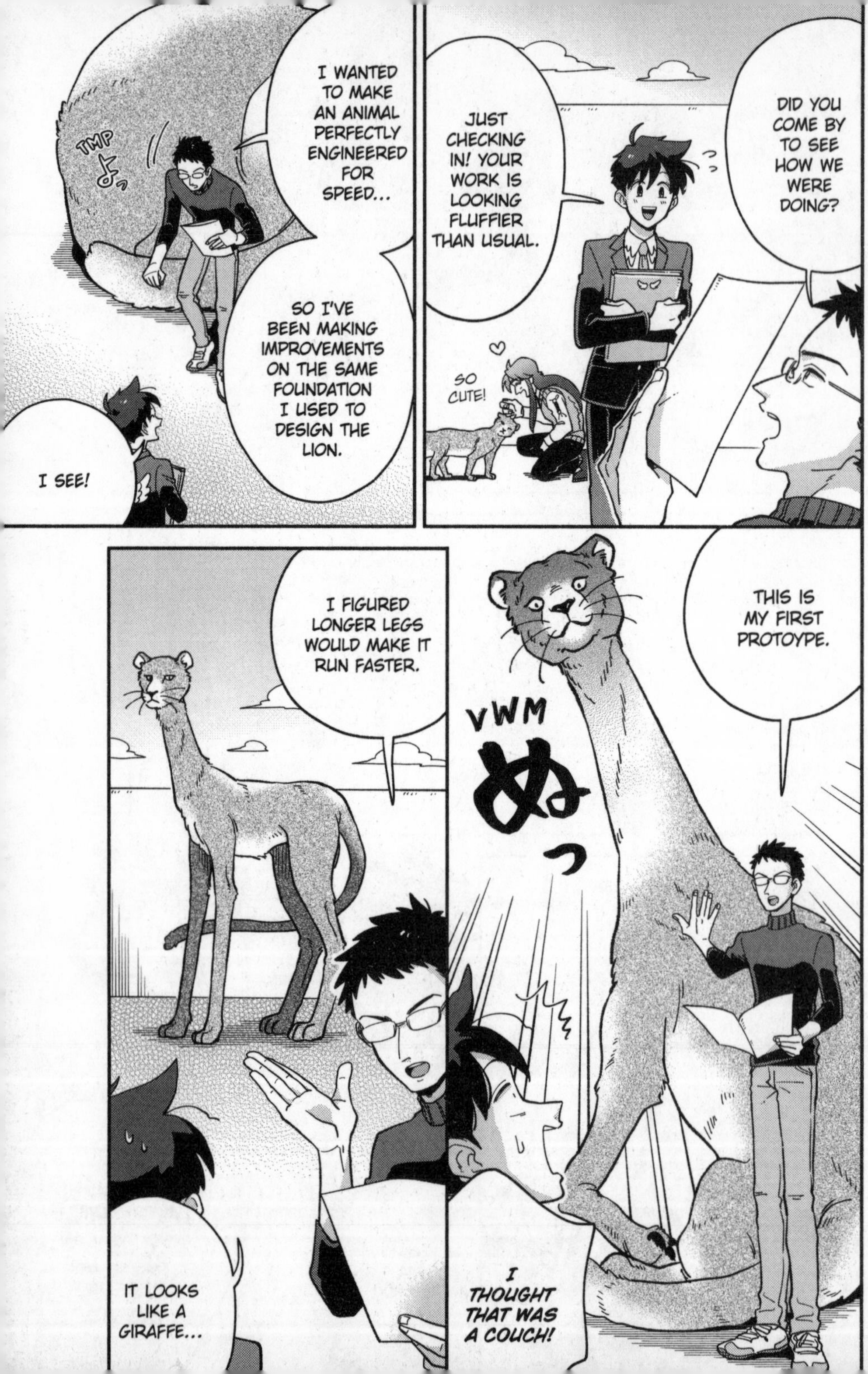
DID YOU COME BY TO SEE HOW WE WERE DOING?
JUST CHECKING IN! YOUR WORK IS LOOKING FLUFFIER THAN USUAL.
SO CUTE!
I WANTED TO MAKE AN ANIMAL PERFECTLY ENGINEERED FOR SPEED...
TMP
よっ
SO I'VE BEEN MAKING IMPROVEMENTS ON THE SAME FOUNDATION I USED TO DESIGN THE LION.
I SEE!
THIS IS MY FIRST PROTOYPE.
VWM
ぬっ
I THOUGHT THAT WAS A COUCH!
I FIGURED LONGER LEGS WOULD MAKE IT RUN FASTER.
IT LOOKS LIKE A GIRAFFE...

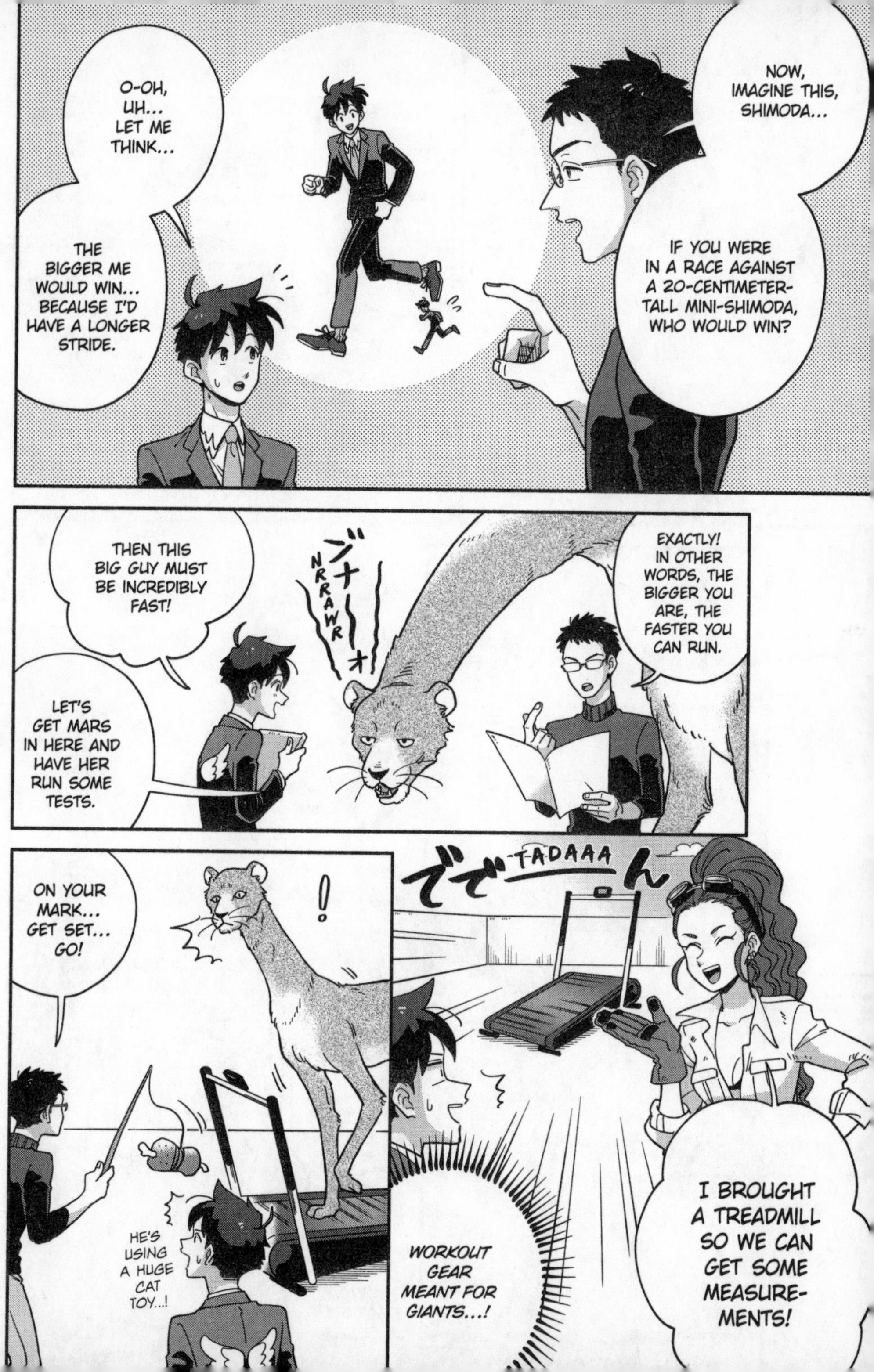
NOW, IMAGINE THIS, SHIMODA...
IF YOU WERE IN A RACE AGAINST A 20-CENTIMETER-TALL MINI-SHIMODA, WHO WOULD WIN?
O-OH, UH... LET ME THINK...
THE BIGGER ME WOULD WIN... BECAUSE I'D HAVE A LONGER STRIDE.
EXACTLY! IN OTHER WORDS, THE BIGGER YOU ARE, THE FASTER YOU CAN RUN.
ゴナーオ
NRRAWR
THEN THIS BIG GUY MUST BE INCREDIBLY FAST!
LET'S GET MARS IN HERE AND HAVE HER RUN SOME TESTS.
でで—ん
TADAAA
I BROUGHT A TREADMILL SO WE CAN GET SOME MEASUREMENTS!
WORKOUT GEAR MEANT FOR GIANTS...!
ON YOUR MARK... GET SET... GO!
!
HE'S USING A HUGE CAT TOY...!

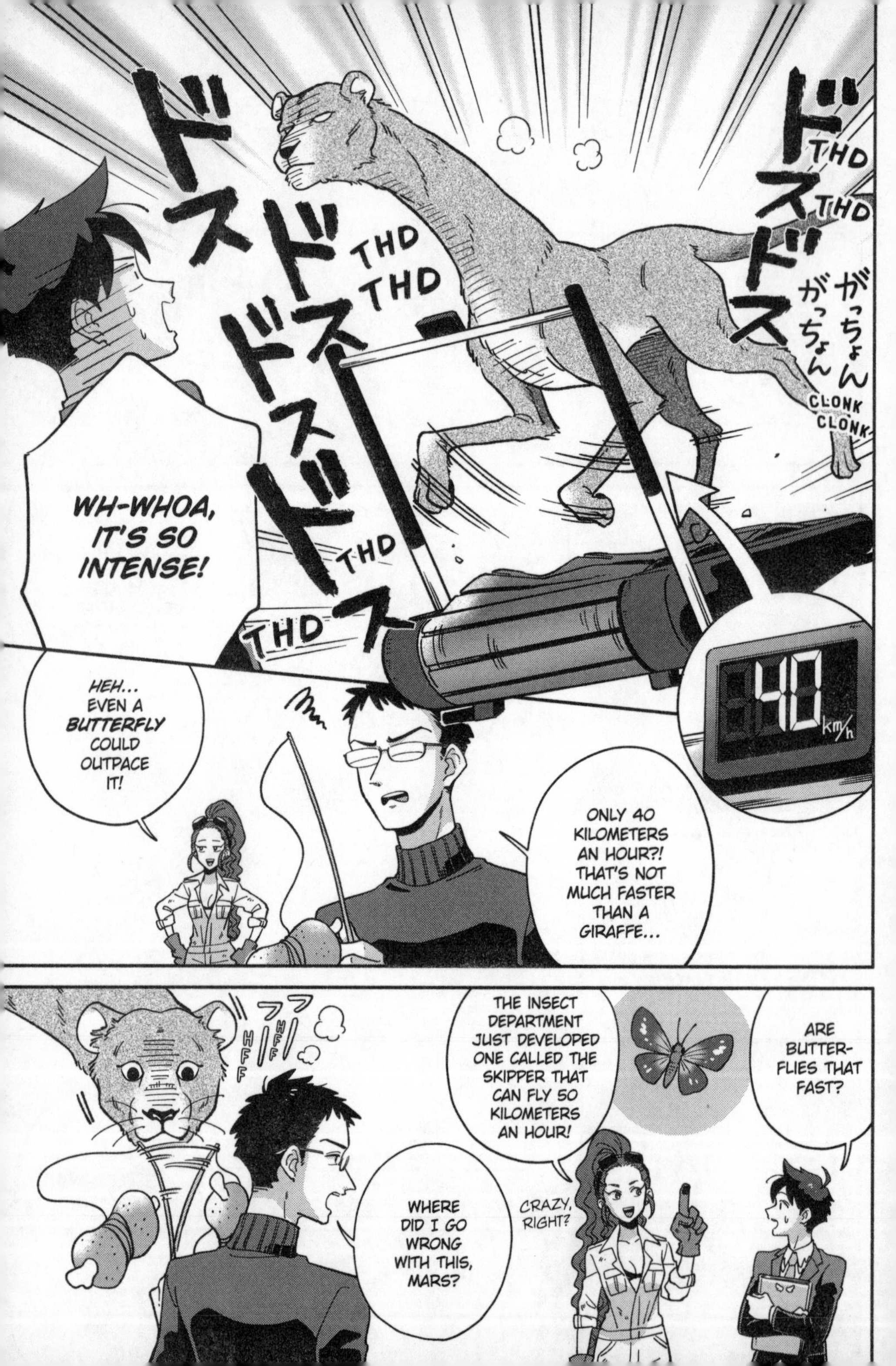
ドスドス
THD THD
がっちょん がっちょん
CLONK CLONK
ドスドスドスドス
THD THD
THD
THD
WH-WHOA, IT'S SO INTENSE!
40 km/h
ONLY 40 KILOMETERS AN HOUR?! THAT'S NOT MUCH FASTER THAN A GIRAFFE...
HEH... EVEN A BUTTERFLY COULD OUTPACE IT!
ARE BUTTER-FLIES THAT FAST?
THE INSECT DEPARTMENT JUST DEVELOPED ONE CALLED THE SKIPPER THAT CAN FLY 50 KILOMETERS AN HOUR!
CRAZY, RIGHT?
フフ
HFF HFF
WHERE DID I GO WRONG WITH THIS, MARS?

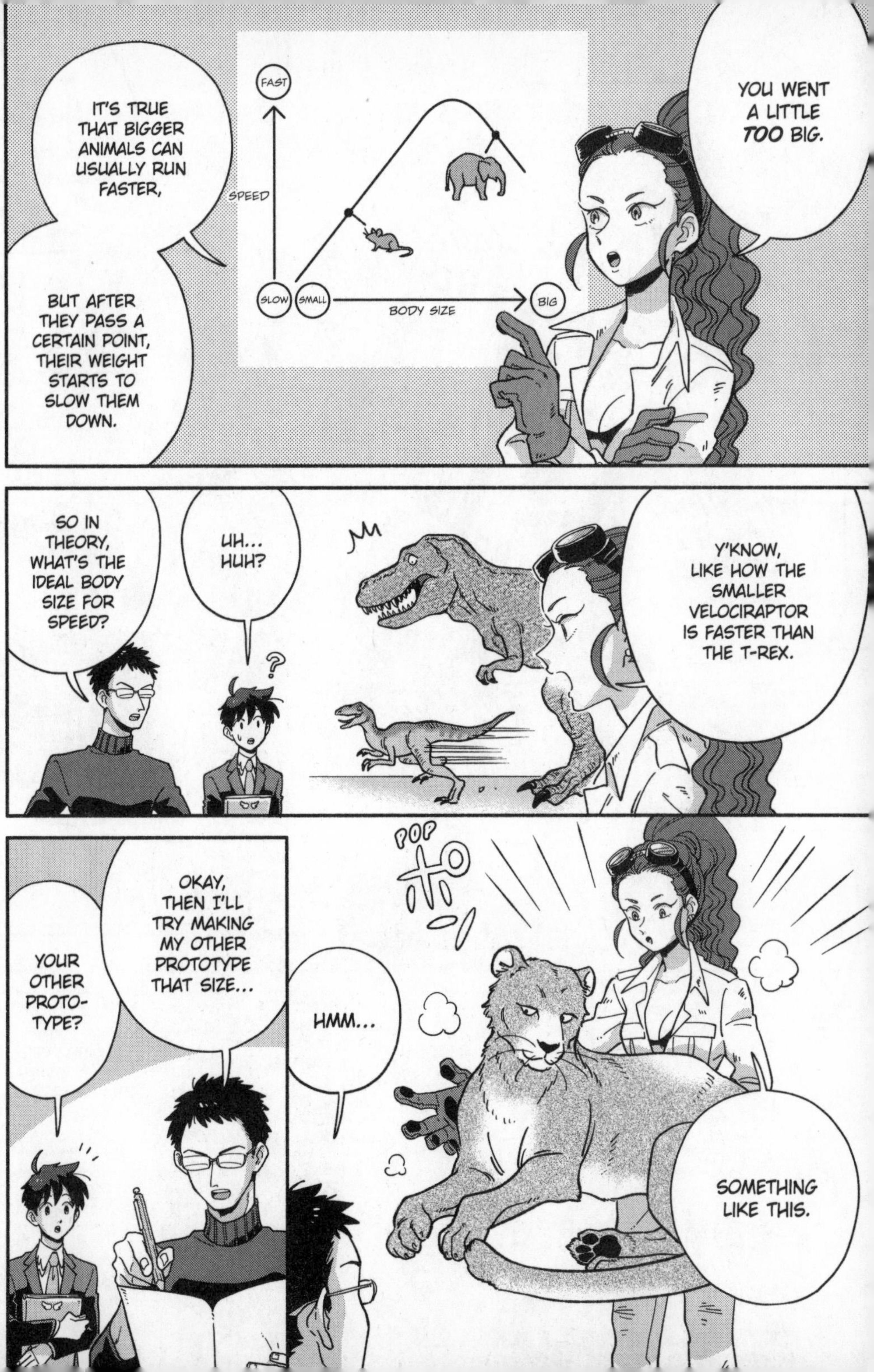
YOU WENT A LITTLE TOO BIG.
FAST
SPEED
SLOW
SMALL
BODY SIZE
BIG
IT'S TRUE THAT BIGGER ANIMALS CAN USUALLY RUN FASTER,
BUT AFTER THEY PASS A CERTAIN POINT, THEIR WEIGHT STARTS TO SLOW THEM DOWN.
Y'KNOW, LIKE HOW THE SMALLER VELOCIRAPTOR IS FASTER THAN THE T-REX.
UH... HUH?
SO IN THEORY, WHAT'S THE IDEAL BODY SIZE FOR SPEED?
POP
HMM...
SOMETHING LIKE THIS.
OKAY, THEN I'LL TRY MAKING MY OTHER PROTOTYPE THAT SIZE...
YOUR OTHER PROTO-TYPE?

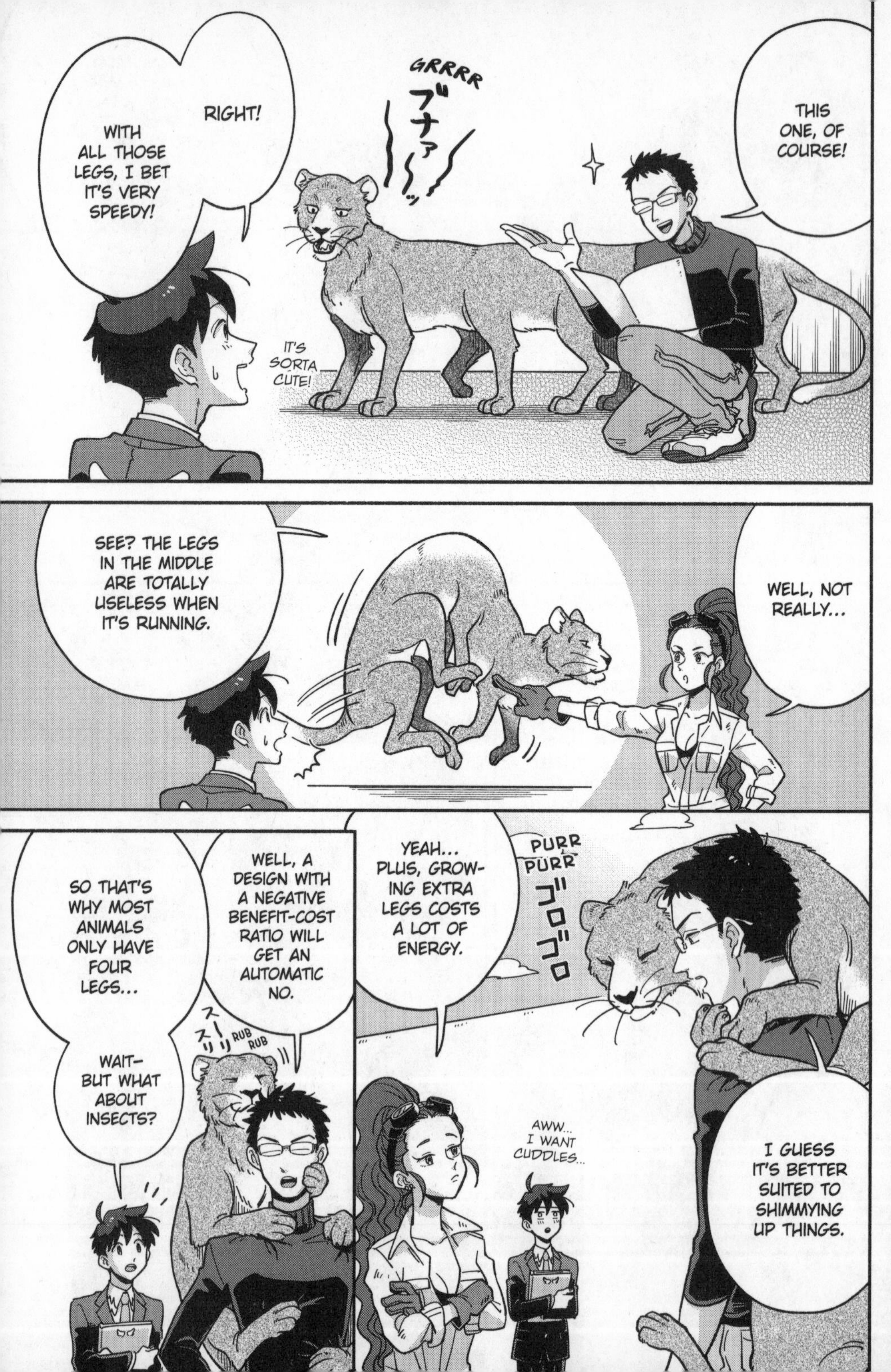
THIS ONE, OF COURSE!
GRRRR
ブナァ〜ッ
RIGHT!
WITH ALL THOSE LEGS, I BET IT'S VERY SPEEDY!
IT'S SORTA CUTE!
WELL, NOT REALLY...
SEE? THE LEGS IN THE MIDDLE ARE TOTALLY USELESS WHEN IT'S RUNNING.
PURR PURR
ゴロゴロ
YEAH... PLUS, GROWING EXTRA LEGS COSTS A LOT OF ENERGY.
I GUESS IT'S BETTER SUITED TO SHIMMYING UP THINGS.
AWW... I WANT CUDDLES...
WELL, A DESIGN WITH A NEGATIVE BENEFIT-COST RATIO WILL GET AN AUTOMATIC NO.
SO THAT'S WHY MOST ANIMALS ONLY HAVE FOUR LEGS...
スーリリ
RUB RUB
WAIT- BUT WHAT ABOUT INSECTS?

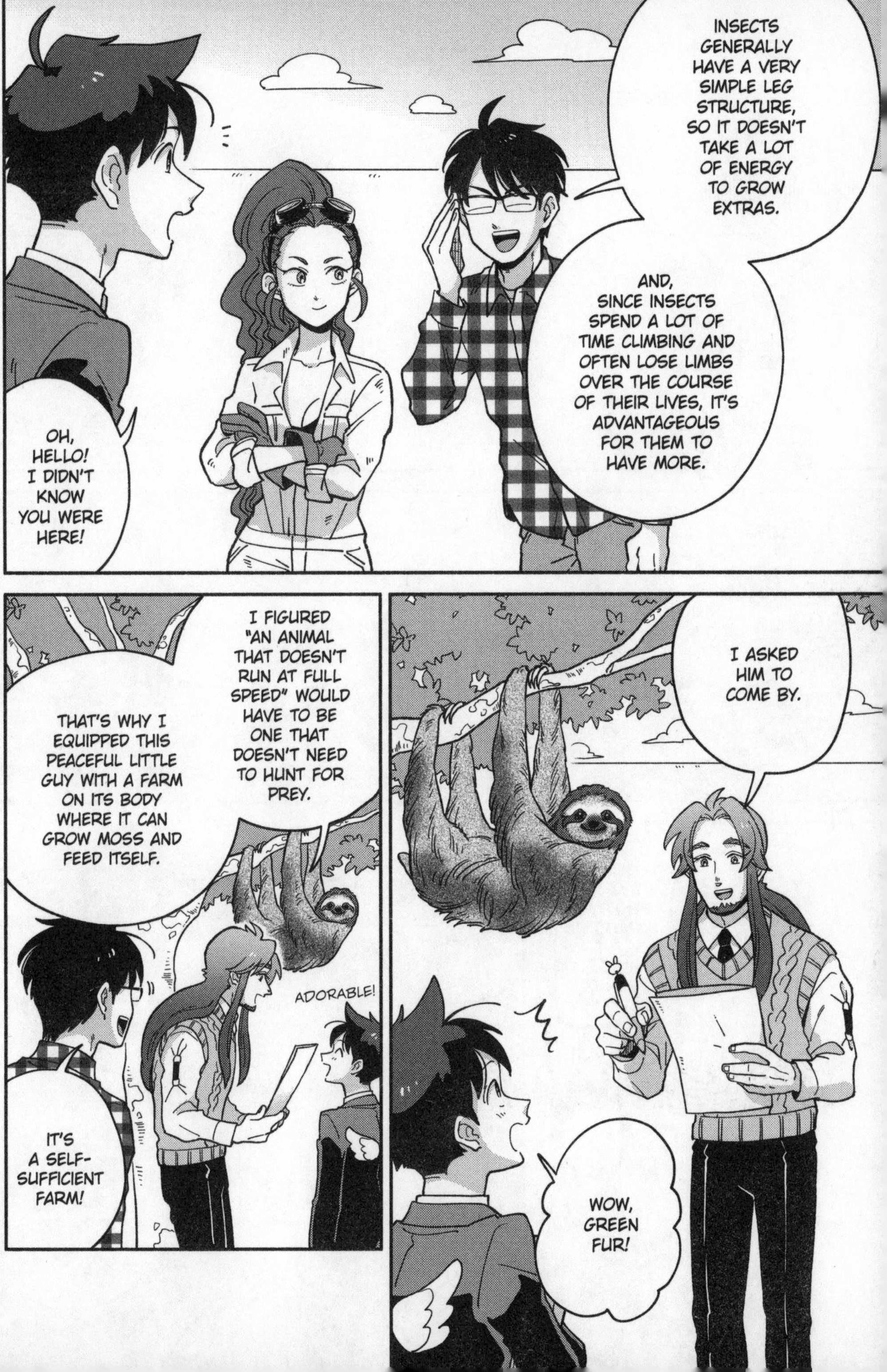
INSECTS GENERALLY HAVE A VERY SIMPLE LEG STRUCTURE, SO IT DOESN'T TAKE A LOT OF ENERGY TO GROW EXTRAS.
AND, SINCE INSECTS SPEND A LOT OF TIME CLIMBING AND OFTEN LOSE LIMBS OVER THE COURSE OF THEIR LIVES, IT'S ADVANTAGEOUS FOR THEM TO HAVE MORE.
OH, HELLO! I DIDN'T KNOW YOU WERE HERE!
I ASKED HIM TO COME BY.
WOW, GREEN FUR!
I FIGURED "AN ANIMAL THAT DOESN'T RUN AT FULL SPEED" WOULD HAVE TO BE ONE THAT DOESN'T NEED TO HUNT FOR PREY.
THAT'S WHY I EQUIPPED THIS PEACEFUL LITTLE GUY WITH A FARM ON ITS BODY WHERE IT CAN GROW MOSS AND FEED ITSELF.
ADORABLE!
IT'S A SELF-SUFFICIENT FARM!

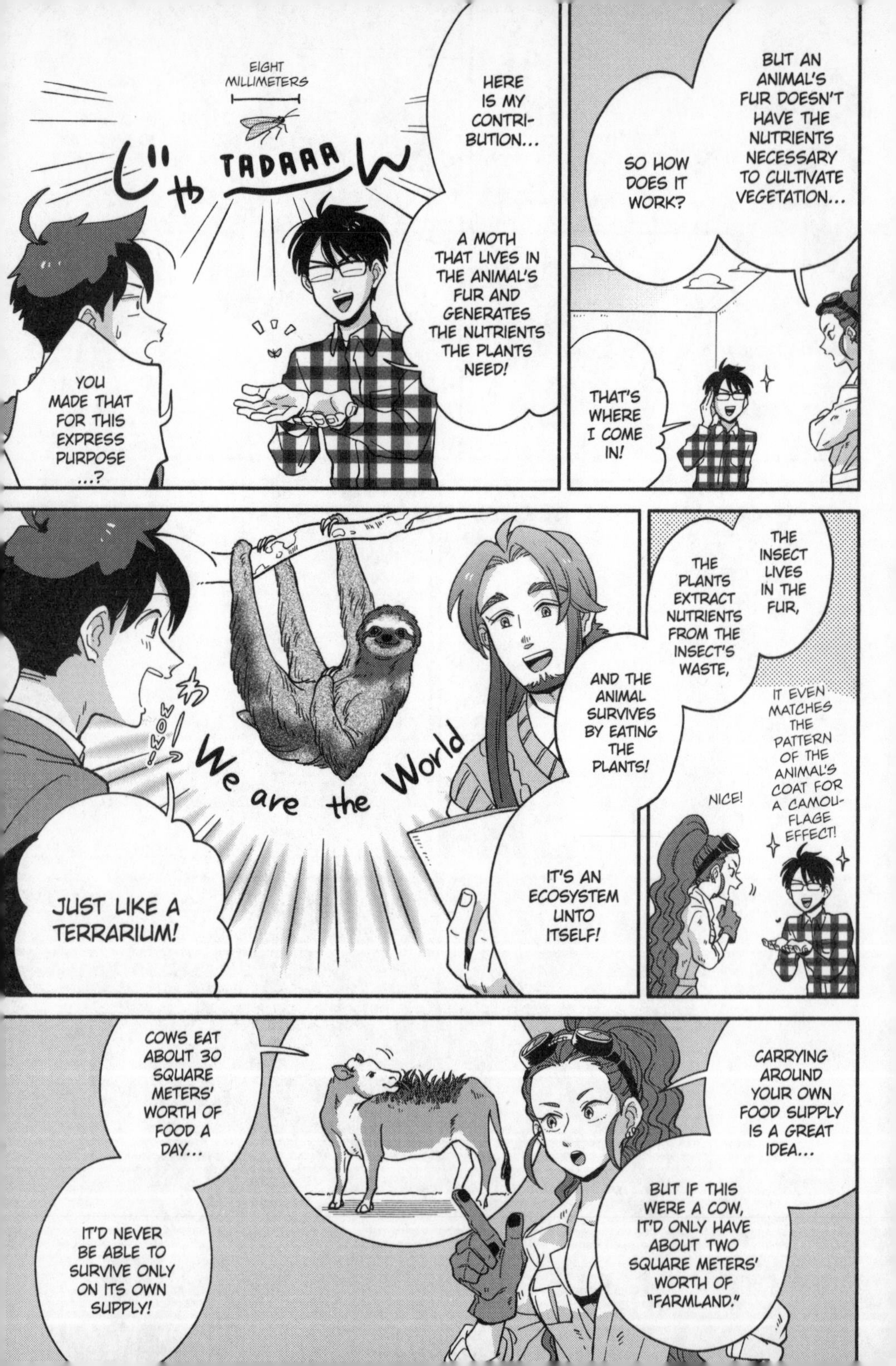
BUT AN ANIMAL'S FUR DOESN'T HAVE THE NUTRIENTS NECESSARY TO CULTIVATE VEGETATION...
SO HOW DOES IT WORK?
THAT'S WHERE I COME IN!
HERE IS MY CONTRIBUTION...
EIGHT MILLIMETERS
じゃ TADAAA ん
A MOTH THAT LIVES IN THE ANIMAL'S FUR AND GENERATES THE NUTRIENTS THE PLANTS NEED!
YOU MADE THAT FOR THIS EXPRESS PURPOSE ...?
THE INSECT LIVES IN THE FUR,
THE PLANTS EXTRACT NUTRIENTS FROM THE INSECT'S WASTE,
IT EVEN MATCHES THE PATTERN OF THE ANIMAL'S COAT FOR A CAMOUFLAGE EFFECT!
NICE!
AND THE ANIMAL SURVIVES BY EATING THE PLANTS!
We are the World
わ WOW!
IT'S AN ECOSYSTEM UNTO ITSELF!
JUST LIKE A TERRARIUM!
CARRYING AROUND YOUR OWN FOOD SUPPLY IS A GREAT IDEA...
BUT IF THIS WERE A COW, IT'D ONLY HAVE ABOUT TWO SQUARE METERS' WORTH OF "FARMLAND."
COWS EAT ABOUT 30 SQUARE METERS' WORTH OF FOOD A DAY...
IT'D NEVER BE ABLE TO SURVIVE ONLY ON ITS OWN SUPPLY!

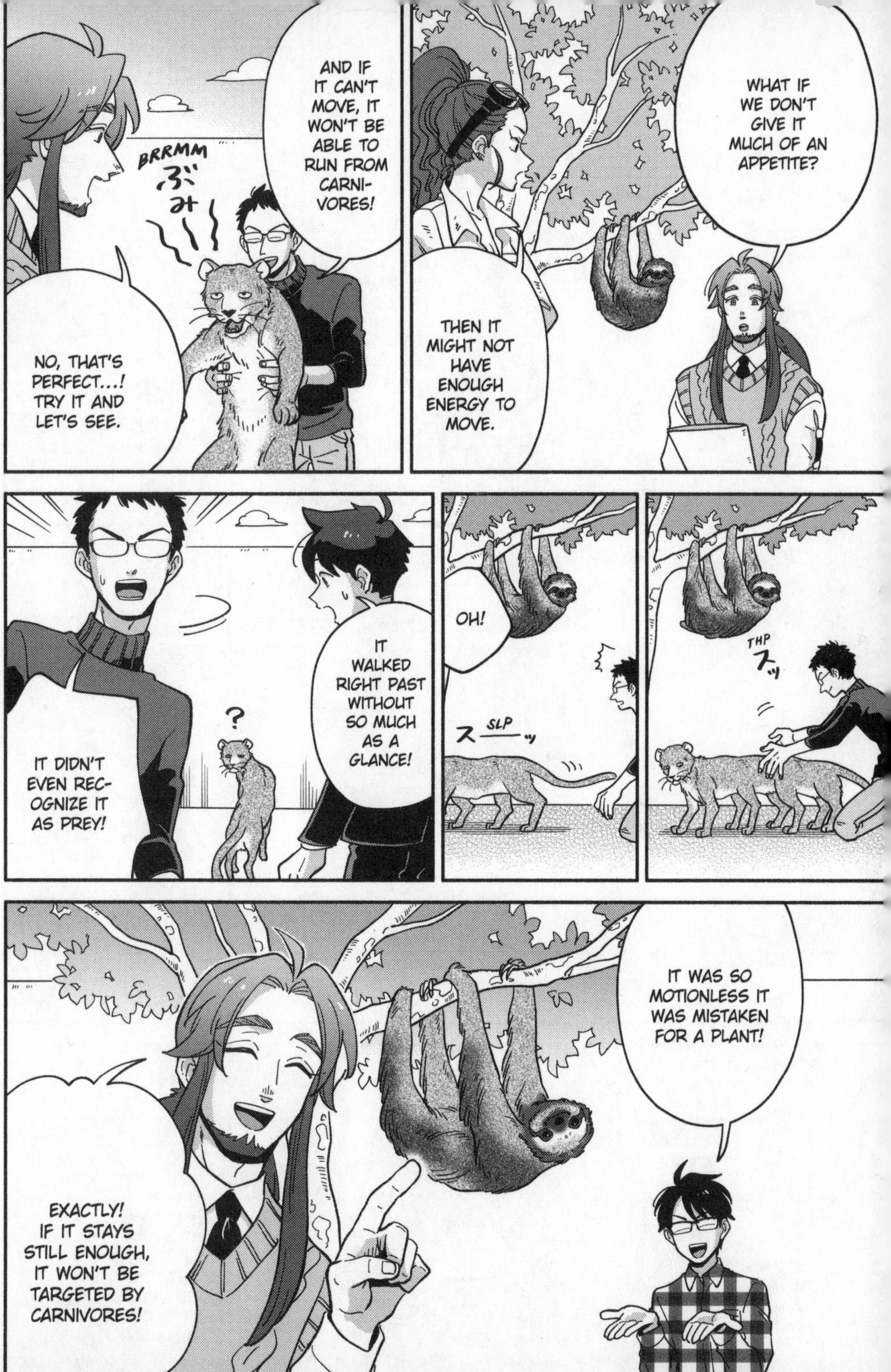
WHAT IF WE DON'T GIVE IT MUCH OF AN APPETITE?
THEN IT MIGHT NOT HAVE ENOUGH ENERGY TO MOVE.
AND IF IT CAN'T MOVE, IT WON'T BE ABLE TO RUN FROM CARNIVORES!
BRRMM ぶみ
NO, THAT'S PERFECT...! TRY IT AND LET'S SEE.
THP スッ
OH!
SLP スーッ
IT WALKED RIGHT PAST WITHOUT SO MUCH AS A GLANCE!
?
IT DIDN'T EVEN RECOGNIZE IT AS PREY!
IT WAS SO MOTIONLESS IT WAS MISTAKEN FOR A PLANT!
EXACTLY! IF IT STAYS STILL ENOUGH, IT WON'T BE TARGETED BY CARNIVORES!

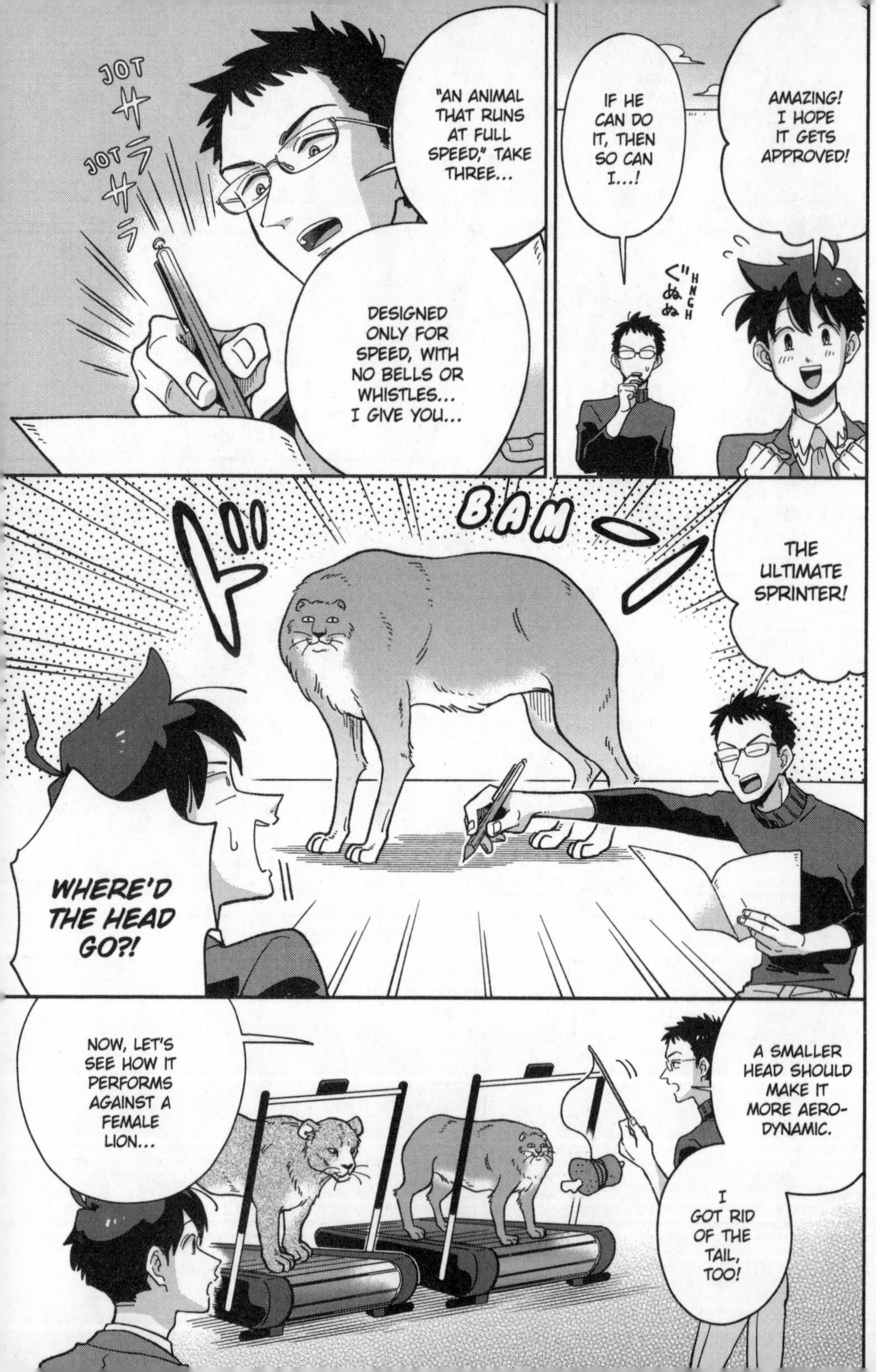
AMAZING! I HOPE IT GETS APPROVED!
IF HE CAN DO IT, THEN SO CAN I...!
ぐぬぬ
HNGH
"AN ANIMAL THAT RUNS AT FULL SPEED," TAKE THREE...
JOT
JOT
サラサラ
DESIGNED ONLY FOR SPEED, WITH NO BELLS OR WHISTLES... I GIVE YOU...
BAM
THE ULTIMATE SPRINTER!
WHERE'D THE HEAD GO?!
A SMALLER HEAD SHOULD MAKE IT MORE AERO-DYNAMIC.
I GOT RID OF THE TAIL, TOO!
NOW, LET'S SEE HOW IT PERFORMS AGAINST A FEMALE LION...

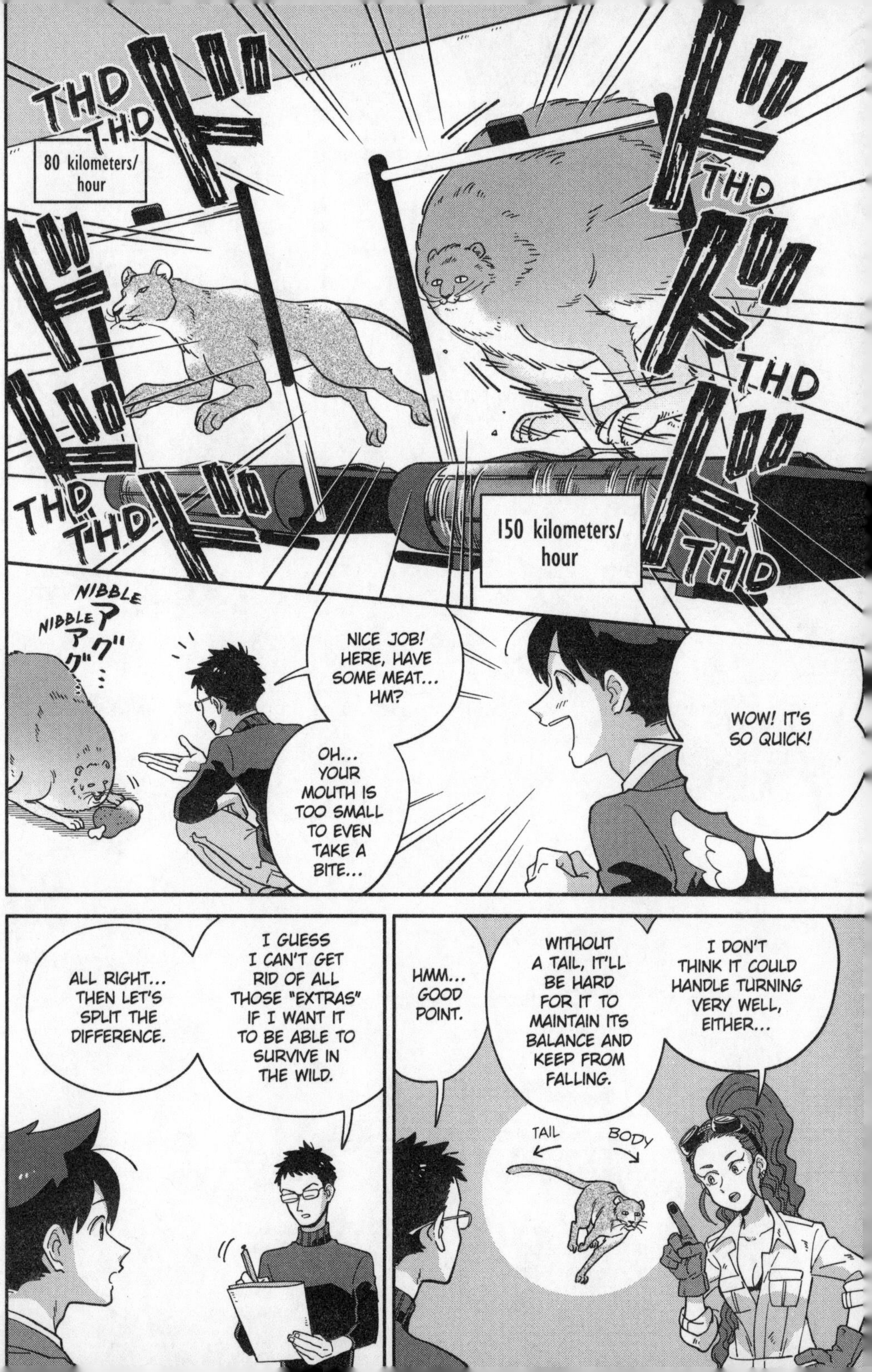
THD
THD
THD
150 kilometers/hour
THD THD
THD THD
80 kilometers/hour
WOW! IT'S SO QUICK!
NICE JOB! HERE, HAVE SOME MEAT... HM?
OH... YOUR MOUTH IS TOO SMALL TO EVEN TAKE A BITE...
NIBBLE NIBBLE
I DON'T THINK IT COULD HANDLE TURNING VERY WELL, EITHER...
WITHOUT A TAIL, IT'LL BE HARD FOR IT TO MAINTAIN ITS BALANCE AND KEEP FROM FALLING.
HMM... GOOD POINT.
BODY
TAIL
I GUESS I CAN'T GET RID OF ALL THOSE "EXTRAS" IF I WANT IT TO BE ABLE TO SURVIVE IN THE WILD.
ALL RIGHT... THEN LET'S SPLIT THE DIFFERENCE.

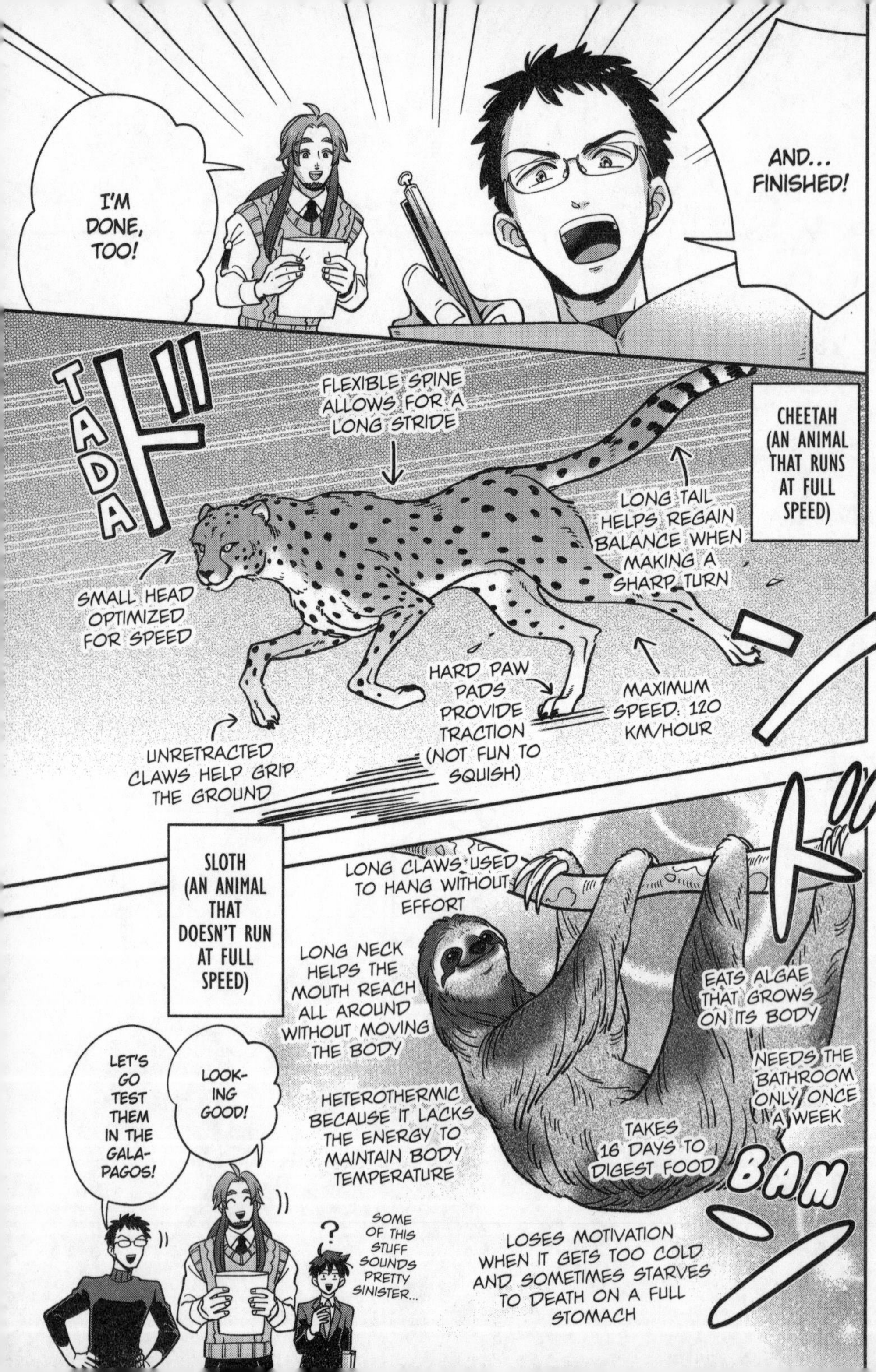
AND... FINISHED!
I'M DONE, TOO!
CHEETAH (AN ANIMAL THAT RUNS AT FULL SPEED)
FLEXIBLE SPINE ALLOWS FOR A LONG STRIDE
TADA
LONG TAIL HELPS REGAIN BALANCE WHEN MAKING A SHARP TURN
SMALL HEAD OPTIMIZED FOR SPEED
MAXIMUM SPEED: 120 KM/HOUR
HARD PAW PADS PROVIDE TRACTION (NOT FUN TO SQUISH)
UNRETRACTED CLAWS HELP GRIP THE GROUND
SLOTH (AN ANIMAL THAT DOESN'T RUN AT FULL SPEED)
LONG CLAWS USED TO HANG WITHOUT EFFORT
LONG NECK HELPS THE MOUTH REACH ALL AROUND WITHOUT MOVING THE BODY
EATS ALGAE THAT GROWS ON ITS BODY
NEEDS THE BATHROOM ONLY ONCE A WEEK
TAKES 16 DAYS TO DIGEST FOOD
HETEROTHERMIC BECAUSE IT LACKS THE ENERGY TO MAINTAIN BODY TEMPERATURE
BAM
LOSES MOTIVATION WHEN IT GETS TOO COLD AND SOMETIMES STARVES TO DEATH ON A FULL STOMACH
LOOK-ING GOOD!
LET'S GO TEST THEM IN THE GALA-PAGOS!
SOME OF THIS STUFF SOUNDS PRETTY SINISTER...

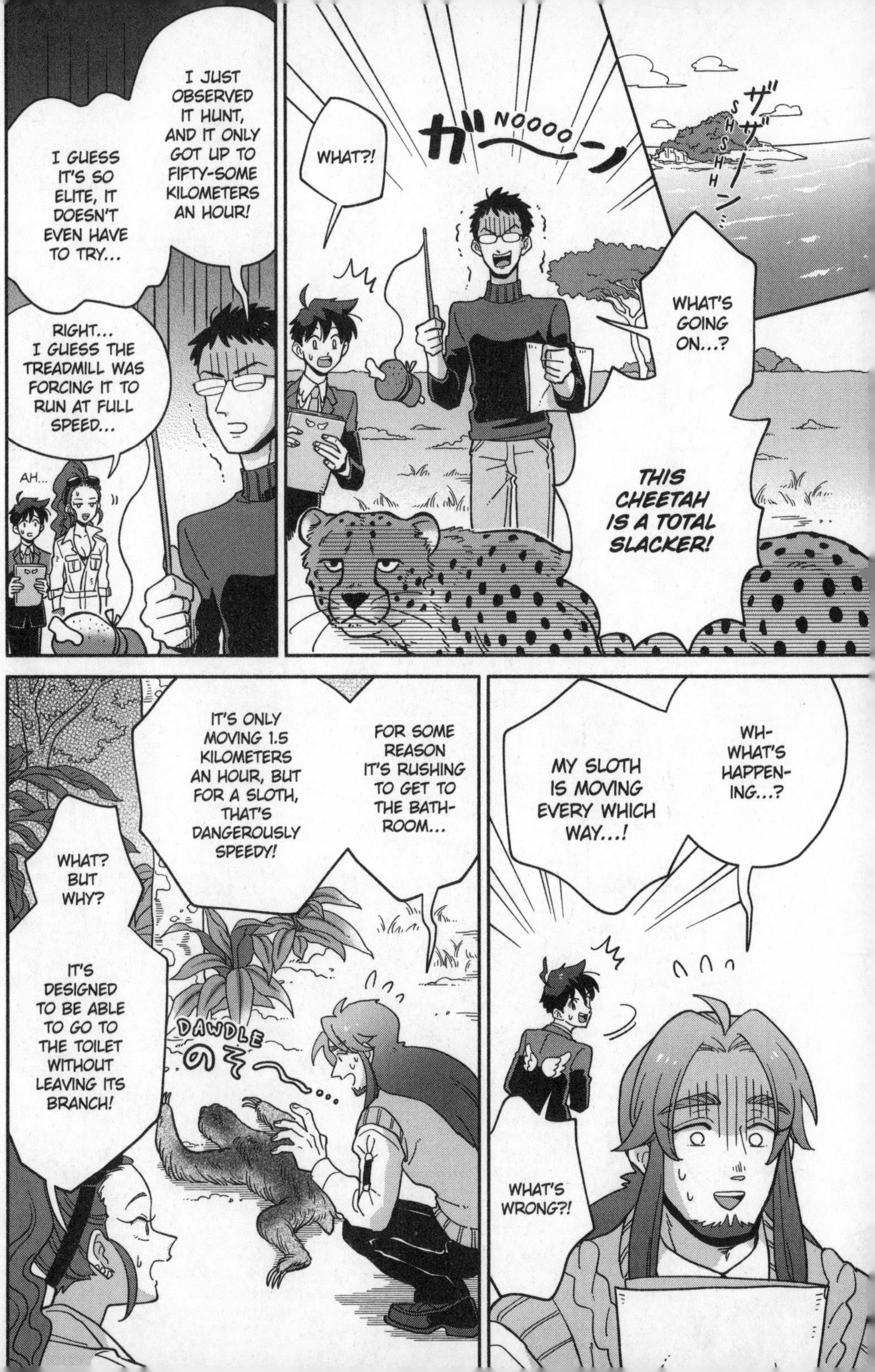
SHSHH
NOOOO
WHAT?!
WHAT'S GOING ON...?
THIS CHEETAH IS A TOTAL SLACKER!
I JUST OBSERVED IT HUNT, AND IT ONLY GOT UP TO FIFTY-SOME KILOMETERS AN HOUR!
I GUESS IT'S SO ELITE, IT DOESN'T EVEN HAVE TO TRY...
RIGHT... I GUESS THE TREADMILL WAS FORCING IT TO RUN AT FULL SPEED...
AH...
WH-WHAT'S HAPPEN-ING...?
MY SLOTH IS MOVING EVERY WHICH WAY...!
WHAT'S WRONG?!
FOR SOME REASON IT'S RUSHING TO GET TO THE BATH-ROOM...
IT'S ONLY MOVING 1.5 KILOMETERS AN HOUR, BUT FOR A SLOTH, THAT'S DANGEROUSLY SPEEDY!
WHAT? BUT WHY?
IT'S DESIGNED TO BE ABLE TO GO TO THE TOILET WITHOUT LEAVING ITS BRANCH!
DAWDLE

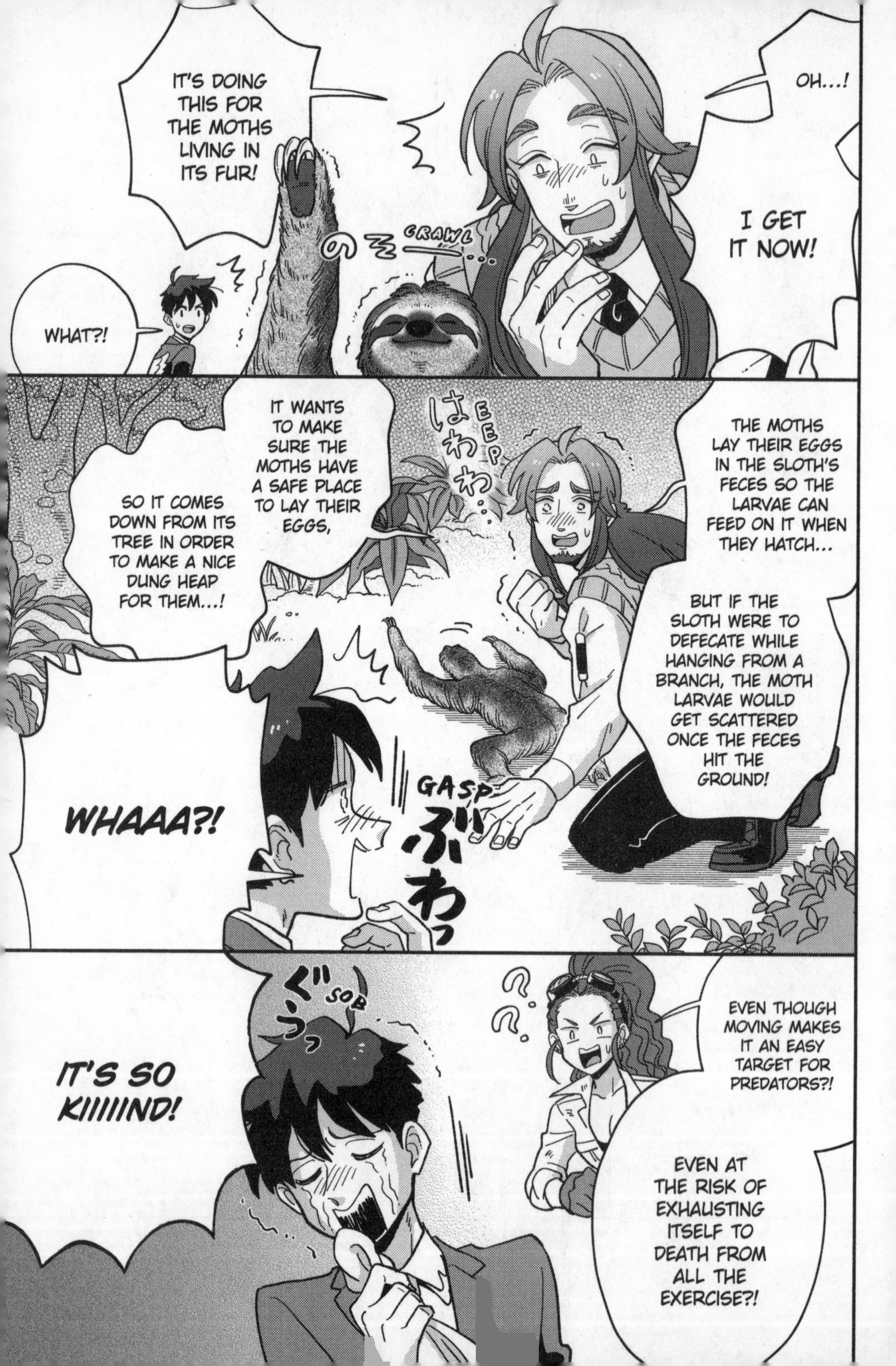
OH...!
I GET IT NOW!
IT'S DOING THIS FOR THE MOTHS LIVING IN ITS FUR!
のそ
CRAWL
WHAT?!
THE MOTHS LAY THEIR EGGS IN THE SLOTH'S FECES SO THE LARVAE CAN FEED ON IT WHEN THEY HATCH...
BUT IF THE SLOTH WERE TO DEFECATE WHILE HANGING FROM A BRANCH, THE MOTH LARVAE WOULD GET SCATTERED ONCE THE FECES HIT THE GROUND!
はわわ...
EEP
IT WANTS TO MAKE SURE THE MOTHS HAVE A SAFE PLACE TO LAY THEIR EGGS,
SO IT COMES DOWN FROM ITS TREE IN ORDER TO MAKE A NICE DUNG HEAP FOR THEM...!
ぶわっ
GASP
WHAAA?!
EVEN THOUGH MOVING MAKES IT AN EASY TARGET FOR PREDATORS?!
EVEN AT THE RISK OF EXHAUSTING ITSELF TO DEATH FROM ALL THE EXERCISE?!
ぐぅっ
SOB
IT'S SO KIIIIIND!

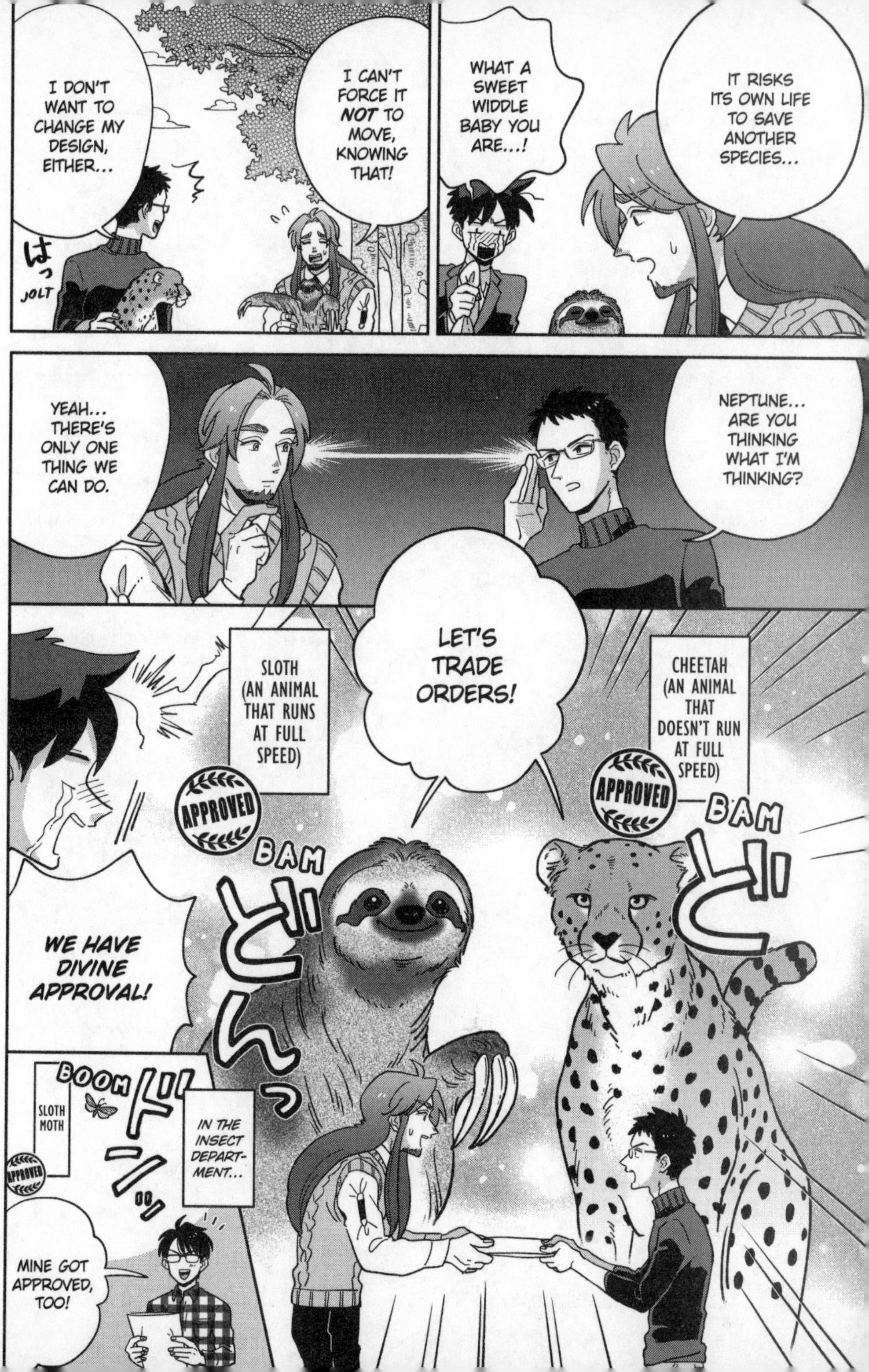
IT RISKS ITS OWN LIFE TO SAVE ANOTHER SPECIES...
WHAT A SWEET WIDDLE BABY YOU ARE...!
I CAN'T FORCE IT *NOT* TO MOVE, KNOWING THAT!
I DON'T WANT TO CHANGE MY DESIGN, EITHER...
はっ JOLT
NEPTUNE... ARE YOU THINKING WHAT I'M THINKING?
YEAH... THERE'S ONLY ONE THING WE CAN DO.
LET'S TRADE ORDERS!
CHEETAH (AN ANIMAL THAT DOESN'T RUN AT FULL SPEED)
APPROVED
BAM
SLOTH (AN ANIMAL THAT RUNS AT FULL SPEED)
APPROVED
BAM
WE HAVE DIVINE APPROVAL!
IN THE INSECT DEPART-MENT...
BOOM
SLOTH MOTH
APPROVED
MINE GOT APPROVED, TOO!

THE ENCYCLOPEDIA OF REAL ANIMALS 41

ANIMAL 96 | CHEETAH

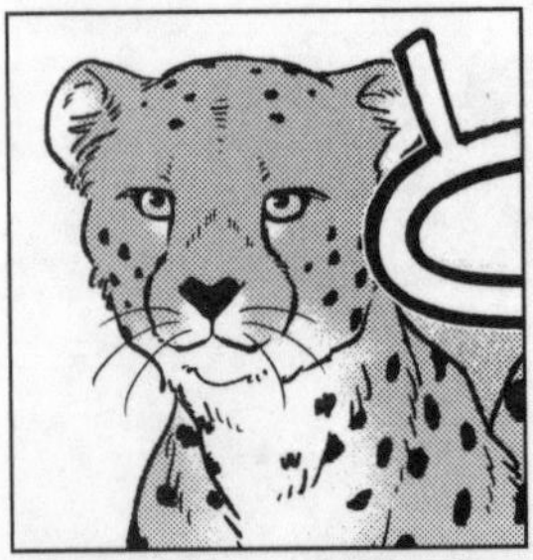

THE REAL THING

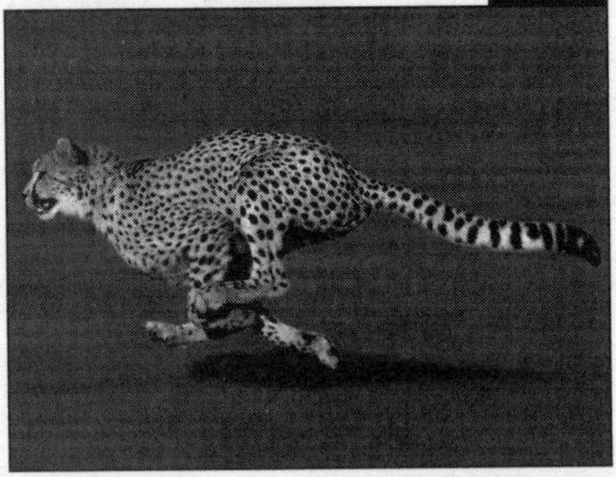

A cheetah flexes its body like a spring to facilitate running.

Photo: Minden Pictures/Aflo

[Name] *Acinonyx jubatus*
[Classification] Class: Mammalia
Order: Carnivora
Family: Felidae
Genus: *Acinonyx*
[Habitat] Africa (excluding tropical zones)
[Length] 110-140 cm (3.6-4.6 ft)

The cheetah is universally known as the world's fastest land animal. It achieves its unparalleled speed with a flexible spine used to manipulate its body like a spring, large claws used to grip the earth, and tough paw pads used to gain traction. A galloping cheetah has a stride length of four to seven meters (13-23 ft) and keeps all four legs in the air for a significant portion of time. The cheetah's long tail is indispensable for maintaining balance when making sharp turns at high speeds, while its large, wide nostrils help it breathe even while gripping prey in its teeth.

In 2012, the fastest cheetah recorded in captivity reached a peak speed of 98 km/h (60 mph), but research has shown that cheetahs hunting in the wild chase their prey at only half that speed. The relatively small head decreases wind resistance, but compromises the ability to bite. As a result, the cheetah sometimes loses its kills to lions and hyenas.

The sloth's survival tactic is to remain as motionless as possible. Its diet consists mainly of very small amounts of leaves, and it has an extremely low metabolism. When temperatures dip, its body temperature follows suit, causing its intestinal bacteria to slow down. This obstacle in absorbing nutrients sometimes leads to the sloth dying of starvation even on a full stomach.

Despite living in a tropical climate, the sloth has a coat of long fur that helps maintain its body temperature and conserve energy. A diverse range of algae, bacteria, and insects living within this coat assists in camouflaging the sloth and provides a supply of nutritious snacks.

A paper published in 2014 asserts that sloths risk their lives to defecate on the forest floor in order to create a safe birthing space for the moths it hosts in its fur. The moths provide the nutrients necessary for cultivating the plants that will then nurture the sloth, resulting in a symbiotic relationship between species.

THE REAL THING

Because its body is optimized for hanging from branches, the sloth crawls when on the ground.

Photo: Minden Pictures/Aflo

[Name]	Sloth
[Classification]	Class: Mammalia
	Order: Pilosa
[Habitat]	Tropical rainforests of Central and South America
[Length]	40-80 cm (1.3-2.6 ft)

HEAVEN'S DESIGN TEAM

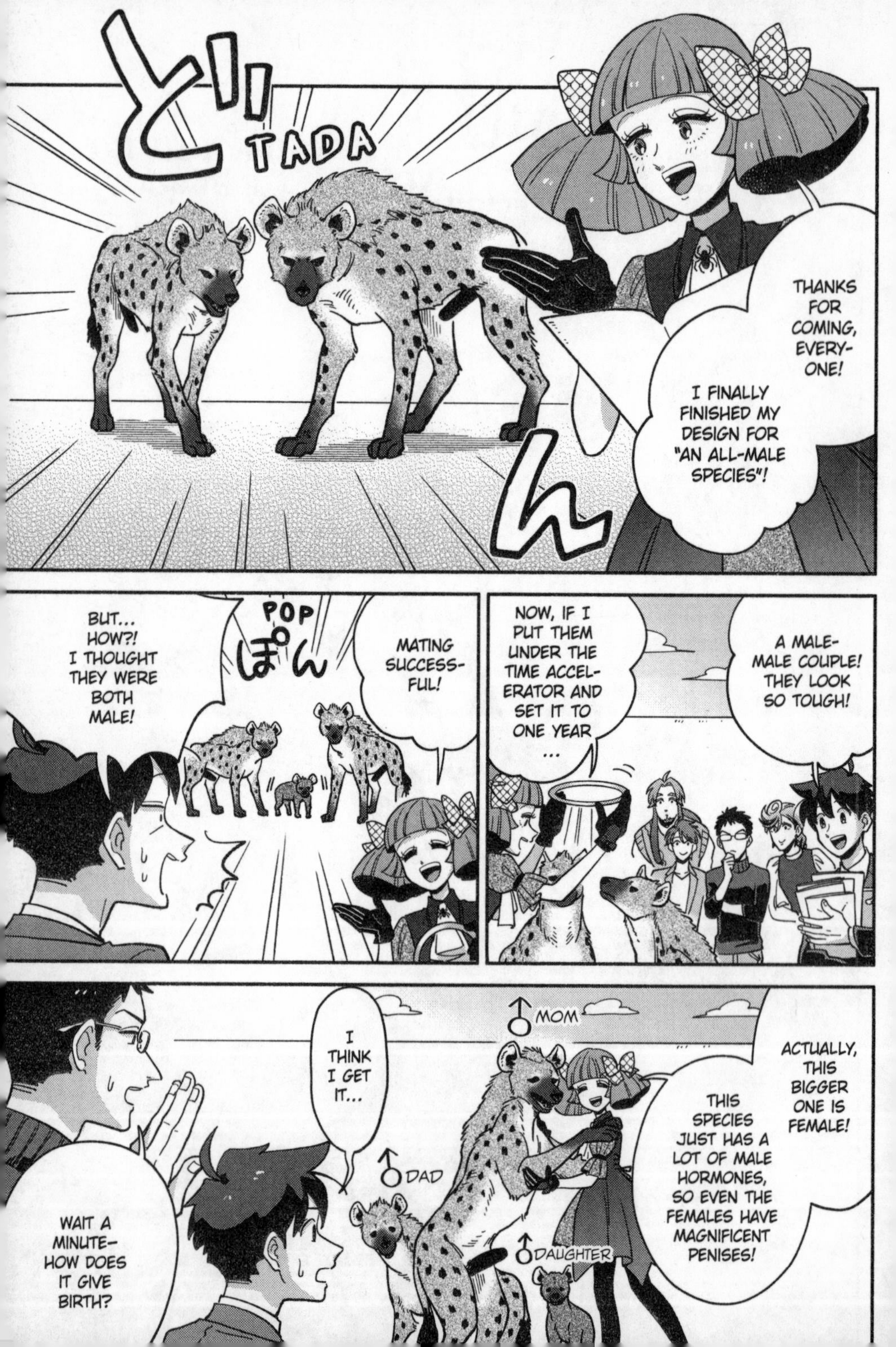
THANKS FOR COMING, EVERY-ONE!
I FINALLY FINISHED MY DESIGN FOR "AN ALL-MALE SPECIES"!
TADA
A MALE-MALE COUPLE! THEY LOOK SO TOUGH!
NOW, IF I PUT THEM UNDER THE TIME ACCEL-ERATOR AND SET IT TO ONE YEAR ...
MATING SUCCESS-FUL!
POP
BUT... HOW?! I THOUGHT THEY WERE BOTH MALE!
ACTUALLY, THIS BIGGER ONE IS FEMALE!
THIS SPECIES JUST HAS A LOT OF MALE HORMONES, SO EVEN THE FEMALES HAVE MAGNIFICENT PENISES!
♂ MOM
I THINK I GET IT...
♂ DAUGHTER
♂ DAD
WAIT A MINUTE— HOW DOES IT GIVE BIRTH?

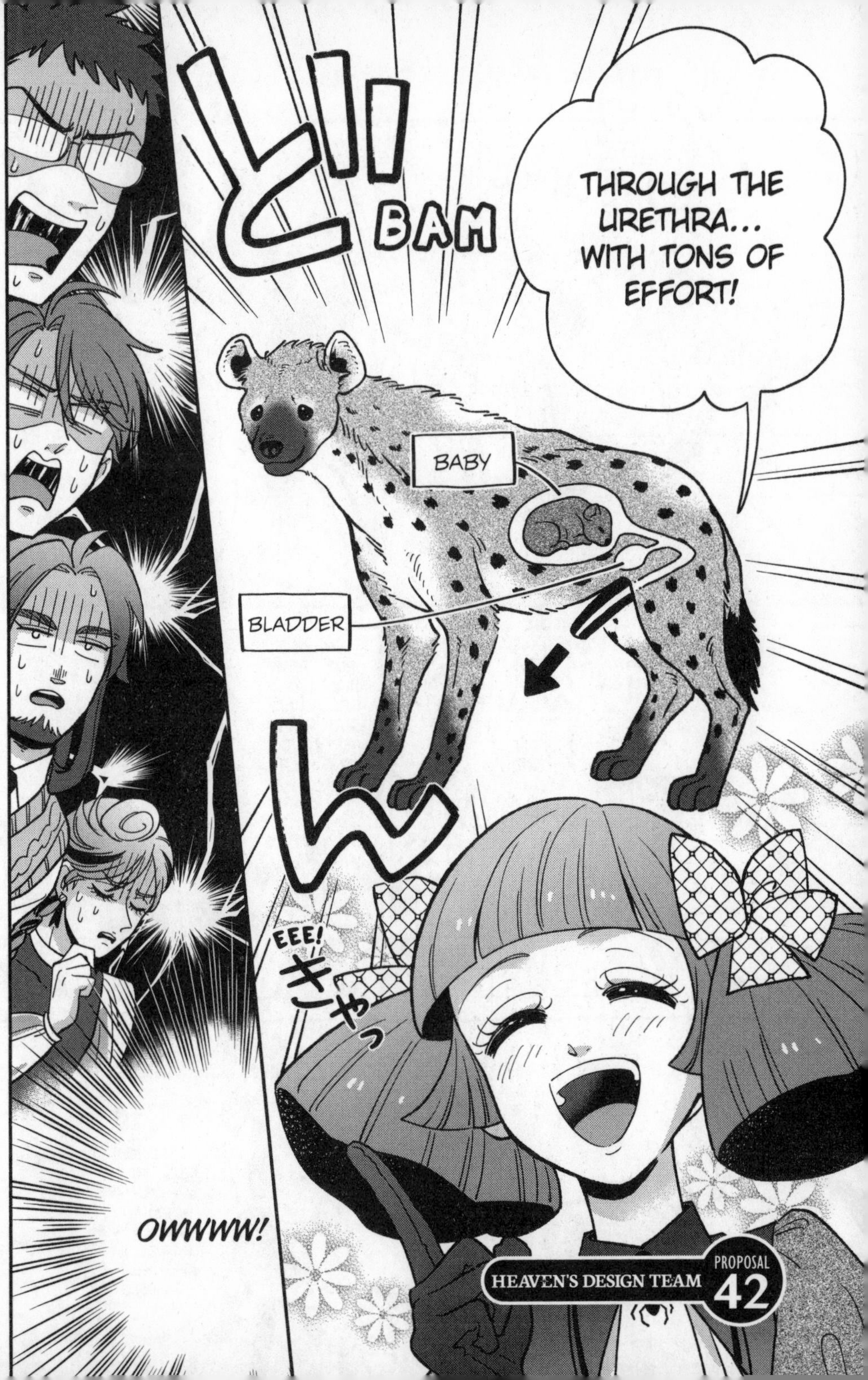
THROUGH THE URETHRA... WITH TONS OF EFFORT!
どん
BAM
BABY
BLADDER
きゃっ
EEE!
OWWWW!
HEAVEN'S DESIGN TEAM
PROPOSAL 42

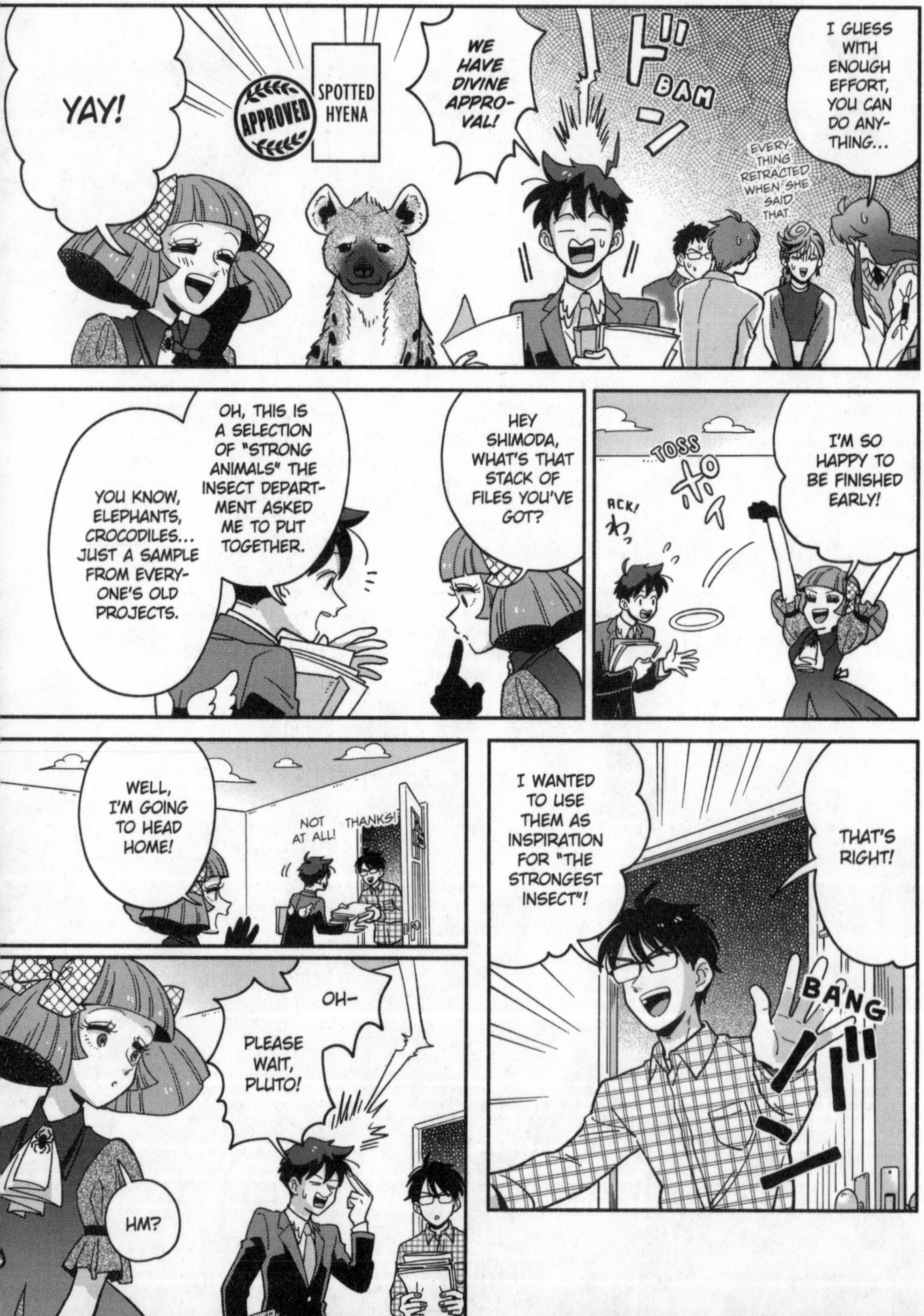
I GUESS WITH ENOUGH EFFORT, YOU CAN DO ANYTHING…
EVERYTHING RETRACTED WHEN SHE SAID THAT…
BAM
WE HAVE DIVINE APPROVAL!
SPOTTED HYENA
APPROVED
YAY!
I'M SO HAPPY TO BE FINISHED EARLY!
TOSS
ポイ
ACK!
わっ
HEY SHIMODA, WHAT'S THAT STACK OF FILES YOU'VE GOT?
OH, THIS IS A SELECTION OF "STRONG ANIMALS" THE INSECT DEPARTMENT ASKED ME TO PUT TOGETHER.
YOU KNOW, ELEPHANTS, CROCODILES… JUST A SAMPLE FROM EVERYONE'S OLD PROJECTS.
THAT'S RIGHT!
I WANTED TO USE THEM AS INSPIRATION FOR "THE STRONGEST INSECT"!
BANG
THANKS!
NOT AT ALL!
WELL, I'M GOING TO HEAD HOME!
OH-
PLEASE WAIT, PLUTO!
HM?

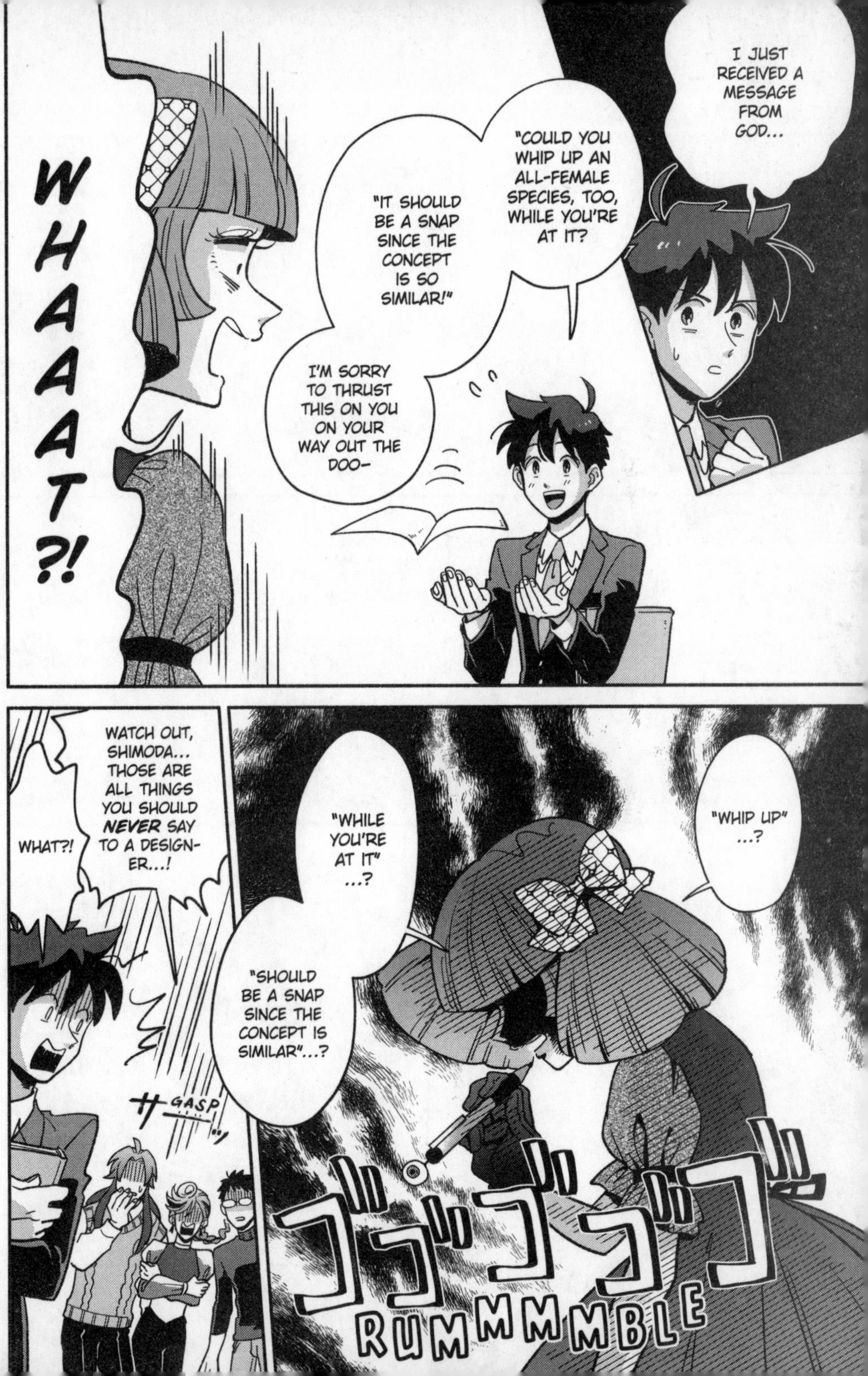
I JUST RECEIVED A MESSAGE FROM GOD...
"COULD YOU WHIP UP AN ALL-FEMALE SPECIES, TOO, WHILE YOU'RE AT IT?
"IT SHOULD BE A SNAP SINCE THE CONCEPT IS SO SIMILAR!"
I'M SORRY TO THRUST THIS ON YOU ON YOUR WAY OUT THE DOO-
WHAAAAT?!
"WHIP UP" ...?
"WHILE YOU'RE AT IT" ...?
"SHOULD BE A SNAP SINCE THE CONCEPT IS SIMILAR"...?
ゴゴゴゴゴ
RUMMMMMBLE
WATCH OUT, SHIMODA... THOSE ARE ALL THINGS YOU SHOULD NEVER SAY TO A DESIGNER...!
WHAT?!
GASP

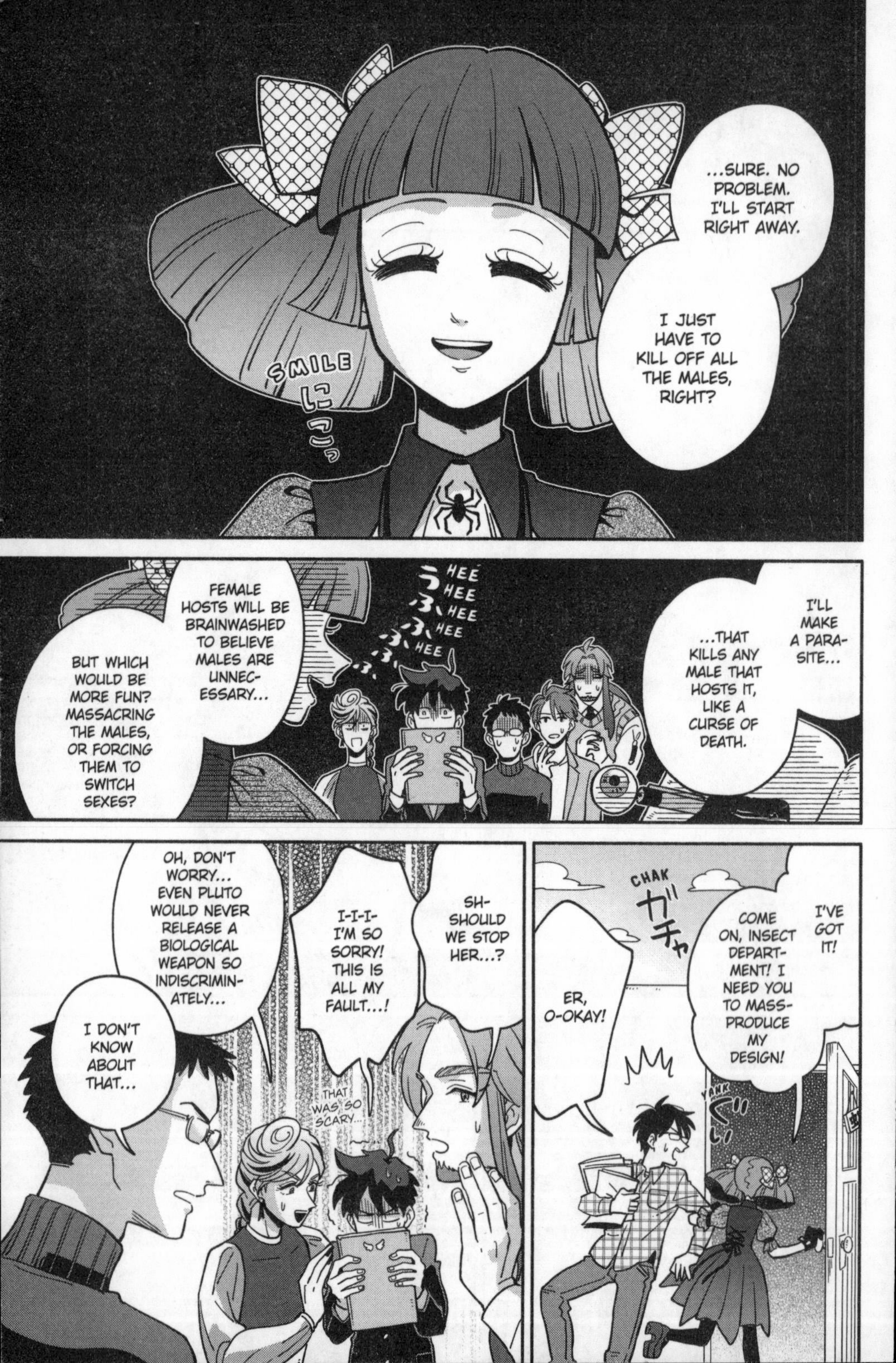
...SURE. NO PROBLEM. I'LL START RIGHT AWAY.
I JUST HAVE TO KILL OFF ALL THE MALES, RIGHT?
SMILE
にこっ
I'LL MAKE A PARA-SITE...
...THAT KILLS ANY MALE THAT HOSTS IT, LIKE A CURSE OF DEATH.
HEE HEE HEE HEE HEE
うふふふふ
FEMALE HOSTS WILL BE BRAINWASHED TO BELIEVE MALES ARE UNNEC-ESSARY...
BUT WHICH WOULD BE MORE FUN? MASSACRING THE MALES, OR FORCING THEM TO SWITCH SEXES?
CHAK
ガチャ
I'VE GOT IT!
COME ON, INSECT DEPART-MENT! I NEED YOU TO MASS-PRODUCE MY DESIGN!
ER, O-OKAY!
YANK
ぐい
SH-SHOULD WE STOP HER...?
I-I-I-I'M SO SORRY! THIS IS ALL MY FAULT...!
THAT WAS SO SCARY...
OH, DON'T WORRY... EVEN PLUTO WOULD NEVER RELEASE A BIOLOGICAL WEAPON SO INDISCRIMIN-ATELY...
I DON'T KNOW ABOUT THAT...

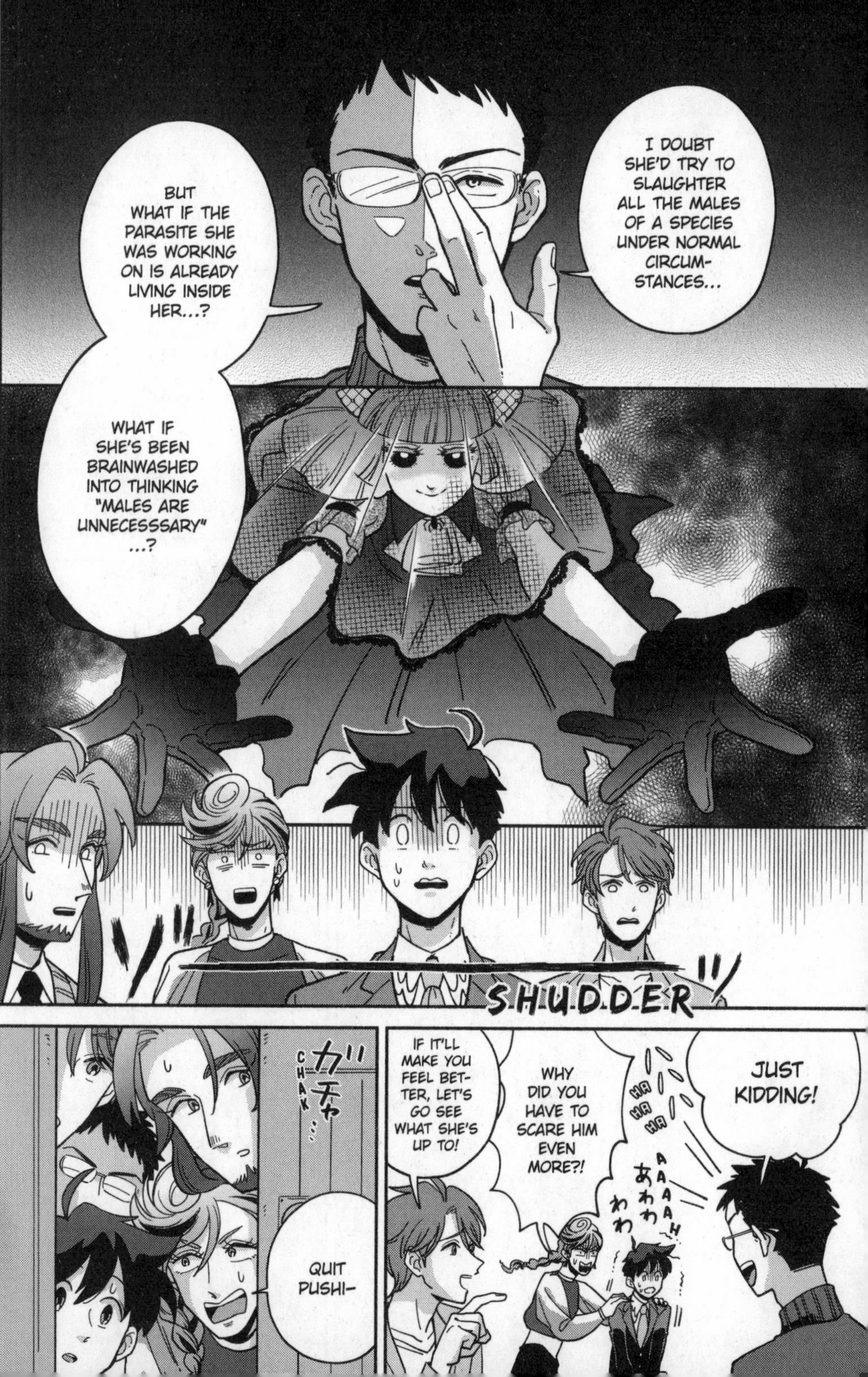
I DOUBT SHE'D TRY TO SLAUGHTER ALL THE MALES OF A SPECIES UNDER NORMAL CIRCUM-STANCES...
BUT WHAT IF THE PARASITE SHE WAS WORKING ON IS ALREADY LIVING INSIDE HER...?
WHAT IF SHE'S BEEN BRAINWASHED INTO THINKING "MALES ARE UNNECESSSARY" ...?
SHUDDER
JUST KIDDING!
HA HA HA
WHY DID YOU HAVE TO SCARE HIM EVEN MORE?!
あわわわ
AAAAH
IF IT'LL MAKE YOU FEEL BET-TER, LET'S GO SEE WHAT SHE'S UP TO!
ガチャ
CHAK
QUIT PUSHI-

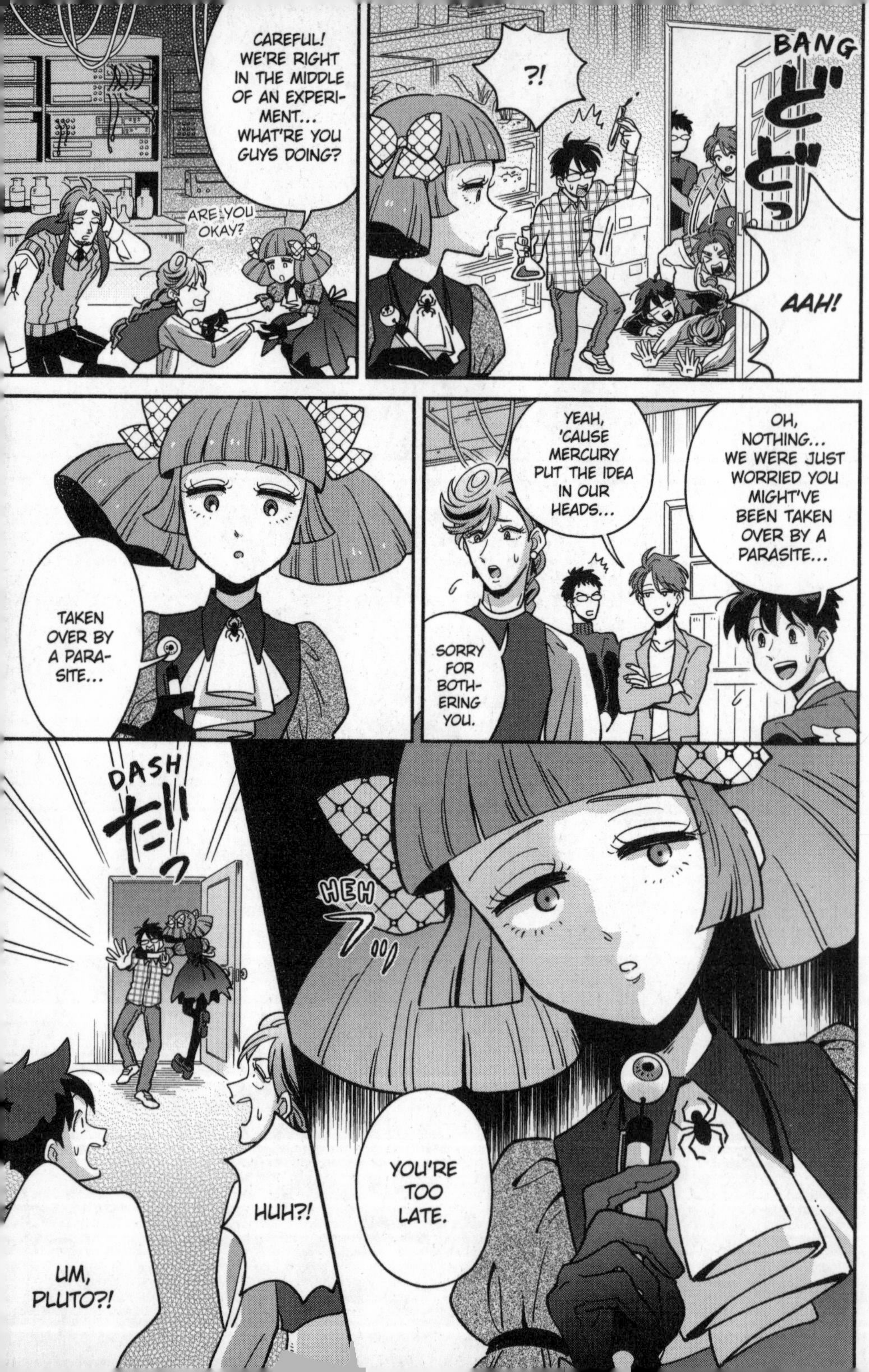
BANG
どどっ
?!
AAH!
CAREFUL! WE'RE RIGHT IN THE MIDDLE OF AN EXPERIMENT… WHAT'RE YOU GUYS DOING?
ARE YOU OKAY?
OH, NOTHING… WE WERE JUST WORRIED YOU MIGHT'VE BEEN TAKEN OVER BY A PARASITE…
YEAH, 'CAUSE MERCURY PUT THE IDEA IN OUR HEADS…
SORRY FOR BOTHERING YOU.
TAKEN OVER BY A PARASITE…
HEH
YOU'RE TOO LATE.
DASH
だっ
HUH?!
UM, PLUTO?!

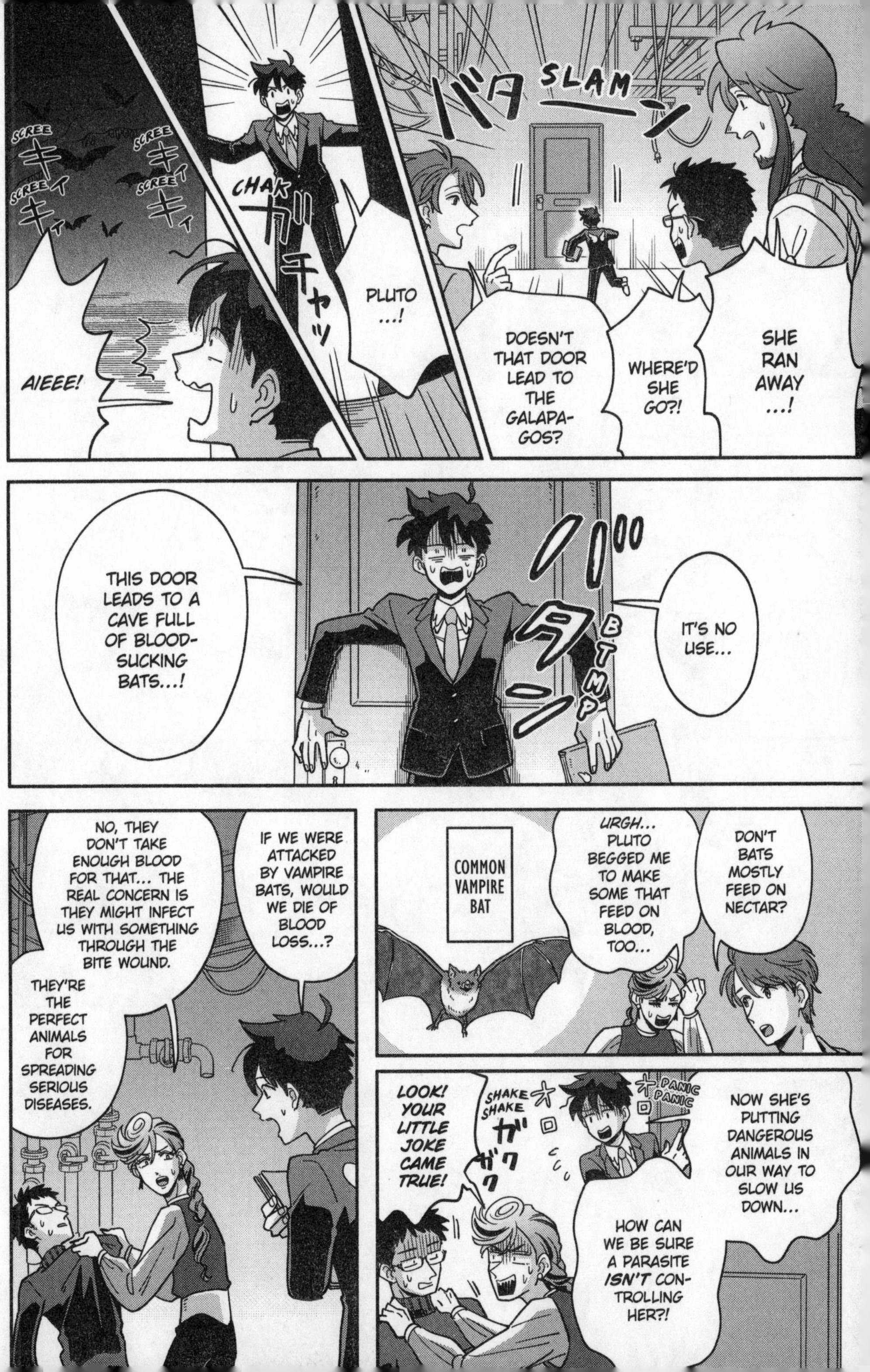
SLAM
SHE RAN AWAY ...!
WHERE'D SHE GO?!
DOESN'T THAT DOOR LEAD TO THE GALAPAGOS?
CHAK
PLUTO ...!
SCREE
SCREE
SCREE
SCREE
AIEEE!
IT'S NO USE...
BTMP
THIS DOOR LEADS TO A CAVE FULL OF BLOOD-SUCKING BATS...!
DON'T BATS MOSTLY FEED ON NECTAR?
URGH... PLUTO BEGGED ME TO MAKE SOME THAT FEED ON BLOOD, TOO...
COMMON VAMPIRE BAT
NOW SHE'S PUTTING DANGEROUS ANIMALS IN OUR WAY TO SLOW US DOWN...
PANIC PANIC
SHAKE SHAKE
LOOK! YOUR LITTLE JOKE CAME TRUE!
HOW CAN WE BE SURE A PARASITE ISN'T CONTROLLING HER?!
IF WE WERE ATTACKED BY VAMPIRE BATS, WOULD WE DIE OF BLOOD LOSS...?
NO, THEY DON'T TAKE ENOUGH BLOOD FOR THAT... THE REAL CONCERN IS THEY MIGHT INFECT US WITH SOMETHING THROUGH THE BITE WOUND.
THEY'RE THE PERFECT ANIMALS FOR SPREADING SERIOUS DISEASES.

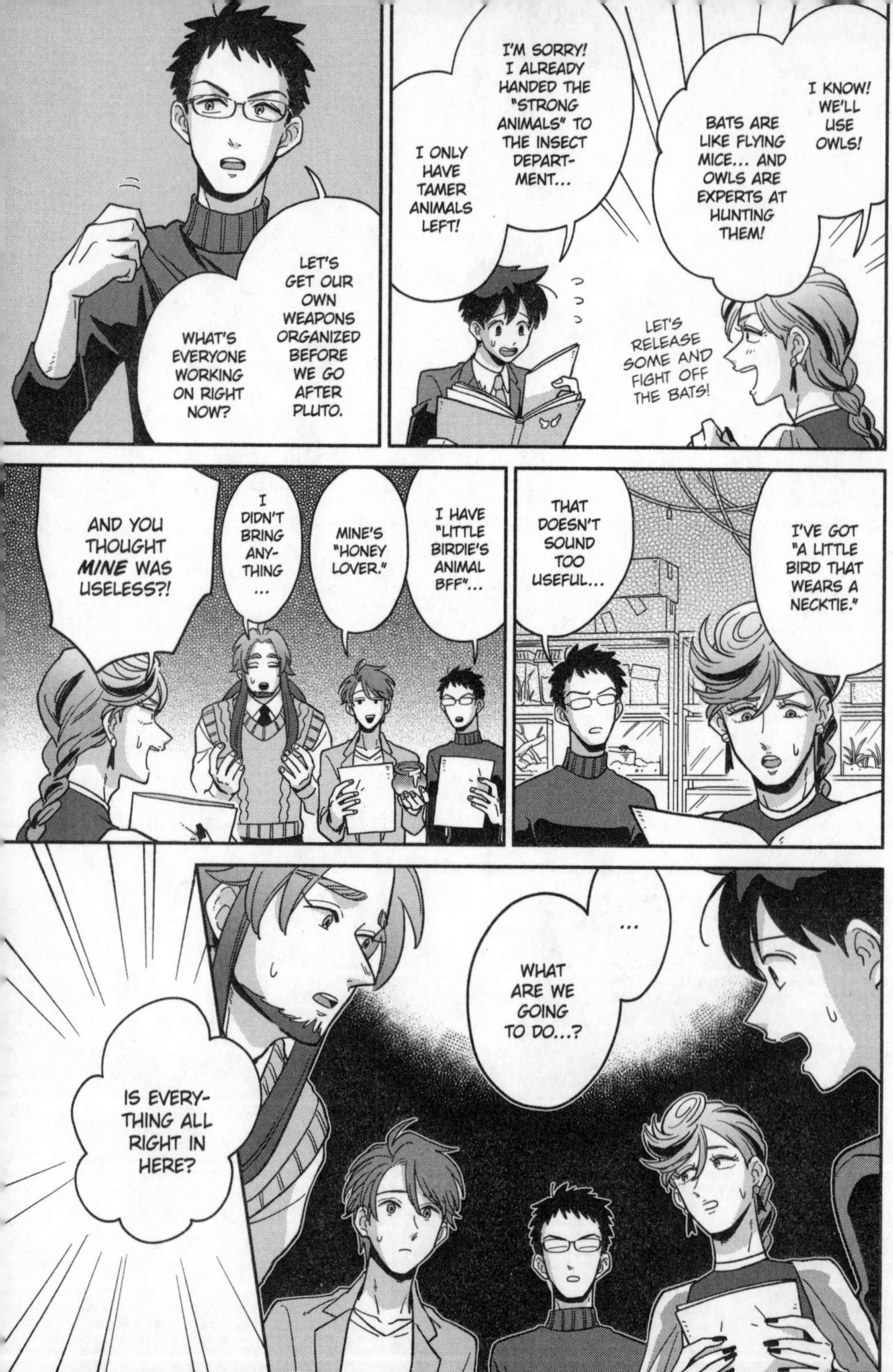

I KNOW! WE'LL USE OWLS!
BATS ARE LIKE FLYING MICE... AND OWLS ARE EXPERTS AT HUNTING THEM!
I'M SORRY! I ALREADY HANDED THE "STRONG ANIMALS" TO THE INSECT DEPART-MENT...
I ONLY HAVE TAMER ANIMALS LEFT!
LET'S RELEASE SOME AND FIGHT OFF THE BATS!
LET'S GET OUR OWN WEAPONS ORGANIZED BEFORE WE GO AFTER PLUTO.
WHAT'S EVERYONE WORKING ON RIGHT NOW?
I'VE GOT "A LITTLE BIRD THAT WEARS A NECKTIE."
THAT DOESN'T SOUND TOO USEFUL...
I HAVE "LITTLE BIRDIE'S ANIMAL BFF"...
MINE'S "HONEY LOVER."
I DIDN'T BRING ANY-THING...
AND YOU THOUGHT *MINE* WAS USELESS?!
...
WHAT ARE WE GOING TO DO...?
IS EVERY-THING ALL RIGHT IN HERE?

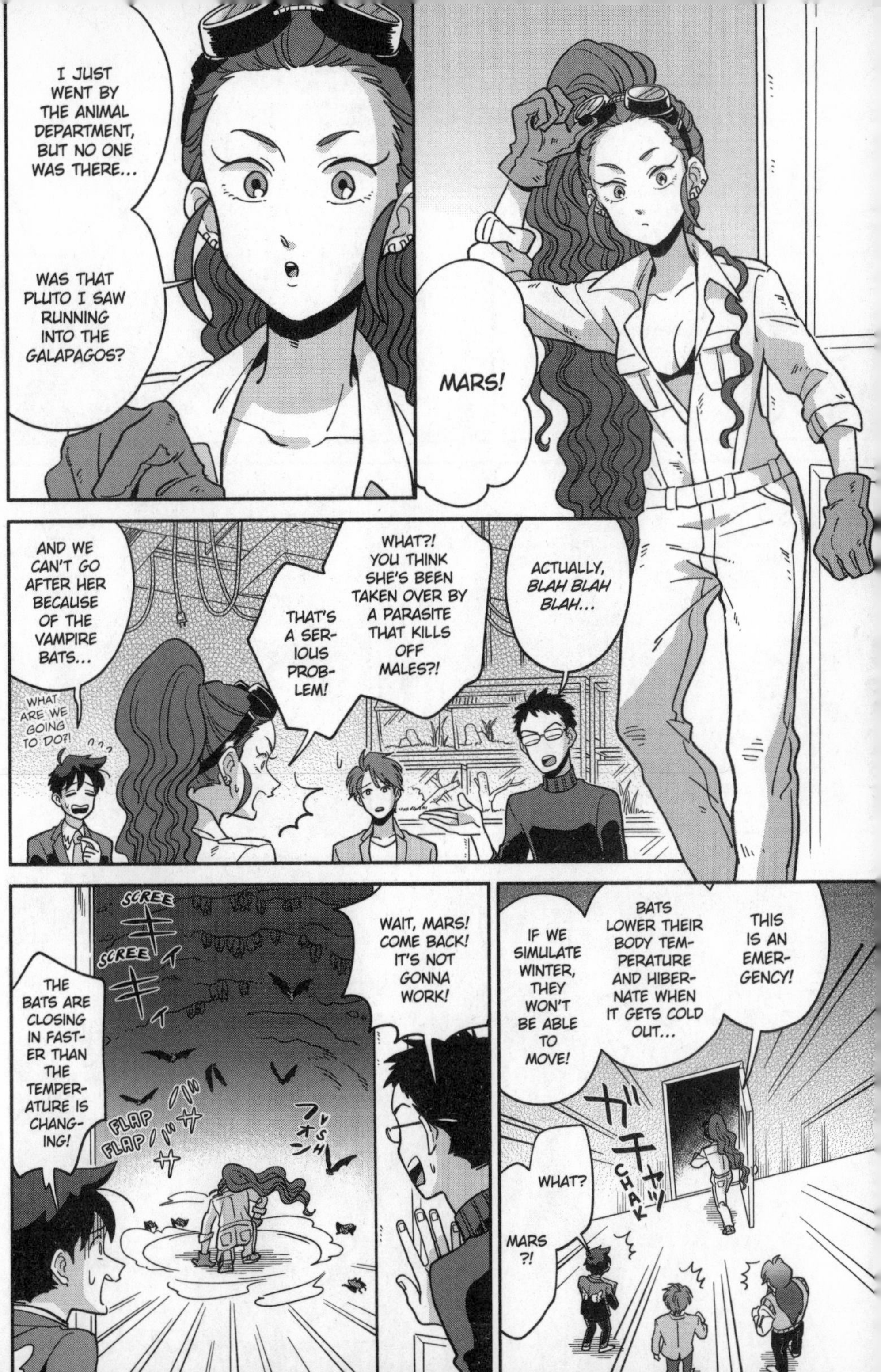
MARS!
I JUST WENT BY THE ANIMAL DEPARTMENT, BUT NO ONE WAS THERE...
WAS THAT PLUTO I SAW RUNNING INTO THE GALAPAGOS?
ACTUALLY, *BLAH BLAH BLAH*...
WHAT?! YOU THINK SHE'S BEEN TAKEN OVER BY A PARASITE THAT KILLS OFF MALES?!
THAT'S A SERIOUS PROBLEM!
AND WE CAN'T GO AFTER HER BECAUSE OF THE VAMPIRE BATS...
WHAT ARE WE GOING TO DO?!
THIS IS AN EMERGENCY!
BATS LOWER THEIR BODY TEMPERATURE AND HIBERNATE WHEN IT GETS COLD OUT...
IF WE SIMULATE WINTER, THEY WON'T BE ABLE TO MOVE!
ガチャッ
CHAK
WHAT?
MARS?!
WAIT, MARS! COME BACK! IT'S NOT GONNA WORK!
SCREE
SCREE
THE BATS ARE CLOSING IN FASTER THAN THE TEMPERATURE IS CHANGING!
FLAP FLAP
VSH

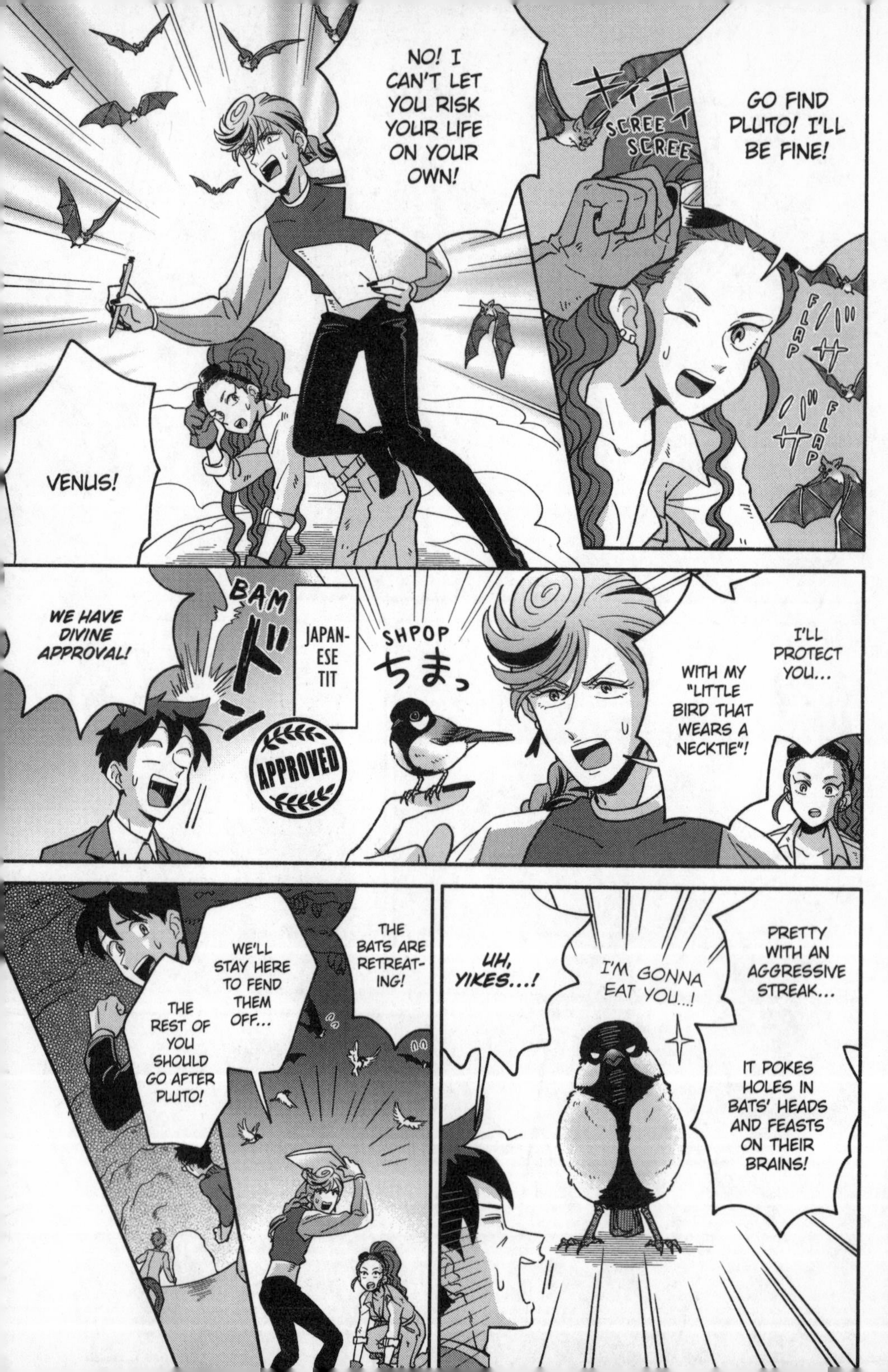
GO FIND PLUTO! I'LL BE FINE!
キィキィ
SCREE SCREE
FLAP バサ
FLAP バサ
NO! I CAN'T LET YOU RISK YOUR LIFE ON YOUR OWN!
VENUS!
I'LL PROTECT YOU...
WITH MY "LITTLE BIRD THAT WEARS A NECKTIE"!
SHPOP
ちまっ
JAPANESE TIT
BAM
ドン
APPROVED
WE HAVE DIVINE APPROVAL!
PRETTY WITH AN AGGRESSIVE STREAK...
I'M GONNA EAT YOU...!
UH, YIKES...!
IT POKES HOLES IN BATS' HEADS AND FEASTS ON THEIR BRAINS!
THE BATS ARE RETREATING!
WE'LL STAY HERE TO FEND THEM OFF...
THE REST OF YOU SHOULD GO AFTER PLUTO!

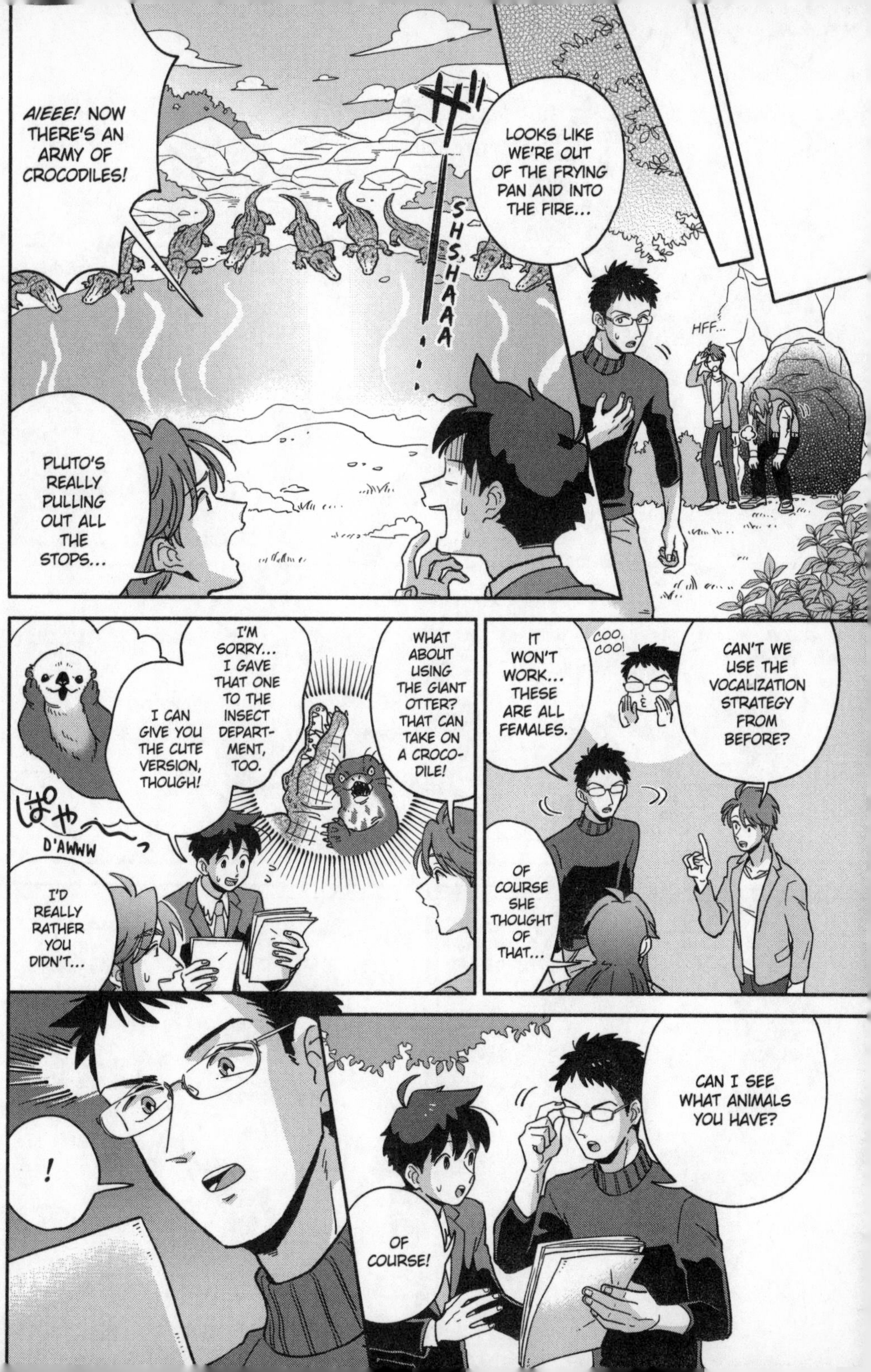
LOOKS LIKE WE'RE OUT OF THE FRYING PAN AND INTO THE FIRE...
HFF...
AIEEE! NOW THERE'S AN ARMY OF CROCODILES!
SHSHAAAA
PLUTO'S REALLY PULLING OUT ALL THE STOPS...
CAN'T WE USE THE VOCALIZATION STRATEGY FROM BEFORE?
COO, COO!
IT WON'T WORK... THESE ARE ALL FEMALES.
OF COURSE SHE THOUGHT OF THAT...
WHAT ABOUT USING THE GIANT OTTER? THAT CAN TAKE ON A CROCODILE!
I'M SORRY... I GAVE THAT ONE TO THE INSECT DEPARTMENT, TOO.
I CAN GIVE YOU THE CUTE VERSION, THOUGH!
ぱや〜
D'AWWW
I'D REALLY RATHER YOU DIDN'T...
CAN I SEE WHAT ANIMALS YOU HAVE?
OF COURSE!
!

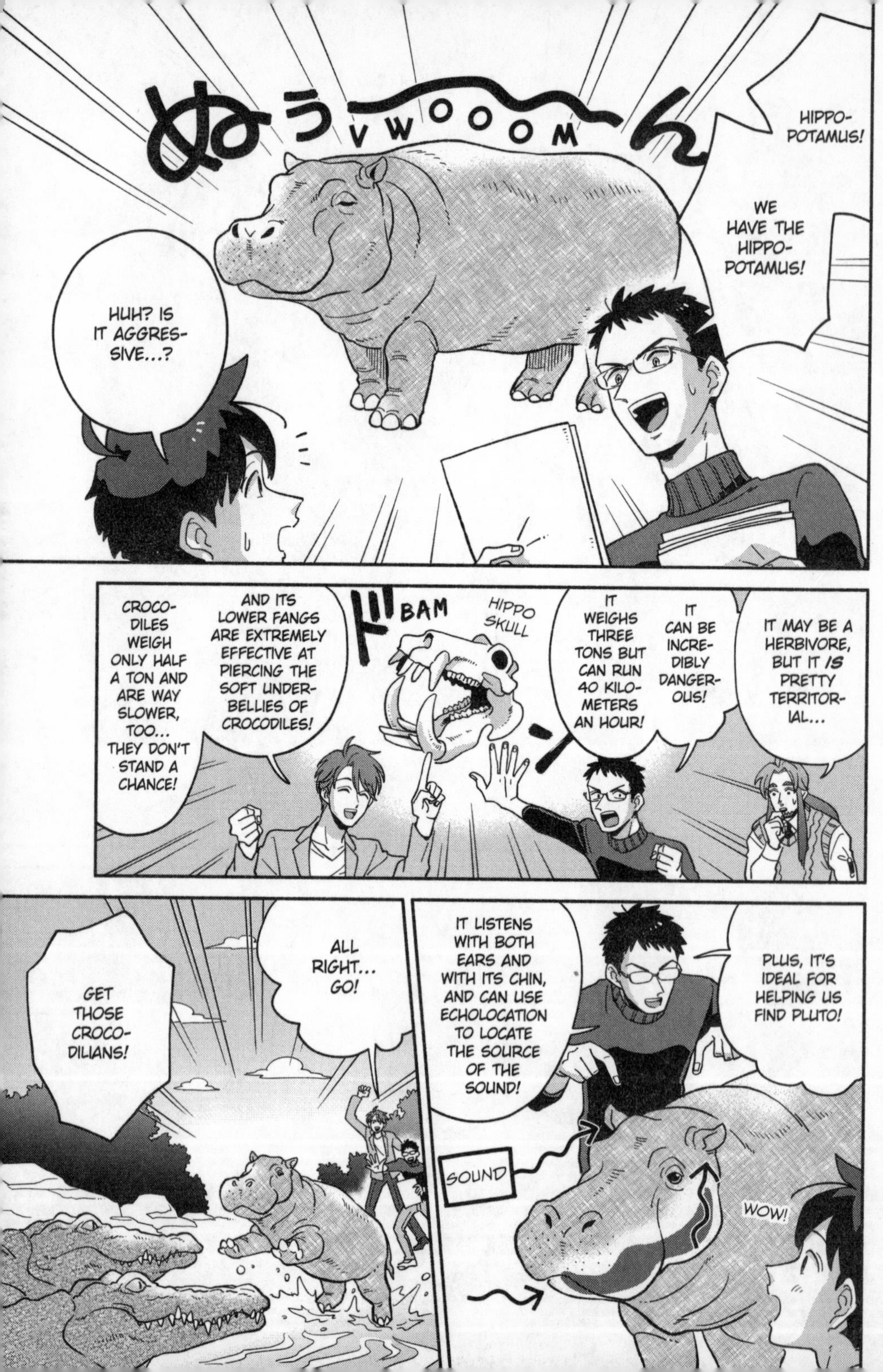
HIPPOPOTAMUS!
WE HAVE THE HIPPOPOTAMUS!
ぬう〜〜〜ん
VWOOOOM
HUH? IS IT AGGRESSIVE...?
IT MAY BE A HERBIVORE, BUT IT *IS* PRETTY TERRITORIAL...
IT CAN BE INCREDIBLY DANGEROUS!
IT WEIGHS THREE TONS BUT CAN RUN 40 KILOMETERS AN HOUR!
HIPPO SKULL
BAM
AND ITS LOWER FANGS ARE EXTREMELY EFFECTIVE AT PIERCING THE SOFT UNDERBELLIES OF CROCODILES!
CROCODILES WEIGH ONLY HALF A TON AND ARE WAY SLOWER, TOO... THEY DON'T STAND A CHANCE!
PLUS, IT'S IDEAL FOR HELPING US FIND PLUTO!
IT LISTENS WITH BOTH EARS AND WITH ITS CHIN, AND CAN USE ECHOLOCATION TO LOCATE THE SOURCE OF THE SOUND!
SOUND
WOW!
ALL RIGHT... GO!
GET THOSE CROCODILIANS!

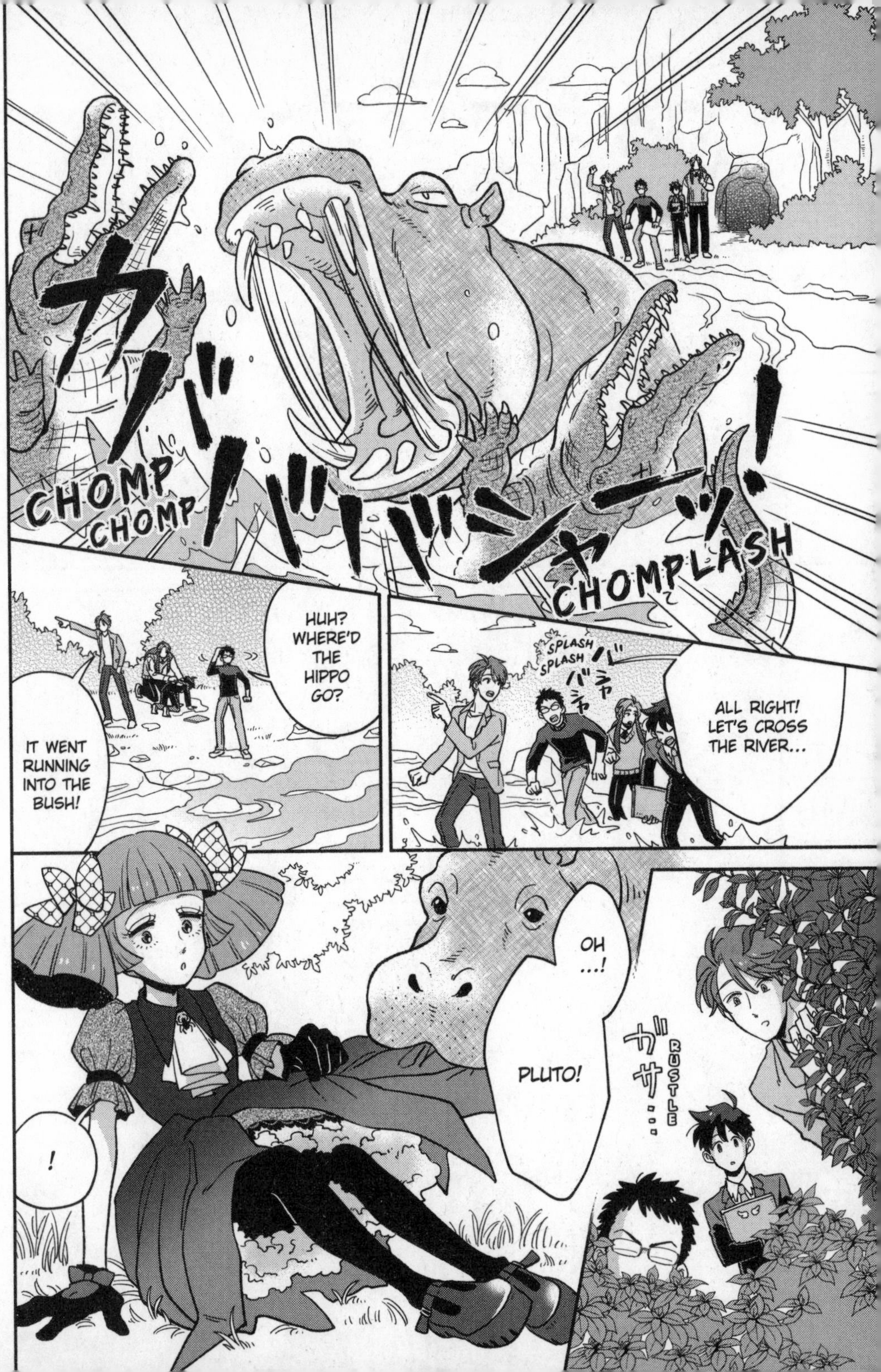
CHOMPLASH
CHOMP CHOMP
SPLASH SPLASH
ALL RIGHT! LET'S CROSS THE RIVER...
HUH? WHERE'D THE HIPPO GO?
IT WENT RUNNING INTO THE BUSH!
RUSTLE
OH ...!
PLUTO!
!

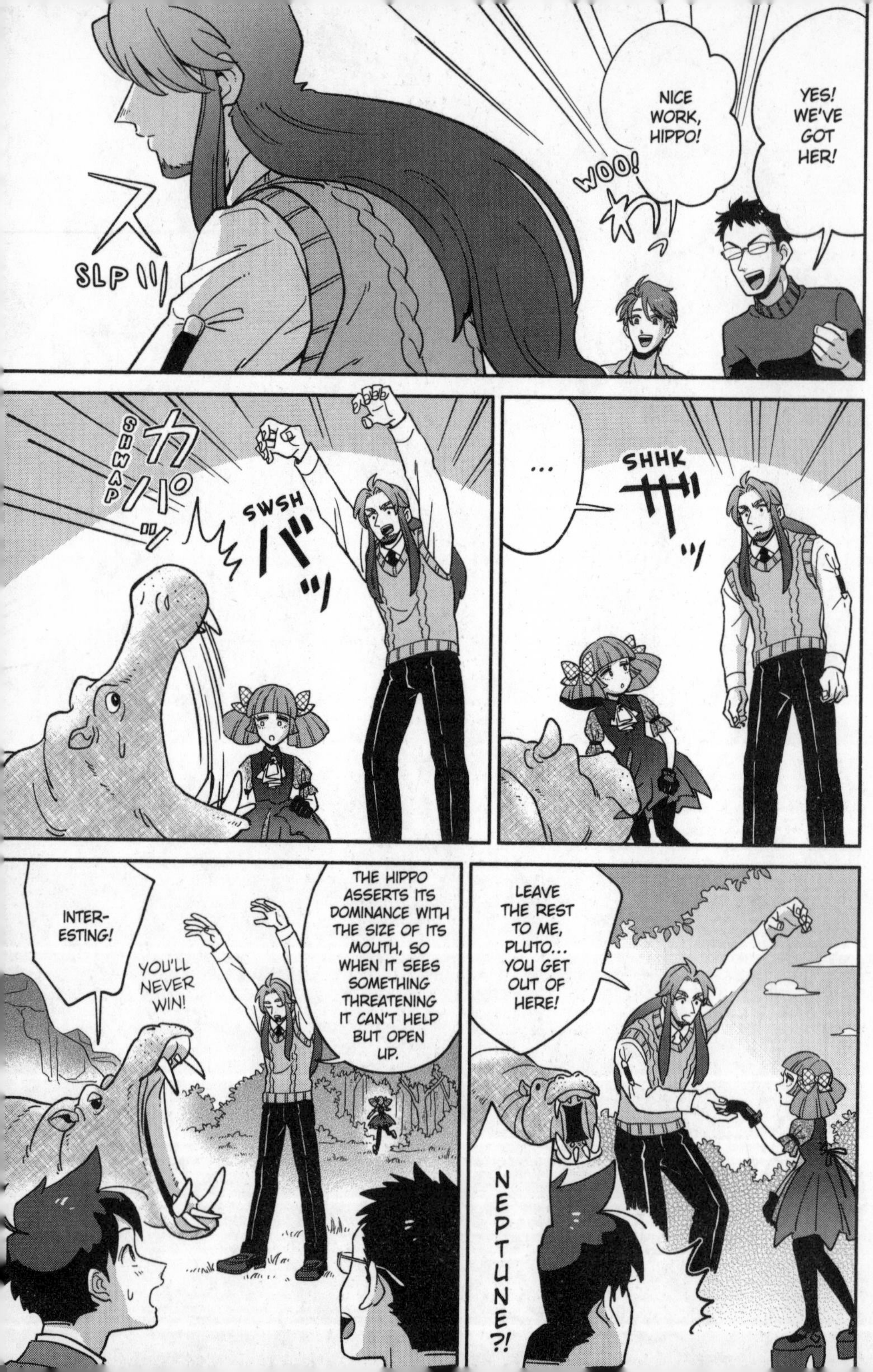
YES! WE'VE GOT HER!
NICE WORK, HIPPO!
WOO!
わっ
スッ
SLP
SHHK
ザッ
...
SWSH
バッ
SHWAP
カパッ
LEAVE THE REST TO ME, PLUTO... YOU GET OUT OF HERE!
NEPTUNE?!
THE HIPPO ASSERTS ITS DOMINANCE WITH THE SIZE OF ITS MOUTH, SO WHEN IT SEES SOMETHING THREATENING IT CAN'T HELP BUT OPEN UP.
INTER-ESTING!
YOU'LL NEVER WIN!

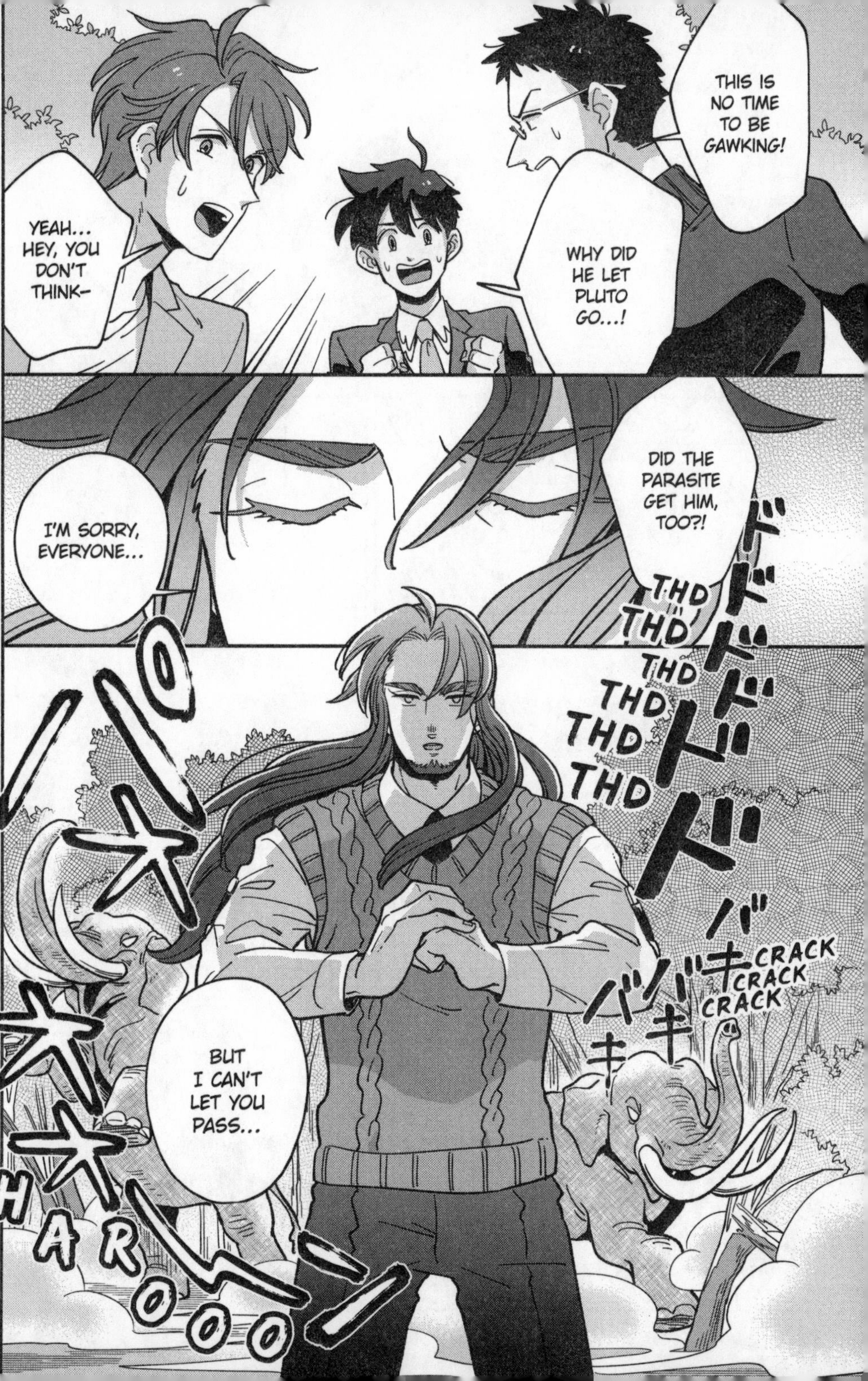
THIS IS NO TIME TO BE GAWKING!
WHY DID HE LET PLUTO GO...!
YEAH... HEY, YOU DON'T THINK-
DID THE PARASITE GET HIM, TOO?!
I'M SORRY, EVERYONE...
THD THD THD THD THD THD
CRACK CRACK CRACK
BUT I CAN'T LET YOU PASS...
HAROOOO

THE ENCYCLOPEDIA OF REAL ANIMALS 42

ANIMAL 98 | SPOTTED HYENA

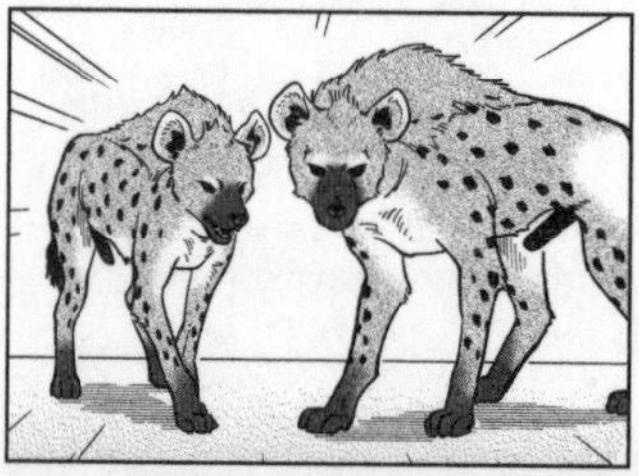

THE REAL THING

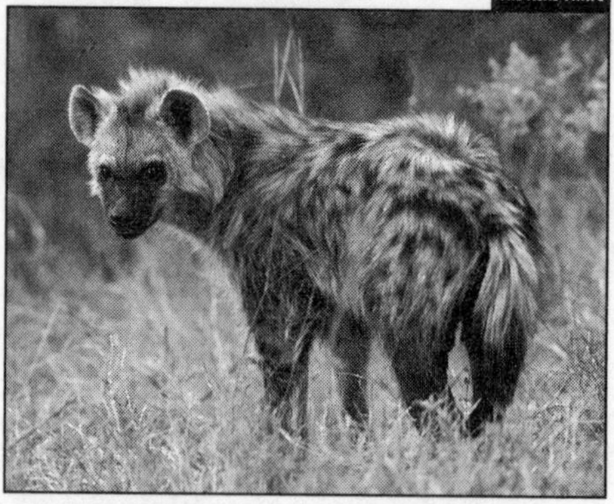

Skilled in both hunting and combat, the spotted hyena is an expert soldier.

Photo: Minden Pictures/Aflo

[Name] *Crocuta crocuta*
[Classification] Class: Mammalia
Order: Carnivora
Family: Hyaenidae
Genus: *Crocuta*
[Habitat] Africa (excluding the Sahara)
[Length] 95-165 cm (3-5.4 ft)

The female spotted hyena's close resemblance to its male counterpart is due to the high concentration of androgens (male hormones) fetuses are exposed to during the final stages of pregnancy. The extreme degree of masculinization means the female gives birth through a pseudo-penis in a difficult labor that ends in death 60 percent of the time. Despite these odds, the female hyena increases its chances of survival with its larger size and aggressive nature.

Although hyenas are often thought to rely solely on scavenging, the spotted hyena actually makes the majority of its own kills. Frequent altercations with lions mean that fighting is a crucial survival tactic. To hone such skills, cubs may attack their siblings shortly after birth, sometimes killing them in the process. The remaining cub is able to monopolize its mother's milk, and grows up to be an elite soldier.

ANIMAL 99 COMMON VAMPIRE BAT

THE REAL THING

The vampire bat is unusual in that it can walk on land using all four limbs.

Photo: Minden Pictures/Aflo

While "vampire bat" is a general term, there are several bat species that feed on blood. When hunting, the bats use thermoception to find a vein to bite. They then make an incision with their sharp fangs and lap up the host's blood. The anticoagulants contained in the bats' saliva keep the host's blood from clotting. Sleeping cows are a common target for these species.

Vampire bats are highly cooperative animals. If another member of the colony is hungry, for example, a bat may regurgitate a small amount of blood to share.

[Name]	Common vampire bat
[Classification]	Class: Mammalia Order: Chiroptera Family: Phyllostomidae
[Habitat]	Forests of Central and South America
[Length]	7-9 cm (2.8-3.5 in)

ANIMAL 100 HIPPOPOTAMUS

The hippopotamus is a semiaquatic animal that can run up to 40 kilometers per hour (25 mph) despite its massive body and short legs. Its sharp teeth are capable of piercing even a crocodile's thick skin.

Aggressive and unpredictable, the hippo will mercilessly attack any animal that dares enter its territory. Many human casualties have been reported, and the animal is responsible for the deaths of approximately 500 people per year. In altercations between members of the same species, the one with the bigger mouth wins.

THE REAL THING

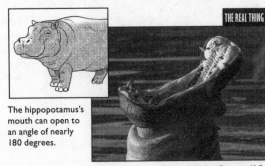

The hippopotamus's mouth can open to an angle of nearly 180 degrees.

Photo: Minden Pictures/Aflo

[Name]	*Hippopotamus amphibius*
[Classification]	Class: Mammalia Order: Artiodactyla Family: Hippopotamidae Genus: *Hippopotamus*
[Habitat]	Sub-Saharan Africa
[Length]	300-400 cm (9.8-13 ft)

References

Inagaki, Hidehiro. *Tatakai Shokubutsu—Jinginaki Seizon Senryaku (Chikuma Shobo)*. Japan: Chikumashobo Ltd. 2015.

Muchhala, Nathan, Patricio Mena V, and Luis Albuja V. "A New Species of *Anoura* (Chiroptera: Phyllostomidae) from the Ecuadorian Andes." *Journal of Mammalogy*, Vol. 86, Issue 3, 2005, pp. 457-461. American Society of Mammalogists.

Muchhala, Nathan. "Nectar bat stows huge tonuge in its rib cage." *Nature*, Vol. 444, 2006, pp. 701-702. Nature Publishing Group.

Inagaki, Hidehiro. *Mijikana Hana no Shirarezaru Seitai*. Japan: PHP Institute, Inc. 2015.

Tada, Taeko and Hajime Tanaka. *Daishizen no Fushigi Souhokaitei Shokubutsu no Seitai Zukan*. Japan: Gakken Plus. 2010.

Matsutani, Shigeru. "Darwin no Ran to Sono Jufun Baikaisha Suzumega to no Kankei." *Kokyuu e-report*, Vol. 2, Issue 2, 2018, pp. 98-104. Respiration Research Foundation.

Nakayama, Hiroyuki. *Juuigaku wo Manabu Kimitachi he: Hito to Doubutsu no Kenkou wo Mamoru*. Japan: University of Tokyo Press. 2019.

"Camel Blood." *The Physiological Processes of Blood*. https://animalcrackerzblood.weebly.com/camel.html.

Zachos, Elaina. "Arabian Camels Eat Cacti With Hardened Mouth Structures." Translated by Kaoru Yonei. *National Geographic*, National Geographic Society, National Geographic Partners, LLC., Nikkei National Geographic Inc. 2018.

Makita, Takashi, Masahiko Fujisawa, Tetsuya Yamane, Cao Guifang, Rai Bou, and Yoshihiro Hayashi. "Rakuda no Kyokusho Kaibou." *The Yamaguchi Journal of Veterinary Medicine*, Vol. 29, Issue 29, 2002, pp. 11-24. Tsukuba Business-Academia Cooperation Support Center, Agriculture, Forestry and Fisheries Research Council Secretariat.

Eitan, Anat, Beny Aloni, and Avinoam Livne. "Unique properties of the camel erythrocyte membrane, II. Organization of membrane proteins." *Biochimica et Biophysica Acta (BBA) - Biomembranes*, Vol. 426, Issue 4, 1976, pp. 647-658. Elsevier B.V.

Doubutsu Daihyakka, Vol. 4, Oogata Soushokujuu. Edited by D.W. MacDonald. Supervised by Yoshinori Imaizumi. Japan: Heibonsha. 1986.

Ewacha, Michelle. "*Oreotragus oreotragus klipspringer*."Animal Diversity Web. Regents of the University of Michigan. 2020. https://animaldiversity.org/accounts/Oreotragus_oreotragus/.

Prakash, Sanjeevi and Thipramalai Thangappan Ajith Kumar. "Feeding behavior of Harlequin Shrimp." *Journal of Threatened Taxa*. Vol. 5, Issue 13, 2013, pp. 4819-4821. www.threatenedtaxa.org.

Doubutsu Koudou Zusetsu—Kachiku, Hanryo Doubutsu, Tenji Doubutsu—. Edited by Shusuke Sato, Seiji Kondo, Toshio Tanaka, Ryo Kusunose, Yuji Mori, and Genichi Idani. Japan: Asakura Publishing Co., Ltd. 2011.

Koyama, Sachiko. *Nioi ni yoru Communication no Sekai—Nioi no Doubutsu Koudougaku*. Japan: Fragrance Journal Ltd. 2008.

Sato, Noriyuki. *Hoya no Seibutsugaku*. Japan: University of Tokyo Press. 1998.

Yamowa, Akira. "*Rafflesia keithii*." Okayama University of Science, Faculty of Biosphere-Geosphere Science Department of Biosphere-Geosphere Science, Kyuu Shokubutsu Seitai Kenkyuushitsu (Hada Lab) Homepage. http://had0.big.ous.ac.jp/plantsdic/angiospermae/dicotyledoneae/choripetalae/rafflesiaceae/rahuresia/rahuresia.htm

Marneweck, Courtney, Andreas Jürgens, and Adrian M. Shrader. "Dung odours signal sex, age, territorial and oestrous state in white rhinos." The Royal Society. https://www.ncbi.nlm.nih.gov/pmc/articles/PMC5247502/

Yamamura, Shinichiro. *Anata no Shiranai Mimizu no Hanashi*. Supervised by Masako Nakamura. Japan: Otsuki Shoten. 2007.

Ishizuka, Kotaro. *Mimizu Zukan*. Japan: Zenkoku Nousonkyouiku Kyoukai. 2014.

Yamada, Tadasu, Toshiaki Kuramochi, Hideki Endo, and Isao Nishiumi. *Kyokuchi no Honyuurui, Chourui*. Supervised by Yasuhiko Naido. Japan: Jinrui Bunka Sha. 2001.

Inagaki, Hidehiro. *Osu to Mesu wa Dochira ga Toku ka? (Shoudensha Shinsho)*. Japan: Shodensha Publishing Co., Ltd. 2016.

de Bruyn, P. J. N., C.A. Tosh, M. N. Bester, E.Z. Cameron, T. McIntyre, and I.S. Wilkinson. "Sex at sea: alternative mating system in an extremely polygynous mammal." *Animal Behaviour*, Vol. 82, Issue 3, 2011, pp. 445-451. The Association for the Study of Animal Behaviour, Elsevier Ltd.

"Chikyuujou ni Mesu 2-tou shikanai Kitashirosai, 3-ko no Juseiran Sakusei ni Seikou." Yomiuri Shimbun Online. https://www.yomiuri.co.jp/science/20200116-OYT1T50255/.

Hirt, Myriam R., Walter Jetz, Björn C. Rall, and Ulrich Brose. "A general scaling law reveals why the largest animals are not the fastest." *Nature Ecology & Evolution*, Vol. 1, 2017, pp. 1116-1122. Springer Nature Limited.

Cunha, Gerald R., Ned J. Place, Larry Baskin, Alan Conley, Mary Weldele, Tristan J. Cunha, Y.Z. Wang, Mei Cao, and Stephen E. Glickman. "The Ontogeny of the Urogenital System of the Spotted Hyena (*Crocuta crocuta* Erxleben)." *Biology of Reproduction*, Vol. 73, Issue 3, 2005, pp. 554-564. The Society for the Study of Reproduction, Inc.

Imaizumi, Tadaaki. *Zukai Zatsugaku Daremo Shiranai Doubutsu no Mikata, Doubutsu Koudougaku Nyuumon*. Japan: Natsumesha Co., Ltd. 2012.

Krausman, Paul. R. and Susana M. Morales. "*Acinonyx jubatus*." *Mammalian Species*, Issue 771, 2005, pp. 1-6. The American Society of Mammalogists.

Watanabe, Shin'ichi, J. de Villiers, J. van der Merwe, and Katsufumi Sato. "Hayaku Hashiranai Cheetah: Namibia Savanna Doubutsu Hogoku ni Okeru Cheetah no Hunting Koudou." *Primate Research Supplement*, Vol. 29, 2013, pp. 110. Primate Society of Japan.

Cooke, Lucy. *The Unexpected Truth About Animals: A Menagerie of the Misunderstood*. Translated by Reiko Kobayashi. Japan: Seidosha. 2018.

Pauli, Jonathan N., Jorge E. Mendoza, Shawn A. Steffan, Cayelan C. Carey, Paul J. Weimer, and M. Zachariah Peery. "A syndrome of mutualism reinforces the lifestyle of a sloth." *The Royal Society*. 2014. https://doi.org/10.1098/rspb.2013.3006.

"Starving to death on a full stomach." *The Sloth Conservation Foundation*. 2016. https://slothconservation.com/starving-death-full-stomach/.

Cliffe, Rebecca N., Ryan J. Haupt, Judy A. Avery-Arroyo, and Rory P. Wilson, "Sloths like it hot: ambient temperature modulates food intake in the brown-throated sloth. (*Bradypus variegatus*)." *Peer*, Vol. 3. https://www.ncbi.nlm.nih.gov/pmc/articles/PMC4389270/.

Glickman, Stephen E., Gerald R. Cunha, Christine M. Drea, Alan J. Conley, and Ned J. Place. "Mammalian sexual differentiation: Lessons from the spotted hyena." *Trends in Endocrinology and Metabolism*, Vol. 17, Issue 9, 2006, pp. 349-356. Elsevier Ltd.

Altringham, J. D. "Bats: Biology and Behaviour." Supervised by Sumiko Matsumura. Translated by Koumori no Kai Honyaku Group. Japan: Yasaka Shobo Inc. 1998.

Wildlife of the World. Supervised by Masao Kosuge. Translated by Atsushi Kurowa. Japan: Nittou Shoin Honsha. 2017.

*All websites were accessed on December 15, 2020.

Special thanks:

Editor/Yoshimi Takuwa-san (Institution for Liberal Arts, Tokyo Institution of Technology)
Illustration Production Collaboration/Izumi Kanchiku-san (Team Pascal)
Kamome Shirahama-san
Saba-san
Ame Toba-san
Tomato-san

CEYA

A Kodansha Comics Trade Paperback Original
Heaven's Design Team 6 copyright © 2021 Hebi-zou&Tsuta Suzuki/Tarako
English translation copyright © 2021 Hebi-zou&Tsuta Suzuki/Tarako
All rights reserved.

Published in the United States by Kodansha Comics, an imprint of Kodansha USA Publishing, LLC, New York.

Publication rights for this English edition arranged through Kodansha Ltd., Tokyo.

First published in Japan in 2021 by Kodansha Ltd., Tokyo as *Tenchi sozo dezainbu*, volume 6.

ISBN 978-1-64651-268-3

Original cover design by SAVA DESIGN

Printed in the United States of America.

www.kodansha.us

9 8 7 6 5 4 3 2 1

Translation and lettering: JM Iitomi Crandall
Additional translation: Jacqueline Fung
Additional lettering and layout: Belynda Ungurath
Editing: Jesika Brooks, Vanessa Tenazas
YKS Services LLC/SKY Japan, INC
Kodansha Comics edition cover design by My Truong

...hiro Sugawara

Director of publishing services: Ben Applegate
Associate director of operations: Stephen Pakula
Publishing services managing editors: Alanna Ruse, Madison Salters
Production managers: Emi Lotto, Angela Zurlo
Logo and character art ©Kodansha USA Publishing, LLC